POLITICS AND SOCIETY

New Governance – New ...

POLITICS AND SOCIETY IN WALES
Series Editor: Ralph Fevre

New Governance – New Democracy?

POST-DEVOLUTION WALES

Edited by

PAUL CHANEY, TOM HALL and ANDREW PITHOUSE

*Published on behalf of the Social Science Committee
of the Board of Celtic Studies of the University of Wales*

UNIVERSITY OF WALES PRESS
CARDIFF
2001

© The Contributors, 2001

British Library Cataloguing-in-Publication Data.
A catalogue record for this book is available from the British Library.

ISBN 0–7083–1678–6

Typeset at University of Wales Press
Printed in Great Britain by Bookcraft Ltd., Avon

Series Editor's Foreword

Not so long ago the most important thing that could be said about Wales was that it was a part of Britain. Wales provided Britain with more than its fair share of coal, iron and steel; and leaders of the opposition, cabinet ministers and prime ministers. Most of the people of Wales expected Wales to be fully integrated into the politics and economics of Britain, and indeed many of them assumed Wales was central to Britain's economic and political system.

In the second half of the twentieth century the British Empire disappeared, cracks appeared in the British welfare state and the nationalized industries went into decline before finally being sold off to the private sector. The assumption that Wales was at the centre of things became even harder to support as, from 1979 onwards, Wales was politically isolated from the centre. For the next eighteen years Wales did not elect very many of the ruling party's MPs and the idea of a prime minister elected from a Welsh constituency was rather too frequently seen as some kind of joke. Echoes of the earlier feeling of being at the heart of a British system could now only be heard in the representations of Welsh history mounted in industrial heritage museums.

Throughout the latter half of the twentieth century employment in agriculture, coal, iron and steel declined while new jobs were created in manufacturing and the service sector. There was some continuity with the past in that central government was responsible for some of the new service-sector jobs. Nevertheless, hardly any of the new jobs could be seen as direct replacements for the jobs lost in the declining nationalized industries. They were mostly in different parts of Wales, particularly the more prosperous parts of south and north-east Wales, and they were more likely to be taken by women than men. Even in the farming areas it was women who sought new opportunities in tourism as agriculture declined. By the time of the 1984–5 miners' strike it was becoming clear just how male the public face of Wales had been up to that point. If male workers were now being superseded by female workers, might the same thing happen to men in other aspects of public life?

The possibility of fundamental changes in the way things had been done over the years also arose in relation to economic development matters. Many of the new jobs were in companies which were based overseas, especially in the United States and Japan. Not only was Wales no longer at the centre of things but there was growing suspicion that Wales might actually be suffering the fate appropriate to an obscure outpost of global

capitalism. There was a genuine fear that Wales was now fit only for
(subsidized) branch plants which offered de-skilled, low-paid, insecure
jobs which were in no sense a fair exchange for the jobs that had been lost
in coal and steel. Moreover, the communities that had been sustained by
heavy industry were suffering. Their physical and social capital was in
decline and their patterns of education and training were adversely
affected. There was serious material deprivation and associated social
dislocation (with escalating drug use and crime). In some places numbers
of people were no longer deriving their identity from work but were
fashioning lives on welfare benefits for permanently sick or disabled
people or as teenage mothers.

In time concerns about social dislocation and deprivation rather over-
came suspicions about inward investment: with social problems like these
it might be thought obvious that any job was better than none. In these
circumstances it is not surprising that great hope, and indeed great trust,
was invested in the development agency responsible for attracting these
jobs to Wales. Although the returns on both investments were sometimes
disappointing, the agency did at least give the impression that Wales was
not content with isolation on the periphery. Elsewhere the messages which
reached the outside world were rather more mixed.

In the nineteenth century Wales had experienced substantial immigration from England which helped to populate the south Wales valleys. In the
first half of the twentieth century Wales became a country of net out-
migration in response to recession. While Wales had a long-established
black population it did not experience the black immigration that
happened in English cities in the 1960s. Immigration did not become a
public issue in Wales until the 1980s when it became an issue because of
language rather than 'race' or ethnicity. The organized campaigns against
the immigration of monoglot English speakers to areas of Wales in which
the Welsh language remained in daily use amongst large sections of the
population were built on earlier protests against the purchase of second
homes in Wales. As in the case of suspicion about inward investment, there
was a widespread revulsion against the changes that were perceived to be
taking place. The Welsh language had been in decline throughout the
century but the changes wrought by immigration were thought to be so
fundamental, so swift and irreversible, that permanent damage was being
done.

There was also a more positive side to cultural nationalism (becoming
increasingly politicized in the second half of the century) which resulted in
the gradual legitimation of the role of the Welsh language in public life.
Moreover, support for the nationalist political party increased and Welsh
nationalism had to come to terms with the opportunity to offer, and indeed

the necessity of providing, alternatives to the isolationism which has often been thought necessary to protect Welsh language and culture. Support for a measure of self-government for Wales has also grown within other political parties. These developments contributed to the creation of an independent Welsh politics which was given further legitimation when the aspiration for self-government was partially satisfied by the limited devolution of power in the shape of the National Assembly for Wales in 1999:

> the devolution of decision-making powers to the National Assembly for Wales signifies political recognition of the distinctiveness of Wales as a place that merits independent representation, which has its own 'voice', and its own problems and concerns. In other words, it is accepted as forming a distinct, although not wholly separate, society with its own history, identity and institutional structure.[1]

This devolution is at least partly responsible for the creation of the 'Politics and Society in Wales' Series. Indeed, devolution will be a central focus of many of the early volumes and the series will provide much of the research and scholarship required to inform an ongoing debate about the constitutional settlement. Devolution also has implications for a variety of social and economic phenomena which the series will explore. Thus theories about the link between local political control and economic success can be pursued by reference to other regions or countries with different levels of local control. For example, the economic and social changes (including the rapid decline in the social influence of religion) experienced in Ireland offer interesting points of comparison.

In a sense devolution has turned Wales into the natural laboratory that some social scientists have always thought it might be. It is not surprising that some of the early experimental findings are disappointing. Devolution has exposed worries about the weakness of Welsh civil society, the ineffectiveness of the new Assembly and the fragility of its legitimacy amongst the electorate. It has also brought to light very many hopes and expectations that these problems will be solved in due course. Amongst these expressions of hope it is surprisingly easy to find visions of a new Welsh politics and society which are not only different from the past but a great improvement on it. People want and expect government and administration to be more effective. They desire a more open and self-confident society which actually achieves the tolerance once claimed (in the absence of any evidence) to be characteristic of Wales. They want generalized prosperity but are increasingly worried about the environmental effects of development strategies and about strategies which simply exacerbate old divisions and inequalities.

Again it is surprising to some, but many of these hopes and aspirations are actually alive in the debates of the National Assembly. A generation ago the idea that leading figures of such an Assembly might share a passionate commitment to equal opportunities and sustainable development would have been a cause for laughter. To add that these politicians would also be women would have invited complete incomprehension. Perhaps this is a temporary phase but, if it is, then our series will document the circumstances of its passing. The writer of a foreword is sometimes allowed to tell a complex and contradictory story as if it were a simple one that was easy to explain in a couple of paragraphs. The 'Politics and Society in Wales' Series will tell the unfolding story of Wales in the twenty-first century in all its complexity and detail.

Ralph Fevre
Cardiff , May 2001

Note

[1]   G. Day, D. Dunkerley, and A. Thompson (2000), 'Evaluating the 'new politics': civil society and the National Assembly for Wales', *Public Policy and Administration*, 15, 2, 25.

Contents

Series Editor's Foreword   v
List of Figures   x
List of Tables   xi
List of Abbreviations   xiii

1. New Governance – New Democracy?
    Paul Chaney, Tom Hall and Andrew Pithouse   1

2. Turnout, Participation and Legitimacy in the Politics of Post-
    devolution Wales
    Richard Wyn Jones and Dafydd Trystan   18

3. Inclusive Government for Excluded Groups: Women and Disabled
    People
    Sandra Betts, John Borland and Paul Chaney   48

4. Inclusive Government for Excluded Groups: Ethnic Minorities
    Charlotte Williams and Paul Chaney   78

5. The National Assembly and the Voluntary Sector: An Equal
    Partnership?
    Bella Dicks, Tom Hall and Andrew Pithouse   102

6. Learning by Doing: Devolution and the Governance of Economic
    Development in Wales
    Kevin Morgan and Gareth Rees   126

7. Devolution and Regulation: The Political Control of Public
    Agencies in Wales
    Rachel Ashworth, George Boyne and Richard Walker   172

8. Reading the Runes
    Paul Chaney, Tom Hall and Andrew Pithouse   213

Bibliography   229

Index   245

Figures

4.1   Early days – the mobilization of democracy?   81–3

7.1   Regulatory arrangements for social services departments   180

7.2   Regulatory arrangements for DSOs   182

7.3   Regulatory arrangements for local authority housing
       departments   185

7.4   Regulatory arrangements for housing associations   187

7.5   Regulatory arrangements for institutions of higher
       education   190

7.6   Regulatory arrangements for the Welsh Development
       Agency   191

Tables

2.1	Results of the 1997 UK general election in Wales and the 1999 National Assembly for Wales election	19
2.2	Turnout in devolution-related polls in Wales	20
2.3	Turnout in selected polls in the UK since 1997	26
2.4	Reasons given for not voting	29
2.5	Sex and turnout	30
2.6	Age and turnout	31
2.7	Place of birth and turnout	32
2.8	Ability to speak Welsh and turnout	32
2.9	National identity and turnout	33
2.10	Self-ascribed class and turnout	33
2.11	Goldthorpe–Heath class schema and turnout	34
2.12	Information deficit and turnout	34
2.13	Partisan identification and turnout	35
2.14	Feelings towards the parties and turnout	36
2.15	Recalled referendum vote and Assembly turnout	37
2.16	Constitutional preference and turnout	37
2.17	Did you care who won the Assembly elections and turnout	38
2.18	Expectations of the Assembly and turnout	38
2.19	Will the UK general election make a difference by turnout	39
2.20	Politicians and parties	39
2.21	Logistic regression model of partisan influence and turnout	40
2.22	Logistic regression model of demographic/identity factors and turnout	41
2.23	Logistic regression model of attitudes to politics and turnout	43
2.24	Logistic regression model of turnout in the 1999 National Assembly election	44
7.1	Survey instrument for assessment of regulatory problems	179
7.2	Number of regulatory mechanisms	196
7.3	Extent of regulatory problems	196

List of Abbreviations

AGW	Auditor-General for Wales
AM	Assembly Member
ASPB	Assembly Sponsored Public Body
AWEMA	All Wales Black and Ethnic Minority Assembly Consultative and Participatory Association
BBC	British Broadcasting Corporation
BME	Black and Minority Ethnic
C+AG	Comptroller and Auditor-General
Cadw	Welsh Historic Monuments Executive Agency
CBI	Confederation of British Industry
CCET	Community Consortia for Education and Training
CCT	compulsory competitive tendering
CETW	National Council for Education and Training in Wales
CRE	Commission for Racial Equality
CVC	County Voluntary Council
CWA	Campaign for a Welsh Assembly
DRC	Disability Rights Commission
DSO	direct-service organization
DSO	local authority direct service organizations
EEP	European Equality Partnership
EOC	Equal Opportunities Commission
ESF	European Structural Fund
ESRC	Economic and Social Research Council
ETAG	Education and Training Action Group for Wales
ETAP	Education and Training Action Plan for Wales
EU	European Union
FSB	Federation of Small Businesses
GDP	gross domestic product
GM	genetically modified
GP	General Practitioner
HEFCW	Higher Education Funding Council for Wales
HEI	higher education institutions
HRA	Housing Revenue Account
IHE	institutions of higher education (*see also* HEI)
IoD	Institute of Directors
LASSD	local authority social services department
MEWN	Minority Ethnic Women's Network
MP	Member of Parliament

NAAG	National Assembly Advisory Group
NAO	National Audit Office
NAW	National Assembly for Wales
NCVO	National Council for Voluntary Organizations
NDPB	non-departmental public body
NEDS	National Economic Development Strategy
NGO	non-government organization
NHS	National Health Service
NPM	new public management
OECD	Organization for Economic Co-operation and Development
OFSTED	Office for Standards in Education
ONS	Office of National Statistics
OPCS	Office of Population, Census and Surveys
PAC	Public Accounts Committee (Parliament at Westminster)
PAF	postal address file
PI	performance indicator
PWC	Parliament for Wales Campaign
RDD	random direct dialling
RDD	Welsh Office Regional Development Division
REC	Racial Equality Council
RNIB	Royal National Institute for the Blind
S4C	Sianel Pedwar Cymru
SCOVO	Standing Council of Voluntary Organizations for people with a learning disability, Wales
SSD	social services department
SSI	social services inspectorate
TEC	Training and Enterprise Council
TQA	Teaching Quality Assessment
VFM	value for money
WAC	Welsh Affairs Committee (Parliament at Westminster)
WCVA	Wales Council for Voluntary Action
WDA	Welsh Development Agency
WLGA	Welsh Local Government Association
WLP	Wales Labour Party
WNAES	Wales National Assembly Election Survey
WWA	Welsh Women's Aid
WWNC	Wales Women's National Coalition

1

New Governance – New Democracy?

PAUL CHANEY, TOM HALL and ANDREW PITHOUSE

Devolution is a great experiment in political reform. It has no comparable predecessor in UK history and, for this and other reasons, it is not at all clear what the outcome of the experiment will be. We do not know whether the experiment will work – for example, whether it will deliver better governance – and we do not even know how the experiment will end. It is conceivable that devolution might lead to independence for Scotland. It is also possible, and some of the contributors to this book would say it is more than likely, that devolution will eventually lead to a Welsh parliament with powers on a par with those already devolved to Scotland.

All of this makes social scientists very excited. Most of them never get the chance to conduct an experiment, and here a great experiment is being conducted in full public view. Instead of wondering, and theorizing, about what the effects of political change might be, they can go out and gather data which will demonstrate what these effects are. In Wales, social scientists have eagerly grasped the opportunity offered by the great experiment of devolution, and this book reports on the findings of the first research projects that they have mounted to explore devolution in action. While much of this research has been to do with different ways of finding out if the experiment is working, all of the researchers involved have also thought about where the experiment will end. Some of their interim conclusions about the direction of the devolution process are included in the chapters that follow, and we will return to a longer discussion of what the future might hold in our concluding chapter.

This book sets out the findings of recent research into the operation of the National Assembly for Wales which was undertaken by five teams of social scientists working within the University of Wales. The book goes to press before the end of the Assembly's second year of governing in Wales and therefore cannot claim to be a definitive study of the Assembly. Instead we attempt to establish some key features of a rapidly changing institutional landscape in the governance of Wales by reporting on five very different projects which have inquired into the impact of the Assembly on key aspects of Welsh society. The five projects covered studies of the

Assembly elections in relation to questions of political participation and legitimacy, devolution and economic development, the regulation of public agencies in Wales, new government and the voluntary sector, and relations between the Assembly and people traditionally under-represented in politics and public life in Wales (women, disabled people and people from an ethnic minority background). These projects combine an inter-disciplinary focus on the political, sociological and economic implications of devolution with a wide variety of research methods. In addition, each of the studies has been informed by a different body of theoretical and empirical literature, and some space will be devoted to discussion of the implications of the various findings for social science.

It was an important component of each of these projects that a record was made of the various hopes and expectations that were held within Wales at the point at which the Assembly came into being. Special attention was paid to the many policy ambitions that helped to forge this new constitutional arrangement. This book therefore functions as a record of the goals that were set for the Assembly at the start of its life as well as an evaluation of some important developments in the Assembly's early days. We hope that the book will therefore provide benchmarks for future studies in each of the five research areas discussed here.

We believe that our approach is the most useful one at this juncture. Given that the Assembly is still in its infancy, we do not believe the time is right for a detailed and comprehensive description of the new polity or for systematic comparison between the Assembly and other similar democratic initiatives in the UK and elsewhere. Rather, the work reported here seeks to establish where and how the Assembly is beginning to have an impact on life in Wales on the basis of rigorous investigation and analysis. One of our goals is to show what can usefully be learned from a social science perspective that seeks to reveal the less obvious effects of a landmark event in the social and political history of modern Wales, particularly those effects which may not have been anticipated by journalists or in wider public debate. We are sure that this approach will produce findings which are of interest to a wider audience interested in devolution and change.

In this introduction we devote some space to discussing the new empirical material arising from the five studies and their various theoretical concerns. We also describe the background to these studies, but we will spend little time discussing the political events which occurred at the time of the referendum in 1997 and the elections to the new Assembly in 1999, since these have already received a great deal of coverage and comment elsewhere. This book is not about the heady moments and big personalities of Welsh devolution, although we will make some mention in this introduction of the key dates and speeches. The architects and events that have built devolution in Wales are described elsewhere (Jones and Balsom, 2000; Morgan and Mungham, 2000) and our interest is in the arrangements and relationships between the Assembly and wider Welsh society, a society which includes many groups and individuals who were, and perhaps still are, unconvinced of the merits of devolution.

Rereading the key speeches made in both Houses of Parliament by major proponents of devolution in 1997 and 1998 reminds us that devolved government for Wales was predicated upon a number of overlapping themes within the broader aim of greater democratization of government in Wales and the development of a new system of governance. Thus it was very frequently claimed that devolved government would be judged by its ability to bring about more accessibility, representativeness, legitimacy, openness, participation, innovation, inclusiveness and accountability. These themes can also be found in the White Paper *A Voice for Wales* (Welsh Office, 1997). They were prominent in the recommendations the National Assembly Advisory Group (1998b) made to government, and they were given legal expression in the Government of Wales Act of 1998. They are not simply part of the formal and rhetorical enunciations of policy and politicians, intellectuals and other opinion-formers but also embody broadly held assumptions about the essential character and benefits of devolved government. The frequency with which these terms crop up in pre-devolution speeches and later policy documents is of course no predictor of their post-devolution appearance as real effects of new governance. Nor was their pre-devolution utterance ever accompanied by a systematic attempt to unpack what these desirable ideas might mean in practice or a forecast of the tangible benefits they might bring.

In Wales, devolution has frequently been cast as a process and not an event. This may help to explain why its advocates have often relied on the persuasive virtue of such ideas, especially when they have been invoked to create a sense of embarkation on a worthy adventure. The virtues of accessibility, representativeness, legitimacy, openness, participation, innovation, inclusiveness and accountability have been used to dissuade us from the more pessimistic view that devolution was an ill-considered journey with few if any clear bearings and no notion of a final destination or arrival time. It is time to give these familiar themes of devolution a more critical airing within the context of recent empirical research. Each of the research teams whose work is reported in this volume has therefore considered the significance of their findings for one or more of these key themes. We shall introduce our contributors and their topics shortly but first we must make some brief commentary on the antecedents to devolution in Wales. Given the complicated history of devolution, we cannot help but oversimplify, and we are conscious that we have not been able to discuss the role of many of the individuals who made key contributions to the devolution process. Whatever part our readers played in this history, we hope they will forgive our rough guide to devolution and enjoy the chapters that follow and that speak to the practice of self-government in Wales. This, after all, is what the long-drawn struggle for governance was all about – or was not, depending upon how one views the findings contained in this first book on the early days of the National Assembly for Wales.

THE BACKGROUND

The establishment of the National Assembly in May 1999 was a historic achievement in that it gave Wales its own executive forum for the first time in six centuries; in effect devolution means 'the application of an all-Wales viewpoint at the point of decision-making for the first time in modern history' (K. O. Morgan, 1999: 212). The movement to establish the Assembly that gathered pace after the 1987 general election has been linked to the common democratic concerns of a strengthened regionalism across Europe and beyond (G. A. Williams, 1988). This is a process whereby, according to some, 'Europe may help to strengthen the national factor' in Wales (Nagel, 1999: 20). At home, UK devolution is an achievement of which some leading figures in New Labour, the governing party that 'delivered' devolution, are proud. Others, mindful of the sometimes bitter and divisive history of earlier attempts to achieve measures of self-government, have called the establishment of the Assembly 'little short of a miracle . . . a triumph of hope over fear' (Morgan and Mungham, 2000: 195).

Since the rekindling of wider national consciousness in the nineteenth century, successive attempts to achieve varying measures of 'self-govern-ment' have had a common outcome in repeatedly exposing divisions in Welsh society. Balsom's 'three Wales model' containing an industrial heartland in the south (Welsh Wales), a linguistic heartland in the west and north (*Y Fro Gymraeg*) and an eastern, more Anglicized border (British Wales) grasps one aspect of these divisions. The relevance of the model seemed to be confirmed in the 1997 devolution referendum vote when British Wales voted 'No', but the underlying realities were more complex. There had been a swing of 15 per cent in favour of devolution between the 1979 and 1997 referenda, and this swing was highest in those areas where support for devolution had been lowest in 1979. Since these areas were amongst the most populous in Wales, there had clearly been a significant shift in opinion, and it is clear that the divisions over devolution can be oversimplified and perhaps overstated (Balsom, 2000b: 159).

All the same, devolution was achieved with an extremely slender popular mandate and, as Wyn Jones and Trystan (1999a: 90) observe, the principal challenge of devolved government will be

> to generate a sense of legitimacy for the National Assembly which is non-partisan and extends to all those who live in Wales. The success or failure of this task seems to largely depend on the ability of those involved in the devolution process to turn the rhetoric of inclusivity that has characterized Welsh politics since the 1997 general election into reality.

Success will therefore depend upon the Assembly developing new and effective structures of governance that engage with all sections of civil society in Wales. This is a development that provides a natural experiment against which many contemporary academic interests can be investigated. At a fundamental level such inquiry is focused upon the nature of democratic representation, participation and power relations that link groups in civil society with decision-making and resource allocation. In Wales we now have a system of governance that aims to revitalize democracy and engage with civil society, and which, as the government's own proposals stated, will liberate energies, spread economic prosperity and improve the quality of life (Welsh Office, 1997: 10).

The case for devolution of (limited) government to Wales and Scotland and Northern Ireland in 1999 was also born of a fundamental crisis of the British state with its tendency to exclusive party government and control of a highly centralized state with few checks on the executive (Hirst and Barnett, 1993: 6). In Wales, such factors came into sharp focus in the late 1980s with the prospect of another term of Conservative government. The Conservatives' share of the vote had fallen consistently from 32.2 per cent in 1979, and 31 per cent in 1983, to 29.5 per cent in 1987 (and after the Labour win in 1997 fell to less than 20 per cent). The centralization of political power in the UK and the growth of the quango state in Wales throughout the 1980s resulted in devolution creeping back onto the political agenda (K. Morgan and Roberts, 1993; Ridley and Wilson, 1995; Gay, 1996). By 1992, with a fourth successive general election win for a Tory Party which failed to win a significant share of the vote in Wales, Labour policy for devolution began to take shape and gather momentum. It built on a growing sense of grievance across Wales (and particularly the industrialized south-east) that the interests of Wales were not recognized by the government, whose mandate, based on votes cast in England, was surely questionable. This was not a shift by Labour towards a nationalist agenda that would steal Plaid Cymru's colours (Plaid's vote remained below 10 per cent during eighteen years of Tory government, Jones, 2000a: 26). Rather, Labour's approach to devolution drew upon a growing concern in local government and industry about the multiple problems faced by a Welsh economy and civil society for which no remedy seemed forthcoming from a Conservative administration in London.

Pressure groups such as the Campaign for a Welsh Assembly (CWA) and the Parliament for Wales Campaign (PWC) made their mark on the long road to devolution. Speaking at the launch of the CWA the late Professor Gwyn Alf Williams described the purpose of the organization as to 'give history a shove' (G. A. Williams 1988: 5). The PWC's subsequent 1994 Democracy Declaration called for a Welsh parliament to place emphasis on economic regeneration, the participation of women and minority groups, the democratic control of Welsh Office functions, quangos and public appointments, 'conformity with the general principle of subsidiarity' and a responsibility to express cultural diversity (Parliament for Wales Campaign, 1994). The first strategy paper of the newly established cross-party Campaign for a Welsh Assembly referred to

> a groundswell of feeling that there is need for urgent debate about the nature of our democracy when Wales is ruled by a government supported by a minority of the Welsh electorate. Concern has been amplified by what has been happening to local government during the 1980s – the only tier of government where a majority view has had an opportunity of expressing itself. (CWA, 1988: 1)

Although the Campaign singled out for attack the Conservative government's economic policies in Wales, the quango state was also seen as lying at the heart of the problem. However, such ambitions over devolution were not always received with full approval amongst all those who opposed the Conservative government. Within the Wales Labour Party (WLP) there had been enduring tensions since the period in the 1950s when co-operation with devolution campaigners was rejected because the leadership felt that 'any kind of devolution required in Wales can be discussed within the confines of the Labour movement' (Prothero, 1982 cited in R. Davies, 1999a: 6). Davies observes that the tradition within the WLP 'to close down debate' was something 'ingrained into the Party's mindset . . . "inclusiveness" was a direct challenge to that instinct' (1999a: 7). So ingrained in fact that history had repeated itself in the 1990s when the WLP Executive 'tried repeatedly to strangle the CWA and prohibit party members from having anything to do with such dangerous liaisons' (K. Morgan and Mungham, 2000: 88).

In May 1990 the WLP conference discussed the results of a protracted three-year consultation exercise that called for the creation of an all-Wales elected body as part of local government reorganization. Such a notion was conspicuously absent from the proposals for local government reorganization in Wales made in the Conservative government's Green Paper (Great Britain, 1991) in July of the following year. The ensuing debate in the House of Commons provided an opportunity for the airing of arguments that would continue throughout the decade. Plaid Cymru, the Liberal Democrats and Labour all called for greater accountability and democratic control of those functions carried out by the Welsh Office. The Conservative government responded that an Assembly would undermine the unitary state and result in the loss of a voice for Wales in the Cabinet, and would adversely effect Wales's position within the United Kingdom.

The 1992 *Conservative Party Manifesto for Wales* set out the basis on which the Tories successfully contested the general election. It defended the status quo and existing levels of accountability: 'Wales should have a strong voice at the Cabinet table. Hence the importance of the office of Secretary of State. The Secretary of State is ultimately accountable for Welsh Office expenditure to Parliament' (Conservative Central Office for Wales, 1992: 8). In response, Labour restated a strengthening belief in devolution in *Opportunity Wales* (Wales Labour Party, 1992: 3), asserting that 'Labour believes that power must be decentralised from Whitehall to local communities in order to create a system of government that is both efficient and responsive to their needs. We will therefore establish a directly elected Welsh Assembly.'

This was an argument that the shadow secretary of state, Ron Davies, advanced with reference to economic development within a wider European framework. According to Davies, the promotion of regional strategies over jobs, industries and regeneration underlined the need for a modern democratic Wales with its own elected parliament (R. Davies, 1992). The WLP's election manifesto promised that a Labour government would establish 'in the lifetime of a full Parliament, an elected Assembly in Cardiff with powers and functions which reflect the existing admin-istrative structure' (1993: 3). This commitment to devolution was boosted by the new Labour Party leader, John Smith, who charged Ron Davies with the task of implementing devolution proposals.

Tony Blair honoured this commitment after the death of John Smith and was faced with the challenge of 'fitting' devolution into the 'New Labour project', or what became known as the 'Third Way'. This was an ambitious scheme that promised

> reforms [that] . . . will transform our politics. They will re-draw the boundaries between what is done in the name of the people and what is done by the people themselves. They will create a new relationship between government and the people, based on trust, freedom, choice and responsibility . . . they are

concerned with the essence of our democracy and how people can exercise power in our society. (Blair, 1996)

In one respect the task of integrating devolution into this plan was easy, since the Third Way programme already made claims for the benefits of decentralization (see Blair, 1998: 7). However, the programme made no mention of devolution to nations within the UK, and this has been rationalized *post hoc* in a number of different ways. For example, devolution has been advanced as a mechanism to protect 'minority rights' within the UK political system; thus Prime Minister Blair (2000a) observed:

> The measures needed to protect a minority are not always the same as the measures needed to protect a majority. England can if it chooses outvote Scotland, Ireland and Wales at any point. English MPs are in an overwhelming majority in voting through the money for Wales and Scotland. It is the recognition of this that makes devolution a fairer settlement for the future.

As chief exponent of the Third Way, Tony Blair has also presented devolution in terms of national partnerships and pluralism:

> devolution at long last offered a sensible modernisation of the partnership in the UK. Let Scotland and Wales do what they do best locally. Let the UK do what it is right to do together . . . this government's progressive programme of constitutional reform is now moving us from a centralised Britain, where power flowed top-down, to a devolved and plural state. (Blair, 2000a)

Similarly, the (Labour) Welsh Office minister Peter Hain advanced the case that an 'inheritance unmistakably rooted in decentralised libertarian socialist community values of solidarity, social justice and cooperation, points to a Welsh Third Way' (Hain, 1999: 6). Devolution, he argued, is the latest strand of this tradition. Through debate and policy initiatives a devolved Welsh polity could reinform and 'reinvigorate' Blair's Third Way. Hain's argument contains a national dimension that Blair's does not:

> the [pre-devolution] old British state – quintessentially centralised, elitist, secretive – is being dismantled. It was not so much a British as an English state, defined above all by hostility to regional or local autonomy. Devolution is absolutely fundamental to its transformation. Wales's National Assembly, Scotland's Parliament and Northern Ireland's Assembly allow Britain to be reconstituted into a modern pluralistic state, with diversity and decentralisation celebrated not suppressed. (Hain, 1999: 20)

The debate in the Wales Labour Party led to action in establishing a Policy Commission (Wales Labour Party, 1993) and publishing an Interim Consultative Report (Wales Labour Party, 1994). In response, the Conservative leader and Prime Minister, John Major, repeatedly attacked devolution proposals on a number of grounds. It was argued that an Assembly would result in higher taxes, and that inward investment would be lost, businesses would move away, local government would have power syphoned off by this extra tier of government, and there would be disunity and the break-up of the UK.[1]

The report *Preparing for a New Wales* presented to the 1996 Wales Labour Party Conference provided the most detailed exposition of the prevailing Labour vision of devolution. This time the pro-devolution argument was founded upon three aims: 'to introduce democratic accountability to the existing decision-making structures; to ensure proper financial control and efficient distribution of government spending in Wales; and, to assist the people of Wales in developing a competitive and prosperous economy' (Wales Labour Party, 1996: 14).

At this critical juncture, with a looming general election when constitutional reform would be a key issue, Ron Davies argued:

> The case for a Welsh assembly is as much about economic renewal as it is about political renewal. Constitutional reform is not about being diverted down a philosophical cul-de-sac; an elected Assembly is about daily realities, most crucially raising economic prosperity. An Assembly will only succeed if it can deliver a better quality of life and higher living standards. (1996: 6)

New Labour's general election victory of May 1997 saw swift action with the publication of its Referendum Bill after just over a fortnight in office. The White Paper *A Voice for Wales* (Welsh Office, 1997) identified priority areas where the core themes of the devolution were to be applied. Tackling the low-growth sectors of the Welsh economy and raising the Welsh per capita GDP to the UK average by making the best use of European structural funds were to be foremost amongst the Assembly's challenges (Bryan and Jones, 2000). The government's devolution proposals declared the aim of establishing 'a new economic powerhouse' where 'the business community at all levels will have easier access to key decision-makers who will be responsible for shaping the economic framework in Wales'. There was to be a revised form of governance in an environment where success would be dependent upon achieving 'a more highly skilled and internationally competitive workforce', which in turn was linked to the need for 'high quality vocational training . . . Wales needs to upgrade the skills of its people if it is to seize the opportunities created by its success in attracting inward investment' (Welsh Office, 1997: 11–13). The proposals concluded that 'the present economic development effort is hampered by the existence of a multiplicity of national and local agencies, with overlapping responsibilities, that are a source of confusion, inefficiency and unnecessary administrative costs. Reform is long overdue.' In setting itself such a task there was an awareness that 'the Assembly will need to be sensitive in discharging its regulatory role' (ibid.: 12–14).

Amongst a number of proposed new partnership arrangements, the Assembly was to 'harness the special contribution which voluntary organisations can make in a wide range of policy areas'. New legal arrangements would ensure that 'the Assembly will be bound by this commitment' (ibid.: 19), whilst at the same time it would take over the funding arrangements extended to the third sector by the Welsh Office. The White Paper also explained how, by establishing the Assembly,

> the Government is committed to establishing a new, more inclusive and participative democracy in Britain . . . in particular, the Government attaches great importance to equal opportunities for all – including women, members of the ethnic minorities and disabled people. It believes that greater participation by women is essential to the health of our democracy. (ibid.: 15–24)

Devolution was viewed by some as 'an unprecedented opportunity to create a new style of politics in Wales' (Prys Jones, 1997: 3), and the move towards democratic renewal also impacted upon internal party structures in Wales. For example, Labour, the Liberal Democrats and Plaid Cymru all paid some attention to the gender balance amongst their candidates and the need for wider participation by members in selection of Assembly candidates, but not without some tensions with the central leadership across these parties (see Bradbury, Bennie, Denver and Mitchell, 2000: 179).

There is no doubt that the low turnouts for both the referendum of 18 September 1997 and the Assembly elections of 6 May 1999 (51.3 per cent and 46.3 per cent respectively), together with the slender majority (6,721 votes) that delivered devolution, presented the devolved body with a daunting task of establishing its popular legitimacy. There had been some concern that Welsh press and TV reporting of devolution, for example during the 1997 referendum, displayed less than enthusiastic interest in all but the more racy aspects of political electioneering and personalities (see K. Williams, 2000; Bellin, 2000). Moreover, 35 per cent of the population in Wales can receive English network TV stations, and many resort to these networks for news (most people get their news from TV, Bellin, 2000). Thus a significant minority of viewers were unlikely to have seen coverage of Welsh political affairs on their televisions. All the same, lack of media interest cannot explain why around three-quarters of the electorate did not vote for the establishment of the Assembly, and half the electorate did not vote in the first Welsh general election. Such facts raise particular problems that cannot be attributed to the late start and setbacks that characterized the sometimes lacklustre referendum campaign (Andrews, 1999). These are also facts that are uncomfortably at odds with both the White Paper's assertion that 'it is to address [the pre-existing] . . . democratic deficit that the Government is now proposing to set up an Assembly for Wales' (Welsh Office, 1997: 7) and the Prime Minister's claim for 'a renewed democracy engaging and inspiring its citizens' (Blair, 2000b). We might agree with Balsom (2000b) that for many voters the elections for an Assembly were perceived as not being a first-order political event such as Westminster elections. Clearly, the new executive has begun life with a limited endorsement by, and engagement with, its citizenry. It has four years to deliver enough change to prove itself an important national institution worthy of attention and support.

BUILDING A NEW DEMOCRACY

The first days of devolution in Wales were marred by Labour's damaging leadership battles between Rhodri Morgan and Ron Davies, and subsequently between Alun Michael and Rhodri Morgan. Nor was the spectacle of arm-wrestling between Labour chiefs in Wales over the cost and location of the new Assembly particularly edifying. Leadership battles are, for the moment at least, settled. The location of the Assembly in Cardiff Bay now also seems to be a settled matter. These early travails have passed, and it is the routine of governance itself that should now receive attention. Reflecting upon the Assembly's achievements in its first eighteen months, Val Feld, the chair of the Assembly's Economic Development Committee, observed that 'it took a thousand years to make the British Parliament, still with many faults but respected throughout the world'. We have already noted that two years is too short a time over which to judge the new Assembly. It certainly deserves time in which to prove itself, but, as K. Morgan (1999a) asserts, this is no reason for us to suspend our critical faculties altogether: '[t]he early days of an institution are the most important, not least because they set the standards for the future' (ibid.). How then might one characterize the Assembly's early days?

Operationalizing the structures and mechanisms of the new Assembly which were intended to facilitate a more inclusive, consensual style of politics in Wales, has proved to be a challenging task; not least for the civil service, which has had to respond to the pressures of a dramatically increased workload and the tensions associated with serving both an executive and a 'body corporate' (see Osmond, 1999b; 2000a; 2000b).[2] In the face of these difficulties, the Assembly has given some ground to a more 'traditional', parliamentary arrangement – for example, in measures taken to create a more independent office of the Presiding Officer (see National Assembly for Wales Review Secretariat, 2000/2001). The minority position of the first Labour administration has also presented practical challenges,[3] and these have not proved to be the spur to inclusivity that some hoped they might. The coalition agreement reached between Labour and the Liberal Democrats in October 2000 may have established a workable platform of support for advancing the policy agenda, but it can also be read as 'a failure of inclusivity' (Balsom, 2000a: 35), a return to a familiar, adversarial politics, with Plaid Cymru now designating itself as the 'official opposition'.

Set against these developments, there are significant aspects of the legislature that nevertheless signal a break with the past and offer the basis for a new mode of governance in Wales. This transition to greater accountability and inclusiveness is reflected both in the Assembly's legal duties and in the pronouncements of key politicians. Thus democratic innovation in law is typified by the Assembly's duty (cf. Government of Wales Act 1998, section 107) not to act in a way incompatible with the European Convention on Human Rights, whilst elsewhere the First Minister has called for a written constitution (Betts, 2000b).

The Assembly has undoubtedly enjoyed some success in pursuing public openness and accessibility: the majority of the Assembly's proceedings are televised, the Assembly website has provided a tool for both dissemination and consultation, and the publication of Cabinet minutes has been a notable step. There are also signs of a growing willingness and capacity on the part of elements in Welsh civil society to engage with the new system of governance. A proliferation of materials is sent routinely to AMs by diverse interest groups in Wales and there has been considerable consultation and dialogue between the Assembly and sectoral organizations. If we are to view peaceful demonstrations as an indicator of democratic health then it can be noted there has been an increasing number of these outside the Assembly building over recent months. However, wider gauges of public opinion present a more mixed picture, indicating some frustration at the rate of progress made towards a new system of governance that will actually make a difference to people's lives. Under half the respondents in a recent poll believed that the Assembly had actually achieved anything in its first year (ICM/*Scotsman*, 2000). In this sense the impact of the Assembly has been limited. The Presiding Officer has defended the legislature against such 'easy criticisms' (Elis Thomas, 2000) by citing the fifty-six Assembly resolutions passed in its first year (see NAW, 2000i). Of course, given the Assembly's limited powers, the legislature's scope for innovation is restricted. As a result, unfavourable comparisons with the Scottish Parliament have sometimes been hard to avoid, thereby damaging further its public approval rating (see Hornung, 2001). As in Scotland, it also remains to be seen just how effective the new majority administration/coalition will be,[4] both in terms of policy outcomes and in the style of politics on offer.

It would nevertheless be wrong to ascribe complacency to the new Assembly. In July 2000 the First Minister, Rhodri Morgan, announced a review of how the Assembly has operated in its first year, and an Assembly Review Group will now present its report in autumn 2001. The group first convened in December 2000, and its remit and principles were agreed whereby it will focus upon the workings of the Assembly rather than matters of policy. It will invite perspectives from inside and outside the Assembly and will make recommendations that the Assembly is capable of delivering and which do not require changes to the Government of Wales Act 1998 or other legislation beyond the competency of the Assembly to change (NAW Review Secretariat, 2000/2001). The Review Group appears to be a weighty and influential political body in that its members comprise the First Minister, party leaders and their business managers, the Presiding Officer and Deputy Presiding Officer. Possible issues for comment include the Cabinet and its relations with the rest of the Assembly; the purpose, content and outcome of plenary debates; the role and operation of subject committees, regional committees and standing committees. Importantly, the remit includes a review of relations outside the Assembly, notably with business, local government and voluntary sectors in Wales. Assembly relations with Westminster, UK government, European Union and other national and regional governments are also issues for consideration.

The review stems in part from criticism that Assembly deliberations, and plenary debates in particular, sometimes lack focus and have no obvious outcome other than an expression of opinion. Behind this lack of focus there seems to be uncertainty over what are appropriate matters for discussion and the appropriate place for these discussions. Thus the Review Group will look at the function of the plenary sessions to set direction of policy, to approve the budget and subordinate legislation, and to deliberate on matters of relevance to Wales. The latter point is perhaps where much of the difficulty lies, for a key issue is whether the Assembly should spend valuable time on matters over which it has no devolved authority but which may none the less affect the country. Is there, for example, any merit in passing resolutions that cannot be actioned or have any useful impact? In examining these questions the Review Group will also be concerned to ensure that, where action can be taken, systems for reporting progress to the Assembly are effective and, more generally, that the work of committees is properly overseen and published. Judging the appropriate balance of business time allocated to subject committee work and to plenary sessions, where full debate can be very time-consuming, will also tax the Review Group. In brief, Assembly workings with regard to key relationships, legitimate interest, accountability and business management will define much of the Review Group's focus. While there may be much to adjust and enhance in the way the Assembly operates, the fact that it has quickly and publicly undertaken this level of self-scrutiny is encouraging and would appear to be in tune with the ideals of democratic openness and renewal.

AN OVERVIEW

In achieving its democratic potential this evolving new layer of governance will doubtless require further change – a point well noted by the First Minister who declared that 'it will be perfectly natural for the National Assembly to grow in status and authority with the full hearted support and consent of the people of Wales' (R. Morgan, 2000a). Wales is at the beginning of a new history, marked by the arrival of an Assembly with procedures and structures that will have to cope as best they can with the priorities and issues of the day. It is too early to say whether the many (and competing) ambitions for this new executive look like being realized. However, we can offer some valuable insights into the impact of the Assembly on life in Wales from studies undertaken in the universities of Cardiff, Aberystwyth and Bangor (all of which presently remain constituent institutions of the federal University of Wales). Most of this research was funded by the UK's Economic and Social Research Council (ESRC). Indeed, three of the studies reported here were funded as part of the same ESRC programme, which was specifically intended to fund social scientific research on the first months of the devolution experiment. In addition, the study reported in chapters 3 and 4 was funded by the University of Wales itself through the university's Board of Celtic Studies.

Each chapter that follows is based upon one of these studies and sets out a specific problematic in respect of new governance in Wales. Each chapter addresses this problematic in the context of research findings that in turn connect with wider contemporary economic, social or political debates. In chapter 2, Wyn Jones and Trystan use data from the 1999 Welsh Assembly

Election Survey to explore aspects of participation, legitimation and public knowledge and awareness in relation to the first elections to the National Assembly. A central element of the Labour Party's justification for its devolution policy was that it would create a more legitimate form of government in Wales, thus remedying some of the perceived problems created by the so-called 'democratic deficit' of the Thatcher and Major years. However, the relatively low turnouts at the 1997 referendum and first Assembly elections – and, of course, the wafer-thin 'Yes' majority in the former – have all called the public legitimacy of the new structures of governance into serious question. The chapter considers participation in these key elections in relation to various social and geographical cleavages, and asks searching questions about the likelihood of an informed citizenry playing a full part in a more participative democracy.

Chapters 3 and 4 explore notions of 'inclusive' government for tradition-ally excluded groups. Chapter 3 by Betts, Borland and Chaney draws upon extensive interview data to address the central question of whether the Assembly has begun to produce new gender and disability settlements which more adequately meet women's and disabled people's needs and facilitate their engagement in the democratic process. In answering this question the authors explore women's and disabled people's expectations of the Assembly, their experience of the May 1999 elections, and the way in which gender and disability issues have been dealt with by the fledgeling government body during its first months.

In chapter 4, Williams and Chaney examine the expectations that people from an ethnic minority background in Wales held of the recent historical changes. Taking the debates and discussions leading up to the National Assembly elections as a starting-point, the chapter explores the structures and examines the early actions of the devolved institution. Williams and Chaney discuss what the discourse of inclusiveness means for people from an ethnic minority in Wales and explore how this concept relates to issues of identity and notions of a participative democracy.

In Chapter 5, Dicks, Hall and Pithouse examine the evolving relationship between the National Assembly and the voluntary sector in Wales, and question whether recent changes represent a democratization of relations through inclusive governance. The Assembly aims to draw on the institu-tions and energies of civil society in order to broaden and revitalize demo-cracy in Wales. It is for this reason that the voluntary sector – typifying civil society and linked with attendant values of democracy, equity and inclusiveness – figures prominently in the Assembly's ambitions for inclusive government. The chapter focuses on those negotiations leading to the establishment of the required Voluntary Sector Scheme, which sets out how the Assembly proposes to provide assistance to and consult with the voluntary sector. The chapter draws on wide-ranging interviews with politicians, Assembly officers and voluntary-sector staff to trace the expectations and experiences of those directly involved in developing new consultative structures. Data from a telephone survey of voluntary agencies across Wales also reveal different responses (and capacities to respond) to these new consultative mechanisms, and suggest that participation by the voluntary sector in these mechanisms is much more problematic than is allowed for in public pronouncements.

In chapter 6, Morgan and Rees examine the implications of devolution for the governance of economic development. The former Welsh Office and its associated bodies, in particular the Welsh Development Agency, facilitated economic development policies in Wales that operated in a more regionally decentralized manner than similar policy-making and policy action in English regions. The chapter begins by outlining the regime prior to devolution and then draws on theoretical debates concerning the nature of the 'regional state' and emergent forms of regional governance along 'post-Fordist' or 'associationist' lines. Against this conceptual background the authors analyse a series of interviews with key respondents undertaken immediately before and after the establishment of the Assembly. Findings from these expert sources find comparison with key debates in the Assembly, and an account of the early impact of the Assembly on the governance of economic development is developed.

Chapter 7 by Ashworth, Boyne and Walker examines the political control of public agencies in Wales within the overall context of devolution and regulation. A major purpose of devolution was to bridge the 'accountability gap' in Wales by giving Assembly members power to regulate a range of public bodies. The chapter raises a number of important issues concerning regulatory practice, and notes that the Assembly will inherit established policy networks and patterns of working which include strategic planning, financial resource allocation, policy evaluation and review. This research draws on theoretical perspectives of regulation in the public sector to generate an analysis that anticipates possible challenges for the Assembly in the establishment of new regulatory channels. The operation of pre-Assembly channels and mechanisms is investigated through a number of case studies. These comprise public bodies such as the Welsh Development Agency and the Higher Education Funding Council for Wales, local government services such as housing departments, direct-service organizations, social services and providers such as housing associations. Analysis of secondary sources and interviews with civil servants, politicians and regulators allows tentative conclusions to be drawn about the impact of a devolved framework on the regulation of public bodies.

In the conclusion (chapter 8) to this volume the editors offer a brief overview of emerging issues highlighted by the five research studies in the context of the core themes that formed the basis of the devolution argument. This is done with the object of stimulating discussion and debate about the prospects of devolution in Wales achieving some of those worthy, but often vaguely specified, aims of accessibility, represent-ativeness, legitimacy, openness, participation, innovation, (better) regula-tion, inclusiveness and accountability. Such considerations inevitably lead to thoughts about the research agenda for further studies. The editors close by offering some suggestions for further research and by raising some important conceptual and analytical issues which arise in relation to our understanding of devolution and the prospects for new governance and new democracy in Wales.

Notes

[1] Hansard, column 1180, prime minister's questions, 2 March 1995.

[2] This led to some controversy with some subject committees, and, most prominently, the Presiding Officer searching out 'independent' legal advice (Betts, 2000a).

[3] James and Mathias (1999: 32) observe that the poor showing of the WLP in the Assembly elections heightened the need for a 'new politics': 'if Labour had secured an overall majority of seats, they could have dominated th[e] con-sultative process. In that sense, the much vaunted inclusivity and consensual politics would have been optional for the governing party. Now that Labour is in a minority, it is not optional but essential if they are going to get their business through the Assembly.'

[4] It may be that the limited scope of the devolution settlement in Wales, and concomitant difficulties in defining the Assembly's legal powers, will continue to hamper the Assembly's effectiveness (see Rawlings, 1998; 2000).

2

Turnout, Participation and Legitimacy in the Politics of Post-devolution Wales

RICHARD WYN JONES and DAFYDD TRYSTAN

Observers might be forgiven for concluding that, since the summer of 1997, the Welsh electorate has developed a taste for confounding expectations and undermining received wisdom. Both the devolution referendum on 18 September 1997 and the first election to the National Assembly on 6 May 1999 produced political theatre of a high order which left the whole political class in Wales, and many at the UK level too, struggling to make sense of the electorate's views. The wafer-thin pro-devolution majority in the referendum has now been subject to much debate and considerable academic scrutiny (for the latter see, *inter alia*, McAllister, 1998; Wyn Jones and Lewis, 1998; 1999; Evans and Trystan, 1999; Wyn Jones, Trystan and Taylor, 2000). The legacy of the National Assembly election, characterized as it was by a slump in support for Labour and a concomitant, and unprecedented, surge of support for Plaid Cymru, has been all too apparent in the new body's first term. It is arguable that the credibility of Labour's first First Secretary, Alun Michael, already weakened by the circumstances surrounding his selection as Labour's prospective leader in the Assembly, was fatally undermined by the humiliating defeats in the totemic constituencies such as Rhondda, Islwyn and Llanelli (for varying 'internal' accounts of Labour's difficulties see Flynn, 1999; Morgan and Mungham, 2000; Wales Labour Party, 2000). This, coupled with his party's lack of preparedness for the eventuality of being left without an overall majority in the Assembly, meant that Michael's period at the helm was characterized by drift and fragmentation. Rhodri Morgan's subsequent elevation to the post of First Secretary – since October 2000, First Minister – has also been marked by an attempt to regain lost territory. The rebranding of the Wales Labour Party as 'the true party of Wales', and this in the party's centenary year, undoubtedly signalled the continuing reverberations of the Assembly election result – and, of course, represented a remarkable backhanded tribute to the success of Plaid Cymru.

Table 2.1 Results of the 1997 UK general election in Wales and the 1999 National Assembly for Wales election

	General election 1997	%	National Assembly (constituency) 1999	%	National Assembly (regions) 1999	%
Labour	886,935	54.7	384,671	37.6	361,657	35.4
Plaid Cymru	161,030	9.9	290,565	28.4	312,048	30.5
Conservative	317,127	19.6	162,133	15.8	168,206	16.5
Liberal Democrats	200,020	12.3	137,657	13.5	128,008	12.5
Others	54,932	3.4	47,992	4.7	51,837	5.1
Electorate	2,190,722		2,227,336		2,227,336	
Turnout	1,620,044	73.9	1,023,018	45.9	1,021,756	45.9

The drama of the results of the referendum and National Assembly election has, however, tended to overshadow another, and equally significant, aspect of both polls, namely the relatively low voter turnout. As we have noted elsewhere, both sides of the referendum campaign framed the argument in 'make or break' terms (Wyn Jones and Trystan 1999b: 65–6). The result, it was claimed, would be crucial to the future of Wales, as well as the UK as a whole. Yet, despite this, turnout was modest. Similarly, the first National Assembly election, although highlighted in the Welsh Office's publicity material as 'the Welsh general election', was also characterized by relatively low turnout. Unsurprisingly, these low turnouts, taken in conjunction with the grudging referendum majority, have served to cast doubt on the very legitimacy of the devolved body itself. We can confidently surmise that these doubts would have been even more pronounced if the results themselves had not proved to be so striking.

This chapter will explore the validity of these doubts by examining the relationship between the relatively low level of public participation in the National Assembly election – at least as measured by turnout – and the legitimacy of the National Assembly itself. Utilizing data from the Welsh National Assembly Election Survey, the chapter will seek to ascertain the extent to which non-participation in the election

- reflected hostility towards devolution *per se*, or
- was a function of a more general and generalized alienation from the political process.

We will proceed via some initial conceptual ground-clearing and contextualization to a detailed examination of the quantitative data. Following on from this we will consider the likelihood of improved turnout in future Assembly elections, and what practical steps might be taken to achieve this. The chapter concludes with some general remarks about the inter-relationship between participation and legitimacy in the politics of post-devolution Wales.

Table 2.2 Turnout in devolution-related polls in Wales

1997 Welsh Devolution Referendum	50.3%
1999 National Assembly for Wales Elections	45.9%

ON TURNOUT, PARTICIPATION AND LEGITIMACY

First we must address the question of why it is that relatively low turnout in the Assembly elections is widely perceived as calling into question the very legitimacy of the devolved body. There are, after all, political systems that function on the basis of relatively low turnouts without their legitim-acy being challenged in any significant way. While many international critics may cast aspersions on the United States' political system because of the relatively low election turnout, and especially so after the débâcle of the 2000 presidential election, few could seriously doubt that the system enjoys widespread legitimacy (for an interesting recent exchange see Lazare, 1998; 1999; Lind 1999). Closer to home, turnout in local council elections is typically modest. Nevertheless, although there are complaints about this or that aspect of the functioning of local authorities, it is rare indeed for the fundamental legitimacy of local government to be called into question. There does not seem therefore to be a simple correspondence between turnout and legitimacy.

Moreover, it is important to note that there are significant differences at the level of theory as well. That is, there are fundamental differences between theorists about the relative importance and desirability of the various possible forms of political participation in a democratic system, including voting. This in turn reflects different attitudes to the relationship between participation and legitimacy. It is beyond the scope of this chapter to explore these theoretical disputes in detail, but it is important to under-line that at least two broad attitudes towards participation can be identified in contemporary democratic theory. Following Carole Pateman's now classic study *Participation and Democratic Theory* (1970), we can differentiate between the attitudes of proponents of representative government and those of the champions of participatory democracy. For the former, popular participation, while necessary, should be limited in scope; the latter, in contrast, advocate the broadest possible popular participation in the life of the polity.

Theorists of representative government view participation in rather narrow, instrumentalist terms. Pateman summarizes the case from this perspective:

> 'democracy' refers to a political method or set of institutional arrangements. The characteristically democratic element in the method is the competition of leaders (élites) for the votes of the people at periodic, free elections. Elections are crucial to the democratic method for it is primarily through elections that the majority can exercise control over their leaders . . . through the sanction of loss of office . . . [T]he function of participation in the theory is solely a protective one; the protection of the individual from arbitrary decisions by elected leaders and the protection of his private interests. It is in the achievement of this aim that the justification for the democratic method lies. (1970: 14)

There are of course variants of this viewpoint, with important differences between them. Advocates of rather limited popular participation can be found not only among classical liberal theorists, such as Jeremy Bentham and James Mill, and such giants of post-Second World War political science as Joseph Schumpeter and Robert Dahl, but also among left-leaning thinkers associated with the Frankfurt School such as Otto Kirchheimer and Franz Neumann (on the first two groups see Pateman, 1970; for the latter see Scheuerman, 1994). But while there may be very different reasons underpinning their distrust – ranging from fear of expropriation of property owners on the one hand, to fear of the potential of fascist dema-goguery on the other – the fact remains that, for all, popular participation in the political system is to be limited in both its role and scope.

For theorists of representative government, therefore, there is no particular intrinsic merit associated with securing high turnouts at elections. All that is necessary is for the turnout to reach 'the minimum necessary to keep the democratic method (electoral machinery) working' (Pateman, 1970: 14). The success or otherwise of the system itself is to be judged on policy outputs rather than on the grounds of popular inputs via participation. Legitimacy is similarly closely linked with the stability and efficacy of the system.

For advocates of participatory democracy, in contrast, ensuring wide participation is viewed as an end itself. Indeed, they regard a system in which participation is limited to the placing of a cross on a ballot paper every few years as representing a pretty hollow version of democracy. Rousseau was characteristically caustic in his dismissal of those who equate the occasional election of representatives to constituent assemblies with a free society. Commenting on the United Kingdom, then considered by many continental radicals as a paragon of good government, he charged that 'The English [*sic*] people believes itself to be free; it is gravely mistaken; it is free only during the election of Members of Parliament; as soon as the Members are elected, the people are enslaved; it is nothing' (Rousseau, 1968: 141). But even J. S. Mill, a less rebarbative classical advocate of participatory democracy, was keen to underline the deep limitations of the model of participation characteristic of modern liberal democracies. He argued that 'A political act, to be done only once in a few years, and for which nothing in the daily habits of the citizen has prepared him, leaves his intellect and his moral dispositions very much as it found him' (cited by Pateman, 1970: 30).

Mill's comment serves to underline a key aspect of the participatory-democracy credo. For its advocates, a system based on broad democratic participation is not simply the most effective way of producing good government, although this is certainly claimed as one of its benefits. Rather, it is the means by which human capacities – our 'intellect' and 'moral dispositions' – can be most fully developed. Participation plays a pedagogic role above and beyond any benefits accruing from efficacious decision-making.

As was the case with theorists of representative government, there are also significant differences among proponents of more participative models of democracy. Some of these differences are concerned with the extent of participation. Until recently most advocates of participative democracy, from Rousseau through Mill, to syndicalism and guild socialism, have advocated the extension of participation into the economic realm. Thus, in the Welsh context, the syndicalist *Miners' Next Step* (Unofficial Reform Committee, 1912) famously advocated a strategy of 'encroaching control' that would lead to the establishment of an 'economic commonwealth' (see also Industrial Committee of the South Wales Socialist Society, 1919); Plaid Cymru's D. J. Davies drew up a detailed and ambitious plan for the future trajectory of Welsh society under the title *Towards an Economic Democracy* (1949); while Aneurin Bevan argued that 'industrial democracy is the counterpart of political freedom' (1952: 105). But, more recently, many advocates of enhanced participation have scaled back their vision of what degree of participation is either feasible or desirable (see, for example, Baynes, 2000). So for those thinkers associated with so-called 'deliberative democracy', for example, the focus should be on delimiting more clearly the social realm from that of the economic, so as to ensure that the market mechanisms that are effective in regulating the latter are not allowed to encroach on the former, a realm that is properly susceptible to greater participation (for a critical account of the social theory underpinning these ideas see the discussion of Jürgen Habermas in Wyn Jones, 1999: 53–90).

Another key point of contention is the type of elections found in contemporary liberal democracies. In the past, many of the more radical advocates of participatory democracy have tended to be very hostile towards these manifestations of 'bourgeois democracy' – often with utterly calamitous consequences (Femia, 1993). At best, their attitude has been one of indifference. Other advocates of participatory democracy, especially more contemporary theorists, have, however, adopted a very different view. For them, the election of members to some form of parliament or constituent assembly is viewed as a necessary although not a sufficient condition for a properly democratic society. While in their view there is more to democracy than simply elections, and more to participation than voting, these are the cornerstones of democratic society. So, while democratic participation may well need to be deepened, it is also clearly of tremendous importance that it should be as wide as possible. In this context, ensuring high election turnout comes to be viewed as an end in itself. High turnout is associated with a healthy political system – a system that is not only an effective deliverer for the public good but also enjoys a high degree of public legitimacy.

If there is no consensus at the level of theory about the relationship between turnout and legitimacy, and if practice also suggests that it is unwise to conclude that there is some straightforward correspondence between high turnout and legitimate government, then we clearly need a context-specific explanation of why relatively low turnout in the Assembly elections is so widely perceived – and certainly not only by opponents of devolution – as raising questions of legitimacy.

Clearly the closeness of the referendum vote is an important part of that explanation. By any standards the majority in favour of the government's proposals for a devolved Assembly was narrow – 6,721 votes; 0.6 per cent of the votes cast, or 0.3 per cent of eligible electorate (Wyn Jones and Trystan, 1999b). That result has cast a shadow over the National Assembly and will doubtless continue to do so for a long time to come.

DEVOLUTION AS AN EXERCISE IN PARTICIPATORY DEMOCRACY

The referendum result is not the whole story; rather, relatively low turnout strikes at the very heart of official justification for devolution. The establishment of the National Assembly for Wales has been accompanied by the rhetoric of participatory democracy (in its modern, apparently more sophisticated guise). Seen in this context, the relatively low levels of public involvement in the first elections to the National Assembly, as measured by turnout, are almost inevitably rendered problematic.

Devolution was 'sold' to the Welsh electorate by the Labour Party as a means by which the government of Wales could be made more 'accountable' and more 'inclusive'. Devolution was intended to generate a 'new politics' for Wales as part of a 'modernized' constitutional structure for the UK as a whole. The participative goals of the devolution programme are apparent in Ron Davies's *post hoc* account *Devolution: A Process not an Event*. He argues, for example, that

> It is incumbent on the members of the Assembly . . . to reach beyond the political classes and extend the sense of ownership to the many who currently feel excluded or alienated from the political process . . . The support and involvement of the public at large is vital to the achievement of a new inclusive society in Wales. (R. Davies, 1999a: 15)

In Peter Hain's Tribune pamphlet, *A Welsh Third Way?*, devolution is explicitly associated with the development of 'participatory democracy' (Hain, 1999: *passim* but especially 14–15). So while 'nationalist' concerns with giving institutional expression to national identity certainly formed a subtext to *some* of Labour's pro-devolution rhetoric – they certainly feature in Davies's analysis, and are not entirely absent from Hain's pamphlet – even where present, they played a subsidiary or secondary role to the main argument. The stress is rather on the possibility of ensuring better governance through creating structures that are more inclusive, more transparent, more accessible: in a word, more participative.

This concern with participation has been no mere rhetorical trope. Rather, the desire to facilitate multiple forms of participation has been a key influence in the design and development of the structures and practices of the National Assembly (National Assembly Advisory Group, 1998b; I. B. Rees, 1999). One strand of this concern with participation has involved a conscious attempt to encourage individuals from backgrounds that have not been well represented in Westminster to put themselves forward for election in the Assembly. So, for example, the National Assembly's operating procedures embrace so-called 'family-friendly' working hours, while the timing of recesses coincides with school holidays. Furthermore, three of the four main political parties in Wales made a conscious attempt to attract party members of different social backgrounds to put themselves forward as candidates for election to the Assembly (Bradbury, Bennie, Denver and Mitchell, 2000).

The Assembly's complex committee structure is designed, in part at least, to give ordinary Assembly Members more input into policy-making than is enjoyed by backbench MPs. But in addition attempts have been made to widen participation in the governmental process. Again, the committee structure is important in this context, as its openness and transparency are also intended to allow civil society groupings to be far more intimately involved in the policy-making process than is usually the case at the UK level. Similarly the introduction of a more proportional electoral system for Assembly elections in place of the traditional first-past-the-post method is also intended to encourage participation (turnout) by reducing the number of 'wasted' votes, and the risk of one-party domination.

Of course it would be naïve to view the introduction of the various innovations that characterize the Assembly simply in terms of a desire on the part of certain political leaders to encourage a more participative political system. Self-interested calculation, as well as simple political expediency, played a role in the shaping of the Assembly. It is not impossible, for example, to explain the establishment of the Assembly's regional committees in the light of the perceived need to placate the editor of the north-Wales-orientated newspaper, the *Daily Post*, in the run-up to the referendum. Neither has an intellectually satisfactory explanation even been advanced to justify giving Wales a less proportional electoral system than the one introduced simultaneously in Scotland. This is not surprising, given that it is the result of expediency, pure and simple.

Most fundamentally, it is arguable that the very constitutional underpinnings of the National Assembly militate against the development of the kind of participative polity desired by the champions of devolution (for the most penetrating account of the constitutional settlement see Rawlings, 1998). Specifically, the chronic lack of clarity in the division of powers between the National Assembly and Westminster/Whitehall must make it extremely difficult for citizens to know which body is responsible for what, and whom, therefore, to hold accountable. The Assembly's status as a body corporate serves further to muddy the waters. It is difficult to conceive how participation can be maximized in a context in which responsibility, and hence lines of accountability, are so opaque. Surely clarity in these areas is a prerequisite for any political system that aspires to be participatory?

Be that as it may, and setting aside further consideration of the National Assembly's constitutional foundations for a moment, it seems clear from this discussion that on its own terms – that is, in light of the arguments around participation used to justify its establishment – turnout in Assembly elections is of vital significance. For, whatever the results of the various measures designed to attract candidates and members from 'non-traditional' backgrounds, or of attempts to draw various civil society groups, or indeed business, into the work of the Assembly, election turnout must remain the starting-point for any assessment of the National

Assembly's success as a body to encourage political participation in Wales. For, in a context in which participation is particularly prized, the voting booth is quite simply the clearest point of interaction between the Assembly and the citizen *qua* citizen. The act of voting is inevitably, therefore, interpreted as an act that legitimizes the institution itself, whether the voter is conscious of this or not: conversely, non-voting is perceived as its denial.

But, however plausible the interpretation, does low turnout really signify some kind of legitimation crisis for devolution? Is it antipathy towards devolution that is causing voters to stay at home? There is after all the wider context to consider, and when participation at the Assembly elections is viewed in the light of rates of participation at recent polls in the United Kingdom more generally, the Welsh case takes on a rather different complexion.

TURNOUT AFTER NEW LABOUR

Table 2.3 reports the turnout figures for several polls held since the 1997 UK general election. With the exception of the Scottish parliamentary elections, the Welsh elections of 1999 compare relatively favourably with the others. Given the low profile of the 1999 European election campaign, it is perhaps not all together surprising that the UK-wide turnout reached a historic low of 24 per cent. However, despite massive publicity in the main-stream UK media, turnout in the London mayoral and assembly elections was only 35 per cent – more than ten percentage points below the turnout at the National Assembly elections.

Table 2.3 Turnout in selected polls in the UK since 1997

Election	Turnout
Scottish Parliament elections 1999	59%
National Assembly for Wales elections 1999	46%
London mayor and Assembly 2000	35%
Referendum London mayor 1999	34%
European elections Wales 1999	28%
European elections UK 1999	24%

Viewed in this context, another equally plausible interpretation of the relatively low turnout in the Assembly election is foregrounded, namely that the figures may be more a reflection of a wider malaise in the UK body politic than some kind of specific rejection of Welsh devolution *per se*. That is, the modest turnout in the National Assembly election may be best understood as forming part of a wider pattern which suggests that voters in the UK are apathetic about, or alienated from, the political system in general. To determine which of these explanations is supported by the available evidence, we will now turn to the detailed analysis of the reasons why electors did not turn out to vote as evinced by the 1999 Welsh National Assembly Election Survey.

We will first present the data from the survey's direct inquiries about why the respondents did not turn out to vote. Then we shall consider patterns of participation amongst various demographic and partisan groups, and assess also the impact of patterns of media consumption. Following from this we will utilize statistical modelling techniques to identify the most significant factors impacting upon respondents' propensity to turn out and vote.

Before proceeding with the analysis, however, it is important to clarify some issues surrounding the source of data that will be used in the remainder of this chapter. Funded by the Economic and Social Research Council (grant number R000238070), the Welsh National Assembly Election Survey (WNAES) is the most detailed survey ever undertaken of the Welsh electorate, based on in-depth interviews with 1,251 individuals aged eighteen and above. As part of the project, a methodological experiment was conducted in order to test the feasibility of utilizing telephone survey techniques for other UK electoral surveys (for full details see Nicolass, Thomson and Lynn, 2000). Thus 522 of the interviews were conducted face to face with the sample being drawn via the Postal Address File (PAF). The remaining respondents were contacted by telephone, with the telephone sample being drawn through two different techniques, namely Random Direct Dialling (RDD) and PAF. The experiment found some mode effects, that is, differences in response between those who responded face to face and those who responded on the telephone. For the sake of clarity, therefore, we shall utilize only the face-to-face sample in the following tables. However, in developing the regression modelling, we will use the whole sample but include also a sample variable in order to control for these mode effects.

WHY ELECTORS DID NOT VOTE

WNAES respondents who reported that they had not voted at the Assembly elections were asked the reasons for their non-participation. These responses may be problematic at one level, in that electors will seek to rationalize the decision not to vote, and therefore may be more likely to present a deliberate decision rather than admit to straightforward disinterest. Nonetheless, they do provide some useful pointers. Questions were organized in such a way as both to allow respondents to explain in their own words why they had not voted, and to generate numerical data. Before we turn to the latter, it is worth noting briefly at least some of the individual responses in order to gain a flavour of types of individual-level decisions that led to the aggregate outcomes.

There are indications that hostility towards devolution did play a role in influencing some voting decisions. So, for example, we find the following responses from two Labour identifiers: 'I didn't agree with the Assembly and so I refused to vote.' 'Didn't agree with the Assembly in the first place. A con from start to finish.' In a similar vein, according to one Conservative identifier, there is: 'Enough government in London. We do not need another.'

More striking, however, is the number of respondents who report that practical considerations impacted on their ability to turn out and vote. Some reported being away on the day of the Assembly elections, while other respondents reported being unable to get to the polling station owing to work, ill health or commitments arising from their role as carers. Another Conservative-identifying respondent, for example, replied that she was elderly and that no one offered to take her to the polling station, consequently making it impossible to vote.

A third broad category of response seems to reflect a generalized disillusionment with politics and politicians:

'I wasn't enthusiastic about any of the candidates. I didn't want to choose one – they were all the same' (Labour identifier).
'Loss of faith in them I suppose' (Labour identifier).
'None of them would help me solve my problem about parking outside my flat' (Liberal Democrat identifier).
'Don't believe any of them' (Labour identifier).

Another category of responses reflected a specific disenchantment with the Labour Party among some electors who identified themselves as Labour identifiers:

'At the moment Labour is as bad as the Conservatives.'
'I didn't feel anybody represented my socialistic Labour feeling.'
'Don't like Alun Michael.'

Other voters stayed away from the polls for reasons related to their perceptions of the Labour Party:

'I thought it was too controlled by the Labour party' (Green identifier).
'I was pulled between Plaid Cymru and Labour' (Labour identifier.)

Somewhat more idiosyncratically, one Plaid Cymru identifier cited the following reason for not voting: 'Because of what they have done to Rhodri Morgan.'

When these and other individual responses were coded we found the following to be the most often cited reasons for not voting.

Table 2.4 Reasons given for not voting

	Per cent
Couldn't be bothered/not interested	18.1
Other answer	12.4
Work prevented me	11.0
Away on election day	10.7
Other commitments/no time	9.6
Don't believe in Assembly	7.6
Sickness prevented me	6.2
Deliberately abstained	5.8
Was not eligible to vote	5.1
Polling card/polling station problem	4.6
Respondent had moved	2.8
Couldn't decide between the candidates	2.5
Vote wouldn't have affected who won	2.1
Religious reasons for not voting	0.4
Never vote/have never voted in my life	0.4
Electoral system too complicated	0.3
Don't consider myself Welsh	0.1
Don't know/refused	0.3
Total (N)	539

These data confirm the impression of the individual responses. Of those who did not vote, 6 per cent explained their non-participation in terms of hostility towards the Assembly. Another 5.8 per cent of non-voters deliberately abstained, although it would almost certainly be wrong to attribute this to hostility towards the Assembly *per se*, given that it is impossible to establish from these data whether or not this reflected a regular pattern of abstentionism in all or most elections. As for the rest, lack of interest was the most often cited reason for non-voting. A number of other respondents cited practical considerations such as work (11 per cent), being away on polling day (10.7 per cent), lack of time or other commitments (9.6 per cent) and sickness (6.2 per cent). Given the concerns expressed in the run-up to the elections about the alleged complexity of the new voting system, it is interesting to note that only 0.3 per cent cited the voting system as a reason for not voting.

All in all, therefore, these data suggest that while hostility to devolution was a factor influencing some decisions not to vote, this was the case for only a very small minority – around 8 per cent of non-voters. The dominant explanations – or, perhaps better, justifications – for non-voting were more practical in nature. Of course, it remains the case that voters are apparently more willing to make the effort to overcome such practical barriers in the context of UK general elections than was the case in the first elections to the National Assembly. Nevertheless, the fact that so few respondents cited hostility towards devolution as an explanation for non-voting is surely significant in terms of how we interpret the relatively low turnout in Assembly elections.

SOCIAL GROUPS AND VOTING BEHAVIOUR

Having established that respondents gave a wide range of reasons for not turning out to vote, the following section will analyse whether any particular groups in society were more or less likely to be amongst the 54 per cent[1] of the electorate who did not turn out and vote.

Table 2.5 Sex and turnout[2]

	Voted %	Didn't vote %	N
Male	49.0	51.0	249
Female	55.6	44.4	266
N	270	245	515

The data relating to sex suggest that women were slightly more likely to report turning out to vote than men, although the difference is not statistically significant. But while sex does not seem to have an impact on turnout, this is emphatically not the case when we consider age.

Even though previous research on elections at the British level has demonstrated that the younger members of the electorate are less likely to turn out and vote at UK general elections than those in older age groups (Jowell and Park, 1997), the degree of difference discovered by the WNAES is still surprising – indeed shocking. Fully three-quarters of respondents in the age group 18–24 did not vote, while almost two-thirds of those aged 25–34 did not vote. Conversely, almost two-thirds of 55–64 year-olds, and three-quarters of those aged 65 and above, turned out to vote.

Table 2.6 Age and turnout[3]

	Voted %	Didn't vote %	N
18–24	25.0**	75.0**	56
25–34	35.1**	64.9**	94
35–44	47.3	52.7	91
45–54	54.9	45.1	91
55–64	63.8*	36.2*	69
65+	75.0**	25.0**	112
N	268	245	513

Note: Throughout this chapter * in a table will denote significant at the 0.05 level; ** will denote significance at the 0.01 level.

There is clearly, therefore, a significant relationship between age and turnout, but how is this to be interpreted? Data from the 1997 Welsh Referendum Survey suggested that younger members of the electorate were more likely to be supportive of devolution than those in older age groups (Wyn Jones and Trystan, 1999b). This in turn appeared to be related to differing patterns of identity, with the younger generations tending to identify themselves more to towards the exclusively Welsh end of the national identity spectrum, compared with older voters who were more likely to identity themselves as British. Given these findings, the data relating to age and turnout in the Assembly election would seem to cast doubt on the hypothesis that those who did not vote regarded devolution as in some way illegitimate.

In order to probe the relationship between national identity and turnout further, we shall first consider the impact of place of birth and seek to ascertain whether respondents born in Wales were more likely to turn out and vote. Secondly we shall consider whether respondents who are Welsh-speaking were more likely to turn out and vote. Our previous work has suggested that both place of birth and linguistic competence are closely implicated with national identity (Wyn Jones and Trystan, 1999b). But we will also consider the relationship between more direct measures of national identity, namely self-ascribed identity as measured on the so-called Moreno scale, and propensity to turn out and vote.

Table 2.7 Place of birth and turnout[4]

	Voted %	Didn't vote %	N
Wales	53.7	46.3	367
England	48.4	51.6	122
Elsewhere	56.0	44.0	25
N	270	244	514

Let us begin therefore by considering the data relating to place of birth and turnout. The potential significance of these data is underlined by the fact that 24 per cent of those surveyed by the WNAES were born in England (this is consistent with the 1991 census, which found that 19 per cent of the population as a whole was English-born). The overall pattern that emerges from this table is that there was no significant relationship between where electors were born and their propensity to turn out and vote. This represents a change from the pattern of voting in the 1997 devolution referendum as uncovered by the 1997 Welsh Referendum Survey (Wyn Jones and Trystan, 1999b).

Table 2.8 Ability to speak Welsh and turnout[5]

	Voted %	Didn't Vote %	N
Yes, fluently	63.9	36.1	61
Yes, but not fluently	57.1	42.9	77
No	49.5*	50.5*	376
N	269	245	514

When the relationship between turnout and the ability to speak Welsh is examined, we find that, although these data overall do not satisfy formal significance tests, there is evidently a relationship between the ability to speak Welsh and turnout. While almost two-thirds of fluent Welsh-speakers voted, one in two of those who do not speak Welsh reported having not turned out to vote. These data are consistent with the constituency results where the highest turnout at the National Assembly elections was seen in the areas with the highest proportion of Welsh-speakers.

Turning to a more direct measure of national identity, we find that the relationship between national identity and turnout is perhaps somewhat less clear than might have been anticipated. There is certainly no consistent pattern across the spectrum. The potential significance of this finding is that previous analysis of the referendum suggested that a more exclusively Welsh sense of national identity was associated with support for devolution, and conversely that voters at the other end of the spectrum tended to be more opposed (Wyn Jones and Trystan, 1999b). The lack of a clear pattern at the time of the Assembly election may therefore be taken as an indication that non-voting should not necessarily be taken to reflect hostility to the Assembly *per se*.

Table 2.9 National identity and turnout[6]

	Voted %	Didn't vote %	N
Welsh not British	59.6	40.4	89
More Welsh than British	49.1	50.9	110
Equally Welsh and British	59.3*	40.7*	167
More British than Welsh	43.2	56.8	44
British not Welsh	49.3	50.7	69
Other description	31.4**	68.6**	35
N	270	244	514

When we consider class, and in the first instance the respondents' self-ascribed class descriptions, although the data presented in the following table marginally fail to meet formal statistical significance tests owing to the comparatively small number of cases, a clear relationship between class and turnout is nevertheless evident. Those defining themselves as middle class are more likely to turn out and vote than those defining themselves as working class.

Table 2.10 Self-ascribed class and turnout[7]

	Voted %	Didn't Vote %	N
Middle class	59.3	40.7	135
Working class	50.0	50.0	360

This finding is confirmed when we consider class as measured on the Goldthorpe–Heath class schema. These data demonstrate that respondents engaged in more middle-class occupations are more likely to turn out and vote than working-class respondents.

Table 2.11 Goldthorpe–Heath class schema and turnout[8]

	Voted %	Didn't vote %	N
Never had job	33.3	66.7	21
Salariat	58.5	41.5	130
Routine non-manual	53.1	46.9	96
Petty bourgeoisie	67.3*	32.7*	55
Manual foremen and supervisors	55.3	44.7	38
Working class	40.4**	59.6**	136
Insufficient information	75.0	25.0	4
N	250	230	480

THE INFORMATION DEFICIT AND TURNOUT

We have previously argued that, given the nature of political culture in Wales, one of the likely consequences of devolution is the creation of a substantial minority of the population who suffer from an 'information deficit' (Wyn Jones and Lewis, 1999; Wyn Jones and Trystan, 1999b). This argument is posited on the fact that substantial sections of the Welsh electorate have few discernible sources of information on developments in Wales. After all, only a small minority of the Welsh population read Welsh-based newspapers, while a substantial minority receive their television programmes from English transmitters, with the result that they receive no Wales-focused news and current affairs programming. The strong version of this thesis would be that as Wales and England become increasingly distinct as a result of devolution, this 'information deficit' could well lead to the creation of a minority within Wales who are increasingly alienated from its structures of governance. A weaker version would expect that minority to show less propensity to participate in Welsh elections, and for their patterns of political alignment more closely to resemble the English pattern than that of the rest of the population.

Table 2.12 Information deficit and turnout

Channel	Voted	Didn't vote	N
BBC1 Wales	58.2**	41.8**	388
BBC1 Other	46.9	53.1	160
HTV Wales	54.4	45.6	373
ITV other	48.2	51.8	112
S4C	56.7	43.3	171
Channel 4	52.0	48.0	102

For the purposes of this chapter, let us consider the relationship between television viewing and turnout. As table 2.12 demonstrates, a number of interesting points emerge from such consideration. In the first instance, we find that between a quarter and a third of the Welsh electorate report watching terrestrial broadcasts other than BBC Wales and HTV Wales on a regular basis, a finding that is consistent with previous surveys. Further, we find that respondents regularly watching 'Welsh' output are more likely to have voted than those who do not regularly watch 'Welsh' output. The data are not particularly striking. Nevertheless, a difference of between 5 and 10 percentage points does suggest that media consumption may well have some impact on propensity to turn out and vote. Clearly this is an issue that requires further research and consideration.

PARTISAN ALIGNMENT AND TURNOUT

In our brief examination of the individual explanations of non-voting, we noted that some respondents reported specifically party-related reasons for not turning out to vote. The survey as a whole does indeed confirm that individual feelings towards the particular parties had a significant impact on their propensity to turn out and vote. As the following table demonstrates, those with no party affiliation were very unlikely to vote, while Plaid Cymru and Liberal Democrat identifiers were the most likely. Amongst the four main parties, Labour fared worst, with only one in two voters who identified themselves with the Labour Party reporting that they had voted.

Table 2.13 Partisan identification and turnout[9]

	Voted %	Didn't vote %	N
None	29.1**	70.9**	55
Labour	50.4	49.6	256
Conservative	54.3	45.7	92
Liberal Democrat	63.2	36.8	38
Plaid Cymru	73.2**	26.8**	56
Others	53.8	46.2	13
N	267	243	510

The WNAES also allows the impact of more general feelings towards the political parties to be investigated. Two patterns emerge from these data. In the first instance, it is apparent that those who have favourable opinions regarding the political parties are more likely to turn out and vote than those who are hostile or indifferent. However, there are differences within this pattern, in that again we find that those in favour of Plaid Cymru and the Liberal Democrats are more likely to turn out and vote.

Table 2.14 Feelings towards the parties and turnout

Party/feelings	Voted %	Didn't vote %	N
Labour			
Strongly in favour	55.4	44.6	258
Neither in favour nor against	48.2	51.8	164
Strongly against	50.0	50.0	92
Plaid Cymru			
Strongly in favour	65.5**	34.5**	200
Neither in favour nor against	41.2**	58.8**	194
Strongly against	48.5	51.5	101
Conservatives			
Strongly in favour	55.8	44.2	95
Neither in favour nor against	45.5*	54.5*	178
Strongly against	55.6	44.4	239
Liberal Democrats			
Strongly in favour	68.1**	31.9**	141
Neither in favour nor against	48.8	51.2	285
Strongly against	38.8**	61.3**	80

The potential significance of these data lies in the fact that it suggests that hostility or indifference towards the political parties is linked to non-participation. This in turn lends support to the argument that the relatively low turnout in the Assembly election was a function of negative attitudes towards the political process in general rather than specific hostility towards the National Assembly. These rival explanations can be more directly addressed by examining in turn the respondents' attitudes towards devolution and setting these against their propensity to vote, and the relationship between turnout and various measures of more general attitudes towards politics.

ATTITUDES TOWARDS DEVOLUTION AND TURNOUT

Turning first to devolution and to the relationship between how people voted in the 1997 referendum (or, more correctly, said they voted) and turnout in 1999, we find that there is indeed a strong relationship between them, but that this relationship casts further doubt on those interpretations that view the relatively low turnout in the Assembly elections as indicative of hostility to devolution *per se*. As table 2.15 demonstrates, those electors who voted in the referendum were likely to vote again in the Assembly elections whether they originally supported devolution or not. Indeed, the group most likely to vote in the Assembly election was those electors who actually voted 'No'! Conversely, those who did not vote in 1997 tended not to vote again in 1999. This strongly suggests that non-voting in 1999 should be viewed in terms of antipathy or indifference towards the political system as a whole rather than as a rejection of the legitimacy of devolution itself.

Table 2.15 Recalled referendum vote and Assembly turnout[10]

	Voted 1999 %	Didn't vote 1999 %	N
Did not vote/not eligible 97	28.0**	72.0**	207
Voted 'Yes' 97	67.8**	32.2**	183
Voted 'No' 97	74.3**	25.7**	105

This reading gains more support when we investigate the relationship between turnout and respondents' preferences for the constitutional future of Wales. Here we find that constitutional preferences had a limited and uneven impact on respondents' patterns of turnout. So, while those in favour of a parliament or an Assembly were rather more likely to turn out, those who favour a return to the pre-devolution situation were less likely. This clearly suggests that attitudes on the constitutional future of Wales did not have a major impact on the decision of whether to vote or not.

Table 2.16 Constitutional preference and turnout[11]

	Voted %	Didn't vote %	N
Independence	40.9	59.1	44
Parliament	58.8*	41.2*	182
Assembly	54.7	45.3	181
No Assembly	42.4*	57.6*	92
N	263	236	499

While hostility towards devolution does not seem to have been a major factor, there is, however, evidence of widely differing levels of interest in and expectations of the Assembly. This, unsurprisingly perhaps, did affect turnout. So, for example, when respondents were asked if they cared who won the Assembly elections we find some 40 per cent of respondents reported caring a good deal about the result of the election. These in turn were much more likely to vote. On the other hand, of the 60 per cent who did not care very much, only a third voted.

Table 2.17 Did you care who won the Assembly elections and turnout[12]

	Voted %	Didn't vote %	N
Cared a good deal	73.5**	26.5**	238
Did not care very much	33.8**	66.2**	275
Overall	52.2	47.8	513

When we explore the electorate's expectations of the Assembly, two clear patterns emerge. First, it is apparent that expectations are generally low. It is only with regard to giving ordinary people more say in government that the majority think that the Assembly will make a positive difference. With regard to increasing the standard of living and improving the education system, the majority are sceptical. This may well be a rather rational position to hold given the National Assembly's limited powers. Nevertheless, it will clearly be a cause for concern for Assembly Members, in particular because the second finding to emerge from these data is that a significant relationship exists between expectations and turnout. Higher expectations of the devolved body are clearly associated with a greater propensity to vote in the Assembly election.

Table 2.18 Expectations of the Assembly and turnout

Expectations	Voted %	Didn't vote %	N
Give ordinary people more say in government			
Will give people more say	58.0**	42.0**	288
Make no difference	44.6**	55.4**	204
Increase standard of living			
Will increase the standard of living	66.2**	33.8**	142
Make no difference	45.3**	54.7**	311
Increase standard of education			
Will increase the standard of education	60.9**	39.1**	220
Make no difference	44.5**	55.5**	245

ATTITUDES TO POLITICS AND POLITICIANS

The WNAES offers a number of routes for exploring how attitudes to politics and politicians in general are related to turnout. One question asks respondents whether they think it makes a difference which party wins the UK general election. If turnout in the Assembly election were a function of alienation from the political process then we would expect to discover a positive relationship between non-voting and a belief that the result of the general election makes little or no difference. Table 2.19 demonstrates that this is indeed the case. Those who believed that the result of the UK general election does make a difference were more likely to vote in the National Assembly election than those who believed that it makes no, or very little, difference. In other words, non-voting in the Assembly election seems to be associated with a more general lack of faith in the political process.

Table 2.19 Will the UK general election make a difference by turnout[13]

	Voted %	Didn't vote %	N
A great deal/quite a lot	59.9**	40.1**	302
Some	45.5	54.5	77
None at all/not very much	37.7**	62.3**	130
N	265	244	509

This argument is given further support when we consider the respondents' responses to the propositions that MPs lose touch with their constituents, and that parties are only interested in people's votes and not in their opinions. Again we find that those who are least sceptical about politicians and parties are the most likely to vote in the National Assembly election. Conversely, the more sceptical – which is by far the largest group – are less likely to vote.

Table 2.20 Politicians and parties

	Voted %	Didn't vote %	N
MPs lose touch			
Strongly agree	52.3	47.7	363
Neither agree nor disagree	41.7*	58.3*	84
Strongly disagree	67.2**	32.8**	64
Parties only interested in votes			
Strongly agree	48.3**	51.7**	362
Neither agree nor disagree	56.3	43.7	71
Strongly disagree	67.1**	32.9**	79

LOGISTIC REGRESSION MODELLING OF TURNOUT AT THE ASSEMBLY ELECTIONS

Having reviewed the survey data, and explored some of the possible interpretations of non-participation in the National Assembly election, we shall now move to the consideration of the key factors via logistic regression analysis. The aim in what follows will be to test differing explanations of turn-out through an assessment of different models of the key relationships.

We shall begin by considering what may be termed a partisan or party-based model, that is, a model which examines the extent to which people's feelings towards the political parties had an impact on their propensity to turn out and vote. As can be seen from table 2.21, the model demonstrates that partisan identification, and indeed the strength of partisan identification, impacted upon an individual's propensity to turn out and vote. Interestingly, the analysis also suggests that respondents with no strong feelings either way about the political parties were less likely to vote.

Table 2.21 Logistic regression model of partisan influences and turnout

	Turnout[14]	
	B	SE
Partisan identification		
(Labour)		
Conservative	0.50	0.31
Liberal Democrat	0.96**	0.30
Plaid Cymru	1.16**	0.26
Other	0.34	0.35
Feelings about the Labour Party		
(Strongly in favour)		
Neither in favour nor against	−0.59**	0.21
Strongly against	−0.54*	0.25
Feelings about the Conservative Party		
(Strongly in favour)		
Neither in favour nor against	−0.67*	0.28
Strongly against	−0.27	0.29
Feelings about the Liberal Democrats		
(Strongly in favour)		
Neither in favour nor against	−0.39*	0.17
Strongly against	−0.75**	0.22
Feelings about Plaid Cymru		
(Strongly in favour)		
Neither in favour nor against	−0.78**	0.17
Strongly against	−0.11	0.19
Constant	1.28**	0.33

* Significant at 5%. ** Significant at 1%.

When we construct a model of voting/non-voting based on demo-graphic and identity marker, a number of other themes emerge. We find confirmation of a significant relationship between age and turn out reinforcing some of our earlier findings. Further, we find that non-Welsh-speakers were significantly less likely to turn out and vote, as were respondents who described themselves as working class. While country of birth does not appear to have an impact on patterns of turnout, self-ascribed national identity does, with those towards the British end of the spectrum considerably less likely to vote.

Table 2.22 Logistic regression model of demographic/identity factors and turnout

	Turnout[15]	
	B	SE
Age		
(18–34)		
35–54	0.90**	0.16
55+	1.41**	0.16
National identity		
(Welsh not British)		
More Welsh than British	−0.37	0.21
Equally Welsh and British	−0.33	0.19
More British than Welsh	−0.71*	0.30
British not Welsh	−0.96**	0.28
Other	−0.61	0.37
Welsh-speaking		
(Fluent)		
Non-fluent	−0.35	0.24
Non-Welsh-speaking	−0.66**	0.21
Sample[16]		
(Face to face)		
Telephone RDD	0.16	0.16
Telephone PAF	0.38*	0.15
Sex		
(Male)		
Female	−0.00	0.13
Class		
(Middle class)		
Working class	−0.46**	0.14
Place of Birth		
(Wales)		
England	0.16	0.20
Constant	0.53	0.28

* Significant at 5%. ** Significant at 1%.

This model provides some support for both the argument that relatively low turnout in the Assembly election is best understood in terms of generalized alienation from the political process, and an interpretation that regards turnout as a reflection of the National Assembly's specific lack of legitimacy. The former is bolstered by the findings on age and class. As already noted, work on elections in the UK has consistently suggested that both younger and more working-class members of the electorate are less likely to participate in the political process than their older or more middle-class *confrères*. The findings from the WNAES would therefore seem to echo this widely recognized state of affairs. On the other hand, the findings with regard to national identity, as derived from measures of self-ascribed identity and captured in a more mediated form through linguistic competence, may provide sustenance to the argument that low turnout is best explained by Assembly-specific reasons. After all, our previous work has demonstrated that in 1997 national identity was correlated with attitudes towards devolution (Wyn Jones and Trystan, 1999b). Strong or exclusive Welsh identifiers were more supportive of the establishment of an Assembly than those who felt primarily or solely British. Our finding that national identity is related to the decision of whether or not to vote in 1999 may therefore indicate that opposition to devolution is still a factor.

In order to explore further the relative importance of Assembly-specific and more general explanations of turnout, the following model brings together the respondents' degree of partisan identification, their attitudes to the difference made by results of elections (to Westminster, the National Assembly and local councils), referendum vote and constitutional prefer-ence. If turnout did indeed reflect scepticism or hostility towards the Assembly we would expect to find significant relationships between turnout and constitutional preference, referendum vote and the difference made by the results of Welsh elections. If, however, alienation from the political process is more generalized then we would expect the strength of partisan identification and the difference made by local and general elections to be significant. On balance the data presented lend support to the latter thesis. Strength of partisan identification had a significant impact on propensity to vote, as did the perceived difference made by the results of elections. Particularly striking is the lack of any clear correlation between constitutional preference and voting, or, for that matter, voting 'Yes' or 'No' in the referendum. In short, this model provides plausible evidence that the low turnout at the Assembly election reflected a more generalized disillusionment with politics rather than with the Assembly *per se*.

Our final model brings together a number of the key variables identified throughout this chapter and is particularly robust in predicting turnout. We find that those who did not identify strongly with a political party were

Table 2.23 Logistic regression model of attitudes to politics and turnout

	Turnout[17]	
	B	SE
Sample		
(Face to face)		
Telephone RDD	0.09	0.19
Telephone PAF	0.51**	0.19
Difference who wins Welsh elections?		
(A great deal/quite a lot)		
Some	−0.59**	0.21
None at all/not very much	−0.83**	0.21
Difference who wins general elections?		
(A great deal/quite a lot)		
Some	0.55*	0.24
None at all/not very much	0.14	0.21
Difference who wins local elections?		
(A great deal/quite a lot)		
Some	−0.63**	0.21
None at all/not very much	−0.51**	0.18
Strong party identifier?		
(Very strong)		
Fairly strong	−0.73**	0.27
Not very strong	−0.99**	0.28
Referendum vote		
(Yes)		
No	0.03	0.23
Did not vote	−1.22**	0.18
Constitutional preference		
(No Assembly)		
Assembly	0.22	0.21
Legislative, tax-varying parliament	0.48*	0.23
Independence	−0.25	0.36
Constant	1.82	0.35

* Significant at 5%. ** Significant at 1%.

less likely to vote, as were younger and working-class respondents. In contrast, constitutional preference did not have a significant impact on turnout; neither did voting 'Yes' or 'No' in the 1997 referendum. However, those who did not vote in that poll were especially unlikely to vote in the Assembly election. Thus our evidence suggests that rather than reflecting specific sentiment concerning devolution, the low turnout in the National Assembly election reflected a deeper and wider sense of alienation from the political process in general.

Table 2.24 Logistic regression model of turnout in the 1999 National Assembly election

	Turnout[18]	
	B	SE
National identity		
(Welsh not British)		
More Welsh than British	−0.47	0.27
Equally Welsh and British	−0.24	0.25
More British than Welsh	−0.84*	0.38
British not Welsh	−0.63	0.37
Other	−0.20	0.49
Age		
(18–34)		
35–54	0.51*	0.20
55+	1.04**	0.24
Party		
(Labour)		
Conservative	0.26	0.23
Liberal Democrat	1.27**	0.31
Plaid Cymru	1.20**	0.27
Other	−0.18	0.44
Constitutional Preference		
(No Assembly)		
Assembly	0.15	0.22
Legislative, tax-varying parliament	0.37	0.25
Independence	−0.27	0.42
Welsh-speaking		
(Fluent)		
Non-fluent Welsh-speaking	0.09	0.30
Non-Welsh-speaking	0.16	0.28
Referendum vote		
(Yes)		
No	−0.15	0.24
Did not vote	−1.24**	0.21
Difference who wins Welsh elections?		
(A great deal/quite a lot)		
Some	−0.43*	0.21
None at all/not very much	−0.82**	0.20
Strong party identifier?		
(Very strong)		
Fairly strong	−0.55*	0.28
Not very strong	−0.78**	0.28
Place of birth		
(Wales)		
England	0.08	0.25

| | Turnout | |
	B	SE
Sex		
(Male)		
Female	−0.11	0.16
Class		
(Middle class)		
Working class	−0.39*	0.18
Constant	1.34**	0.51

* Significant at 5%. ** Significant at 1%.

THE FUTURE: SOME REFLECTIONS

In the preceding analysis we have established that, given the justifications advanced for devolution, it is certainly plausible to view the relatively low turnout in the National Assembly elections as calling into doubt the legitimacy of the new body. Nevertheless, when we explore the survey data we find that the most plausible reading of the pattern of turnout is *not* that non-voters are somehow rejecting devolution. Rather, their non-voting reflects a wider sense of alienation from – or lack of interest in – the political system as a whole. With relatively few exceptions, non-voters appear to be apathetic rather than antipathetic towards the National Assembly.

These findings clearly have implications which extend far beyond the National Assembly. In particular, the data concerning younger voters should surely be of deep concern to all those committed to the democratic process – and certainly not only to advocates of participatory democracy. For the Labour Party in particular, the challenge presented by the alienation of both the young and the working class, is particularly urgent. That party's spokespersons have tended to dismiss the low turnouts in the various polls held since the 1997 UK general election as reflecting the 'politics of contentment'. If, however, the correct interpretation is, as we suggest in this chapter, that disappointing levels of participation are a manifestation of a general disillusionment with politics, then this could have serious implications for Labour. After all, if those staying away from the polling booth are disproportionally young and/or working class, this will tend to erode the traditional bedrock of Labour's support. More generally, our evidence implies that unless those groups that are now alienated are re-engaged with the political process, low turnouts may yet become the norm rather than the exception – not only for elections to the

National Assembly, but also for local and European elections. Neither should reasonably high turnouts in UK general elections be taken for granted.

What specifically can the National Assembly seek to do in order to improve participation in its own future elections? The first and the most obvious point to make is that, given the practical barriers cited by a significant proportion of non-voters, much more needs to be done to facilitate voting for those electors who may not find it easy to attend a polling station between 7 a.m. and 10 p.m. on a given day. In this regard, the experiments undertaken during a number of local council elections in England in 2000 must clearly be given careful consideration (Bennett, 2000).

It may well also be the case that the rather substantial coverage currently given to the National Assembly's activities by the Wales-based broadcast media will persuade more of the electorate of its significance. Our analysis suggests that this in turn may encourage them to vote. That said, the 'information deficit' will almost certainly reduce any such influence – not only because the London-based media remain resolutely uninterested in the deliberations of the Assembly, but also because of the increasing importance of satellite, cable and various other new media.

The task facing the National Assembly in turning present apathy into engagement is rendered particularly problematic because of the classic catch-22 situation in which it finds itself. As we have seen, expectations of the Assembly are low, and so far even supporters of devolution would be forced to concede that the Assembly has done little to change this. It is only when the National Assembly begins to make a more visible impact on daily life in Wales that voter engagement can be expected to increase. Yet many if not all academic commentators, and apparently an increasing number of those more directly involved in the Assembly's activities, are highly dubious whether the present constitutional settlement will deliver effective governance (see, *inter alia*, Rawlings, 1998; G. P. Davies, 2000; R. Davies, 2000b; Sherlock, 2000; D. Williams, 2000). Legislative devolution is a system of Byzantine complexity which bestows a disjointed and incoherent set of powers on the National Assembly. Furthermore, it depends on unrealistic assumptions about the continued existence of a fund of goodwill towards the devolved body within the Whitehall/Westminster nexus. All of this can only serve to ensure that the National Assembly is likely to be plagued by divisive disputes over its competences and responsibilities. In short, the Assembly needs more power if it is to make the significant and sustained impact needed to establish its credibility. Yet the low turnout, and its apparent corollary, limited legitimacy, may well make it even more difficult to persuade any UK government to extend those powers by granting Wales legislative devolution. So might it therefore be a case of not enough power to persuade the electorate of the importance of turning out to vote, and not enough turning out to vote to justify more power?

Notes

[1]   In this context it is reassuring to note the close correspondence between the reported turnout of respondents to the WNAES and the overall pattern among the electorate at large. Thus the face-to-face sample achieved a turnout response rate of 52.4 per cent, compared with the actual reported Assembly turnout of 45.9 per cent. These data are consistent with the over-reporting of turnout that is characteristic of successive British Election Study samples as well as the 1997 Welsh Referendum Survey.

[2]   Pearson Chi-Square 2.28; df 1; sig. 0.13.

[3]   Pearson Chi-Square 55.82; df 5; sig. 0.00.

[4]   Pearson Chi-Square 1.17; df 2; Sig. 0.56.

[5]   Pearson Chi-Square 5.24; df 2; sig. 0.07.

[6]   Pearson Chi-Square 13.42; df 5; sig. 0.02.

[7]   Pearson Chi-Square 3.38; df 1; sig. 0.07.

[8]   Pearson Chi-Square 18.59; df 6; sig. 0.00.

[9]   Pearson Chi-Square 24.03; df 5; sig. 0.00.

[10]   Pearson Chi-Square 86.82; df 2; sig. 0.00.

[11]   Pearson Chi-Square 9.38; df 3; sig. 0.03.

[12]   Pearson Chi-Square 80.65; df 1; sig. 0.00.

[13]   Pearson Chi-Square 19.60; df 2; sig. 0.00.

[14]   Model Chi-Squared 113.51, degrees of freedom 12; –2 Log Likelihood 1332.40.

[15]   Model Chi-squared 124.94; degrees of freedom 14; –2 Log Likelihood 1419.10.

[16]   As previously noted, the WNAES contained a methodological experiment designed to test the feasibility of using telephone interviews in future election studies in the UK. As this table demonstrates, some mode effects were apparent between the different sampling techniques utilized. This issue is discussed at length in Nicolass, Thomson and Lynn, 2000. The point to note for present purposes is that the direction of the relationships identified here is consistent across all three elements of the overall sample.

[17]   Model Chi-squared 192.42; degrees of freedom 15; –2 Log Likelihood 1048.75.

[18]   Model Chi-squared 190.81; degrees of freedom 15; –2 Log Likelihood 1059.93.

3

Inclusive Government for Excluded Groups: Women and Disabled People

SANDRA BETTS, JOHN BORLAND and PAUL CHANEY

INTRODUCTION

'Inclusiveness'[1] or *gwleidyddiaeth gynhwysol*[2] is a concept that links the language of political rhetoric with the process of social change (cf. Skinner, 1989). Its principal concerns are combating social exclusion (Levitas, 1998) and achieving fair and democratic representation, issues that also featured in the discussions that took place in the Labour Party and elsewhere in the early 1990s. Then it was claimed that 'representation has been conflated to elections, which are increasingly events for professional management at ever vaster cost by a political advertising industry rather than reflecting political choice' (Wright, 1996: 95). Instead, it was argued, there was a need for a democratic system that reflects the complexity of modern society and avoids a form of representation that only promotes the interests of powerful social and economic groups, thereby moving away from a 'Tory tradition which emphasised governing as a specialist activity to be done by those who know how to do it' (ibid.: 106).

This was a concern that was addressed by the concept of 'inclusiveness' advanced by Ron Davies in the Welsh devolution debate of the mid-1990s. At that time 'inclusiveness' was used as a code for cross-party campaigning and the proposed use of proportional representation in Assembly elections.[3] Since then it has grown to be the guiding concept that has been widely regarded as the key to the Assembly's future success. As Wyn Jones and Trystan (1999b: 90) observe, 'the success or failure of this task seems to largely depend on the ability of those involved in the devolution process to turn the rhetoric of inclusiveness that has characterised Welsh politics since the 1997 general election into reality'. Moreover, Day, Fitton and Minhinnick (1998: 300) conclude that 'the establishment of the National Assembly, if really inclusive, could be the most important challenge to all of us as we move into the millennium'.

Over recent years inclusiveness has developed, broadening into a concept that has come to mean a number of things including: cross-party co-operation, the development of a more consensual style of politics and the process by which social diversity is directly reflected in the political process through participation and consultation (see Chaney and Fevre, 2001a). Here the latter strand is developed, for as the First Minister Rhodri Morgan observed, the Assembly was founded on the 'principles of democracy, inclusiveness and openness' (R. Morgan, 2000b). The natural corollary to these founding principles is the need to address the prevailing exclusiveness of contemporary Welsh politics which has resulted in the enduring under-representation of certain sections of society and produced a form of marginalization that labels groups with a combined majority status as 'minorities' (cf. Chaney, Hall and Dicks, 2000).

The following discussion centres upon the areas of gender, disability[4] and (in the following chapter) ethnicity. Whilst the needs of other 'minority' groups defined by age, sexuality, faith and language are also beginning to be addressed,[5] the former have been prioritized both in the legal framework that established the Assembly and in the early actions of the devolved government. Thus the devolution White Paper promised that 'the Government attaches great importance to equal opportunities for all – including women, members of the ethnic minorities and disabled people' (Welsh Office, 1997: 4.7, 24). This principle has resulted in the Assembly having unique and pioneering structures and mechanisms for furthering equality outcomes not found in the other devolved assemblies in the UK (see Chaney and Fevre, 2001a). In particular, the inclusive agenda has been driven by the eleven-strong Standing Committee on Equality of Opportunity[6] (supported by the burgeoning civil service Equality Unit within the Assembly) charged with implementing the Assembly's legal duty under clauses 48 and 120 of the Government of Wales Act. These state, *inter alia*, that the Assembly functions should conform to the principle of equal opportunities for all (Government of Wales Act 1998, 32, v, 120, i). The Committee is required to audit the Assembly's arrangements for promoting equal opportunities (National Assembly for Wales, 1999c: Standing Order 14.1). The Assembly as a whole also has to 'ensure that time is made available' to consider the annual reports of the three main umbrella equality organizations in Wales[7] (NAW, 1999c: Standing Order 6.6), ensure that its actions conform to the European Convention on Human Rights and that its progress towards achieving equality of opportunity is recorded annually in a report that will form the basis of a full plenary debate.

From the outset, leading figures in the Assembly have begun the task of turning the inclusive political rhetoric into reality. Speaking in October 1999, Jane Hutt, Assembly Minister for Health and Social Services, told the Disability Wales Annual Conference:

We all wish to create a society where all people are valued and can live their lives with dignity and respect and make a contribution to their community. The Assembly provides a new opportunity to progress this agenda but we cannot do it alone. Disabled people are already making a direct and positive contribution to the work of the Assembly and I thank them for this. (Hutt, 1999)

During the devolution debate of the past decade many policy-makers and politicians advanced their ideas on how to build a new inclusive system of governance. However, left out of this move to greater democratization all too often have been the views and experiences of women and disabled people themselves. This chapter is an attempt to redress the balance, to help voice the experience of these people and those who represent them. Here we consider: the expectations women and disabled people had of the new form of government in Wales, their experience of the Assembly elections, their observations of the way in which the parties debated disability and gender issues and the way in which these issues have been dealt with by the fledgeling government body. Alongside these accounts we examine the views of the AMs charged with the historic task of creating a devolved system of governance.

Our findings stem from a research project[8] that conducted 200 semi-structured interviews between May 1999 and October 2000 with managers, service users and ordinary members of sixty organizations in the two 'minority' sectors examined here, together with a wide range of AMs, MPs, advisers and officials. In the case of the AMs interviewed, twenty were selected by reference to the criteria of broadly reflecting the party balance in the new legislature and the need to place a greater emphasis on the under-researched aspect of the opinions and aspirations of women elected as representatives. Interviews were recorded, and subsequent qualitative analysis of the transcripts allowed the testing of grounded theories and the exploration of analytical concepts in the data. A theoretical sample was developed of women's organizations and disabled people's groups in Wales in order to reflect the diversity of these sectors as defined by factors such as geographical location, membership size, type of funding and access to resources. Field notes were taken during participant observation of key meetings, and these, together with secondary data sources – such as published interviews, organizations' newsletters and specialist literature, internal correspondence, minutes of meetings, policy and consultation documents – permitted triangulation of concepts relating to the interview data.

We now turn to our project findings that address the research question: Has the Assembly started to produce new gender and disability settlements which more adequately meet women's and disabled people's needs and facilitate their engagement in the democratic process? We begin with an initial overview of recent debates on equality and democratic representation before turning to the views of Assembly Members. This section concludes by contrasting the views from inside the Assembly with the expectations of the members of women's organizations. In the second part of this chapter we follow a similar pattern of inquiry and explore the implications of devolution for disabled people in Wales.

WOMEN, INCLUSIVENESS AND THE ASSEMBLY

Women as a group have been historically disconnected from British politics (Stephenson, 1996; Wilkinson and Diplock, 1996). The interests and voices of women have been marginal to mainstream debates and they have been severely under-represented in formal political structures (EOC, 1998). The reasons for this have been much debated (Norris and Lovenduski, 1995) and there is broad agreement that it is time to expand the role of women in decision-making forums in our society. This will involve more than increased representation of women in formal political structures. It will require more fundamental change and the development of new ways of including women in the political process and providing them with a sense of ownership. A prerequisite to securing such social inclusion for women is the effective development and implementation of equal opportunities policies. The current emphasis on 'mainstreaming' captures this aim – it represents 'a paradigm-shift in thinking' (T. Rees, 1999: 4) whereby equality issues are integrated into the whole process of policy planning and decision-making rather than being a specialist 'tag–on' issue. Main-streaming is both anticipatory and participatory (McCrudden, 1996). Anticipatory in the sense that equality of opportunity is built into the process of policy formation and participatory in the sense of involving meaningful consultation with disadvantaged groups before policies are conceived or put into effect. Mainstreaming tackles issues of organization, culture and practice with a view to integrating equal opportunities into all policies, procedures and processes. It involves finding out the ways in which current systems and ways of doing things are not gender-neutral, and collecting baseline statistics so that the nature and shape of gender inequality within an organization or field of activity can be made familiar to all concerned (T. Rees, 1999: 7). Such information can then be used to rethink how we organize our institutions and to monitor progress and change.

Proponents of mainstreaming draw attention to the fact that we must also take account of the diversity of patterns of gender relations and of differences among women and among men. 'We all have multiple identities and the particular mix of characteristics we have impacts upon the extent to which equal access is a reality . . . Identifying and addressing systematic biases in the distribution of resources, opportunities and realities are essential elements of the mainstreaming agenda' (T. Rees, 1999: 92–3). The mainstreaming agenda is both ambitious and long-term. It involves 'thinking the unthinkable' or 'visioning' (ibid.: 2), imagining other ways of organizing and doing. This can only be achieved by ongoing dialogue, opening up lines of communication and building ownership. This is a case powerfully advanced elsewhere by Mansbridge (1999) in her analysis of 'descriptive representation'. Here representatives are, 'in their own persons and lives, in some sense typical of the larger class of persons whom they represent. Women legislators represent women constituents . . . and so on' (ibid.: 629). For Mansbridge, descriptive representation is a 'deliberative process . . . [one that] furthers the substantive representation of interests by "improving the deliberation", [in turn, this] reduces distrust, and increases democratic legitimacy' (ibid.: 654). Gargarella (1998) concludes that contemporary

> institutional system[s] could be examined in the light of at least two important observations. First, that the diverse groups that comprise society find it difficult to express and defend their particular claims. Second, the system does not provide sufficient guarantees for the protection of the interests of minorities. (1998: 274)

The National Assembly for Wales has at its heart the principle of inclusiveness. In the following section the findings from in-depth interviews with twenty AMs (broadly reflecting the party political balance in the Assembly) suggest that the fledgeling legislature has the *potential* to address these concerns and rebuild and renew political democracy at different levels.

ASSEMBLY MEMBERS: THE VIEW FROM WITHIN

The National Assembly Advisory Group and Consultative Steering Group on the Scottish Parliament proposals for gender balance associated with devolution have been described as one of the 'most radical aspects of the plans for constitutional change' (Brown, 1998: 116). In terms of social representation or the 'politics of presence' (Phillips, 1995) the Assembly would appear to have succeeded in reconnecting women to the political system and 'brought gender equality far closer' (Phillips, 2000: 64). Forty-two per cent of AMs are female, and women comprise a majority in the joint Wales Labour Party/Welsh Liberal Democratic Party administration's Cabinet. This constitutes the second-highest proportion of women members in a national political forum anywhere in Europe.[9] As in the case of elections to the Scottish Parliament (cf. Alexander, 2000: 81), the Wales Labour Party's 'twinning' mechanisms in candidate selection procedures for the Assembly significantly increased the number of women elected. This progress towards greater gender balance was compounded by Plaid Cymru's careful management of their candidacies in respect of regional Assembly seats (Bradbury, Denver, Mitchell and Bennie, 2000: 20; Gill and Tarkowski, 2000). In marked contrast to the other parties, the Welsh Conservative Party singularly failed to field any women candidates in the May 1999 elections.

Despite the overall progress in including more women in the formal political system than ever before, the present evidence of the candidate selection procedures for the 2001 general election suggests that this is a fragile achievement that may well suffer future setbacks. However, significant as the number of female elected representatives is, it should be remembered that it is not simply the number of women in political office that is important, but what women do when they get there. Alice Brown highlights the *potential* of a 'critical mass' of women representatives 'for moving beyond symbolic to substantive differences' in political decision-making in ways that 'will lead to direct change in political agendas and policy outcomes' (1999: 50). However, such a transition is not inevitable, for, as Anne Phillips cautions, 'however plausible it is to say that male-dominated assemblies will not adequately address the needs and interests of women, it cannot be claimed with equal confidence that a more balanced legislature will fill this gap' (1995: 71). It is dangerous to assume that simply increasing the number of women in the legislature will actually work to 'reconnect politics' to women and/or their interests or beliefs. Descriptive representation (the politics of presence) must be integrated with ideological and functional representation (the politics of ideas) if new boundaries of political representation are to be negotiated. This does not mean that the representation of women is not important, but that it cannot be isolated from other forms of inequality and it cannot be assumed that the sheer presence of greater numbers of women means that women's interests will be better recognized. Such an argument rests on the false assumption that women have shared interests that can be represented by other women. Judith Squires draws attention to the inherent difficulties in claiming to speak for another: 'to speak for a group . . . Without silencing some within the group or some aspects of the group is probably an impossibility' (Squires, 1999: 185; see also Alibhai-Brown, 2000). This assertion is now explored in relation to the National Assembly.

Our interviews indicated high levels of optimism discernible among women AMs; there is a strong belief that change is occurring and that the opportunity to achieve genuine equality is there to be grasped. Such optimism is based on both the presence of large numbers of women in the Assembly and the enshrining of equal opportunities into its structure and operation. The fact that several women elected to the Assembly have vast experience of working in equal opportunities groups and organizations links these two issues. One female AM described the key task of the National Assembly as that of 'working towards a more equal society' and suggested that 'it's obviously a very good thing that responsibility for promoting equal opportunities has been written into the Government of Wales Act'. She recognized that a lot would depend on 'the political will to make it happen' but 'looking around the chambers there are a lot of people there who you would expect to have that political will.' In particular there is broad agreement that the high numbers of women in the Assembly would make a difference and would influence the agenda. According to one AM, women in the Assembly were challenging institutions and organizations and raising issues such as childcare and flexible working practices which now got serious consideration, whereas previously they would not have been listened to. Some referred to strength in numbers and women AMs being more 'up front' and challenging because there are now more of them. Some referred to a unity or 'sisterhood' amongst women AMs that cross-cuts party allegiances and seeks to promote a 'women's agenda'. Speaking about women in the Cabinet, one AM noted that

> those women know they have the good wishes of all the other women in the chamber with them, not just the women from their own party . . . I feel there is a sort of sisterhood thing definitely. Not that anybody ever mentioned it to me but I can see it.

Women AMs of all political parties were determined to influence the working practices of the Assembly, and in particular the style of political debate. One observed:

> I think the Assembly . . . is going to operate in a way which probably looks so much more low-key than Parliament in that there will be a distinctive influence of women because there are so many of us here . . . when you get all women debating or a majority of women debating the tone of the debate changes.

Another felt that 'there was a determination to break down tribal, confrontational politics' and to 'relate better to ordinary voters who don't like all this shouting and banging and all the rest of it'. At the same time there was a commitment among women AMs to cross-party working, openness, and transparency, and a belief that the presence of significant numbers of women in the Assembly would lead to greater efficiency. A leading AM said:

> I'm hoping that because the Assembly is going to be able to address issues in very much more depth than has ever been addressed in public before, you know, decisions have previously been made very much by three ministers for the whole of Wales and they've done it in private. Well now these things are going to be addressed and debated and discussed in public and I'm very much hoping that we'll identify problems and solutions in a much more efficient manner than has been done in the past.

Awareness of the way in which gender issues would be addressed varied greatly between male AMs. The comments of a minority indicated that they felt such matters were peripheral and 'largely a matter for the cross-cutting committee'. However, for others gender equality had a higher priority. Expressing his own views and those of male colleagues, one said of the Equality Committee, it is 'not just an "add-on" committee but we recognize it as being *very, very* important'. The majority expressed the view that, as one put it, women's 'concerns are absolutely fundamental to the work of the *whole* Assembly'.

It is incumbent upon the Assembly to work along equal opportunities lines. The legal and economic imperatives for equality of opportunity provide women AMs with a firm platform from which to address their agenda. Nevertheless, it is recognized by some that barriers still remain. One female AM observed that equality issues are not necessarily a priority for all, and that whilst there may be little or no hostility to equal opportunities there remain much apathy and lack of understanding. Among National Assembly civil servants she detected a feeling that the equality issue was yet another burden, yet another task to be added to their already heavy workload. There is a danger that equal opportunities becomes an 'add-on' element to policies and programmes rather than being mainstreamed. Another AM, addressing the Chwarae Teg conference (an independent body established in 1992 to promote and develop women's role in the workforce) in November 1999, recognized this when she claimed that 'we must . . . keep hammering away at equal opportunities . . . we should not feel embarrassed or sidelined . . . we are right, these issues are central to the regeneration of the Welsh economy'. Among women AMs there is a clear political will to bring about change and to pursue the mainstreaming agenda. There is a recognition that this is not going to be an easy task, but also a determination and an optimism that, as one AM put it, 'we now have the opportunity to achieve genuine equality. We are through stage one. We are now in there on the agenda and part of the game. What matters now is what we do with this chance.'

Women AMs are also acutely aware of the need to reach out to the electorate, particularly to marginalized and under-represented groups. Interviews conducted early on in the life of the Assembly showed that the inclusive agenda was high on women AMs' list of priorities, but there were real concerns about how this was to be put into practice. According to one AM, they had 'an obligation to get out there and get involved and to get the organizations . . . to come and see our committees'. In the words of another, 'Being inclusive means allowing people easy access to the political system and making sure that what we're doing is done well and is providing a full service, particularly public services to people out there.' Several AMs recognized the importance of reaching out to voluntary organizations with the message that they wanted to be involved with them and influenced by them. One noted

> I've actually made an effort to go out to visit as many voluntary organisations as possible and say 'look, you know, I want to get involved with you and I want you to influence me in the Assembly, I want us to work together.' And it's very, very important.

This AM had set herself a target of visiting at least two community groups each week.

From the interviewees came recognition of the enormity of the task of achieving inclusiveness and of the barriers and constraints that stood in the way. One AM referred to a barrier of apathy/cynicism, having detected during the election campaign that there had been 'no huge sense that people thought that the National Assembly was going to be different . . . or better'. Another suggested that an Assembly in Cardiff was in some ways as remote as Westminster and that 'any sort of institution is immediately a barrier . . . to most people'. Another AM referred to the need to 'deconstruct the world of politics . . . to make it as down to earth as possible . . . to make it accessible'. Others raised the question of whose voices would be heard by the Assembly. Would it be a case of those who 'shout loudest' reaching in to Assembly business? Would 'ordinary' groups get to be heard? And did some groups, perhaps, have a 'head start'? In the words of one AM, 'We're supposed to be accessible, it just appears to me that some groups are going to be off the starting blocks a little quicker than others.' There were suggestions that this was already the case in that larger groups and organizations had been 'smart to the Assembly' early on, lobbying and providing manifestos, literature and invitations to prospective candidates.

For AMs the target was, as one stated, 'to get to that mass of people out there who are not very well skilled in accessing the political process'. It was generally recognized that inclusiveness was an aspiration and not 'something we've achieved all of a sudden because we've set up an Assembly'. Political will and optimism, particularly among women AMs, was high, but it was felt that there was a long way to go and that many barriers still had to be overcome.

> I have no illusions, it's not going to work perfectly and I will undoubtedly be disappointed in certain ways, but there's one thing you cannot change, you cannot change the sex of those there and that's really going to have an impact, I'm sure of that,

an AM concluded. We now explore whether such certainty is reflected in the interviews with 100 women associated with women's organizations drawn from across Wales.

Women's groups and organizations: the view from without

Women come together in a wide variety of groups and organizations throughout Wales, a significant proportion of which comprise 8 per cent of the country's 25,000 voluntary organizations (Wales Council for Voluntary Action, 1999), although not all operate on a voluntary basis. Some groups are locally based but form part of a national or regional structure; others operate independently within a particular area or community. Some are single-issue groups; others have a wider remit. In addition there are 'umbrella organizations' to which many individual groups are affiliated and which seek to co-ordinate activity on a broader basis, in order, as one manager outlined, 'to take into account the needs of all women regardless of what organization or sphere of life they come from . . . to ensure that the voice of women within Wales . . . is on the political agenda'. Whilst all groups are concerned with what might be termed 'women's issues', the particular focus of concern varies from broad issues of equal rights and equal opportunities to specific issues of funding or support for practical projects. In the early days of the Assembly, representatives of a large number of groups were interviewed about their experience of the election campaign, their expectations for the Assembly and how they saw them-selves relating to the new political process.

There was general agreement that the election campaign had been singularly unimpressive and had not addressed women's issues in any meaningful way. The views of two managers were typical: 'Many of the candidates were pretty ignorant on women's issues.' 'Some of the issues didn't get raised, certainly on the media level.' Nevertheless, despite disappointment with the campaign, representatives expressed high levels of optimism that the Assembly would improve things for women. One project co-ordinator hoped that it would 'make things better and raise women's issues higher up the political agenda'. Several respondents spoke of their high expectations and excitement and looked forward to significant changes. The representative of one leading umbrella organization felt that 'it will be very exciting. I'm sure that because there are so many people, so many women that have been elected, it will reflect a lot of our concerns.' Similar optimism was echoed by the women's officer of a leading trade union who had 'a high expectation that it [the Assembly] could drive the agenda in a very positive way', and also by the representative of a prominent voluntary group who felt that 'it is going to give us a much larger voice . . . I think it's very positive.'

However, there were discernible differences among groups with respect to the framing of expectations and the grounds for optimism. Representatives of some of the smaller, locally based or single-issue groups spoke about their 'hope' that the Assembly would 'prioritize women's issues', 'listen to people who are marginalized', 'look at the rural transport problem', 'set up improved lines of communication', 'reach out to groups like ours', 'back our projects to improve family life' and provide funding for particular activities. Interviewees generally expressed a positive view of the constitutional changes; they felt that, as one interviewee put it, the Assembly 'was bound to make a difference'. However, many were uninformed and uncertain about what the AMs would do. In this respect a businesswoman's comments were typical: 'It's an awful thing to say but y'know with all the election things that happened the other week . . . you just didn't know what their role is really going to be.'

By contrast, representatives of larger umbrella groups and organizations based their optimism on personal contacts with key AMs and prior knowledge about the Assembly structures and purposes. It was not just the number of women AMs that was seen to be important, but who those AMs were. Many of the women AMs elected to the Assembly were already known to them, were referred to on a first-name basis, and were part of an existing network of women active in the field of equal opportunities. According to the representative of one leading women's group, 'there are friends in the Assembly.' These pre-existing contacts and connections were seen to be crucial not only because of the high levels of awareness and expertise that these AMs brought to the Assembly, but also because they provided a way into the Assembly. In the words of one interviewee, 'We are not going in from a zero baseline. Our existing contacts and connections are very important. There are "soft targets" in the Assembly.' A member of another organization echoed this by making the point that 'you have to be in the right groups or else you will get marginalized. You have to network.'

Some of the larger groups had undertaken forward planning prior to the establishment of the Assembly to consider how they might best fit into the new political process. One or two had set up standing committees within their own organizations to liaise with the Assembly and to monitor progress. Others had lobbied prospective candidates through information packs, and established both direct formal links with Assembly committees and indirect contacts through what one termed 'the appropriate channels' such as the EOC Wales (Equal Opportunities Commission), the WCVA (Wales Council for Voluntary Action). In addition, several had specific priorities and agendas for action. The Wales Assembly of Women sought a dialogue with AMs with a view to 'the removal of barriers in education, training and employment in public life, the need for good public transport in both urban and rural areas and the eradication of poverty'. Elsewhere, the Wales Women's National Coalition, an umbrella body comprised of women's organizations such as Wales TUC Women's Advisory Committee and Merched y Wawr, compiled an extensive document on *Priorities for Further Action in Wales* (Wales Women's National Coalition (WWNC), 1999) and viewed its task as one of making sure that the National Assembly fulfilled its role of promoting equal opportunities. To this end it sought 'formal representation in the partnership between the Assembly and the voluntary sector in Wales' (WWNC, 1999: 6,) with a view to ensuring that appropriate action is taken to achieve a range of goals. These include: programmes to increase the numbers of women in senior positions in all sectors, main-streaming of gender equality into economic development, the implementation of the National Association of Carers Charter and a co-ordinated strategy to combat domestic violence and provide rape crisis counselling in Wales. Welsh Women's Aid (WWA) also wanted formal recognition by the Assembly of their expertise and knowledge. They called for an Assembly Select Committee on Domestic Violence, and a commitment to a 'sound and realistic funding base' for Welsh Women's Aid (WWA, 1999: 3).

Umbrella organizations also benefited from personal contacts. A leading figure reflected: 'Many AMs are members of our organization. We feel we know them very well.' Such organizations had been involved in advisory groups and the preparation of consultation documents prior to the setting up of the Assembly and felt they had already had a direct influence. Another manager commented:

> I honestly believe that looking at the way they put things together for the Assembly that a lot of our ideas have come through in that and a lot of our

arguments have been taken on board. I'm very encouraged by that. We've still got a long way to go mind, don't get the impression that everything is hunky-dory, we've got a long way to go, but we're getting there I feel.

These organizations had a head start. They had a knowledge and under-standing of the system and personal contact with key AMs. This enabled them to develop strategies for 'reaching in' to the Assembly in effective and targeted ways. One stated that they intended to be 'very entrepreneurial in approach' and felt that the onus, at least in the early days, was very much on groups and organizations to make themselves heard.

> I think it's up to us at this point to make a noise and make our presence felt because I think they've got so much on their plate that it would be totally unrealistic for us to expect them . . . to contact us. I mean clearly you know, we have got contacts in high places and I don't think we're going to be forgotten, but they have got an awful lot on their agenda at the moment.

Other groups, however, had no 'contacts in high places' and little or no understanding of the political process or channels of communication. They were concerned not so much about being forgotten as about getting to be known. These tended to be the smaller, locally based and single-issue groups. For many their only point of contact with the Assembly was through their local AM, and even this link was somewhat tenuous. The AM was often known by name, but not on a personal basis. These groups confessed that they were, as one member put it, 'a bit vague about the Assembly and its workings . . . It's difficult to understand what's hap-pening in the political process at the moment.' They were not sure that they had, as another interviewee noted, 'any real way of being heard'. Nevertheless, some had been proactive and had written to prospective candidates, and later to AMs, informing them of their groups' aims and objectives.

Evaluations of the success of this strategy of reaching into the Assembly were mixed. Two small locally based groups felt it had been a waste of time. The responses that they had received from AMs were, in their words, 'very bland' or 'contained nothing positive'; and one group questioned whether the AMs actually read their letter in the first place. Another group had targeted letters at what they saw as 'relevant ministers' and key female AMs. Their director was 'encouraged by the responses received', for they had been invited to observe the Committee on Equality of Opportunity and were planning to develop a wider range of contacts among committee members as well as Assembly ministers. Other groups were less proactive and expressed the hope that the Assembly would reach out to them. A project officer said, 'I hope the Assembly would like to meet us and see what we do.' Another urged, 'we would like to have an input and be listened to.' For many groups resources of time, money and personnel were scarce, and it was not practical or possible to mount expensive lobbying campaigns involving literature, questionnaires or glossy brochures. Disadvantaged and marginalized, they nevertheless expressed a hope that the new political settlement would provide them with a voice, but felt that the Assembly had to reach out to them. A volunteer with a small locally based group felt that 'people should come out from the Assembly to the areas to tell us what it's about and what's available'.

Early expectations concerning the Assembly and its potential impact on the lives of women in Wales, as expressed by representatives of a variety of women's groups and organizations, ranged from high optimism to rather vague hopes. The groups which were most positive were the larger groups or umbrella organizations. At the other end of the spectrum were a number of smaller or more locally based groups whose representatives expressed hopes that the Assembly would make a difference and that it would listen to them, but who were unclear as to how to engage with the Assembly and participate in devolved policy-making. One interviewee said, 'I'm just hoping, we live in hope that because it's going to be smaller, and more local, that they're going to be able to address [women's] issues a lot better.' Another added, 'I hope the Assembly would like to meet us and see what we do . . . I'm optimistic, but sceptical . . . I hope I'll be able to say I was wrong, but I'm not really convinced that they are going to be interested in [women's] grass-roots, practical projects.'

It is evident that in the early days there was some measure of uncertainty concerning channels of communication between the Assembly and voluntary groups and organizations. Should women's groups seek to 'reach in' to the Assembly and, if so, how? Or would the Assembly 'reach out' to them and, if so, by what mechanisms? How was the much-publicized principle of inclusiveness to be put into practice? Overall, despite contrasts in the level of expressed optimism, the overriding impression gained from the women interviewed was one of positive expectation that devolution would advance gender equality in Wales. After centuries of marginalization, this was a hope that was founded upon the level of direct representation that devolution had delivered. As the following discussions reveal, it is not a pattern that was repeated for the other 'minority' groups studied. We now consider the views of 100 members and workers with Wales-based organizations that represent people with a variety of psychiatric, learning, sensory and physical disabilities.

DISABLED PEOPLE, INCLUSIVENESS AND THE ASSEMBLY

Official statistics suggest that there are 407,000 'long-term' disabled people of working age[10] in Wales and that they make up 23 per cent of this age group (Disability Rights Commission, 2000). In addition, statistical surveys suggest that there are approximately 225,000 disabled people of retirement age in the country (Age Concern, 2000). Other sources indicate that disabled people are members of 57 per cent of families (John, 1998), comprise one in six voters (John, 1999b: 11) and that 'disability' organizations number 1,487 or 7.9 per cent of the voluntary sector (Wales Council for Voluntary Action, 1999: 5). Many disabled people in Wales are elderly and have an acquired rather than inherited disability. Disability includes a great variety of conditions relating to restricted mobility, sensory impairment and learning difficulties. In some cases these problems will be openly acknowledged and in some cases hidden. Involvement in disability, of course, goes wider than disabled people themselves; it involves carers, family, professional workers, academics and the political allies of disabled people. This complexity and variety is mirrored by a similar diversity of organizations that represent disabled people. Historically the stress has been on care and on the representation *of* disabled people; in recent years the emphasis has been on civil rights and representation *by* disabled people.

The notion of disability is condensed here around two views that can be briefly described as the medical and social models of disability. The former approach 'imposes a presumption of biological or physiological inferiority upon disabled persons' (Hahn, 1986: 89). It emphasizes individual loss and in the recent past has generated labels such as cripple, spastic and retarded, which imply functional loss and inferiority. The social model, which now challenges the medical model, produces a very different view. In this perspective, disability is a form of oppression originating in the power of significant groups in defining the identity of others and reproducing for disabled people disempowerment, marginalization and dependency (Barton, 1996: 8–9). It is the Assembly's ability to widen the understanding and application of the latter model that will, in large measure, determine whether 'inclusive' governance is achieved for disabled people in Wales. We now consider the first stages in this process and examine the expectations that disabled people held of the new Welsh tier of government.

The expectations of disabled people: devolution and the first Assembly elections

Before the Assembly elections, disabled people's expectations of what could be achieved were varied, reflecting those of the population as a whole. Some were very optimistic. One director expressed the wider view of national organizations: 'It can only be for the good. The Equality bodies [including the Disability Rights Commission in Wales] they're going to set up are going to include all the work that's being done by the Assembly and I think it's a wonderful opportunity to influence the Assembly.' At a local level there was a hope that, as one project officer explained, 'they will take more interest in local issues, because north-west Wales is very different to south-west Wales and different areas have different needs and require different services.' At a practical level, one manager expected that disability organizations would 'have the opportunity to influence policy and develop a partnership with the Assembly'. Others were quite hostile, reflecting experience of past failures and suspicions. One project worker added, 'Personally, I don't have any confidence in it at all. I think that it's no more than creating more quangos and jobs for the boys, I think it's going to be pretty damn ineffectual, it's bent on spending money on Cardiff-based initiatives.' One interviewee reflected what was probably the majority view in Wales at the time: 'I haven't got a clue really. I know it will bring decisions closer to the people and there are a lot of people out there, who have opinions.' This uncertainty was tinged with apprehension: 'I think most of the people I work with are very worried that they're going to be sidelined and they're not really going to have a voice.'

The more optimistic thought the Assembly had a wonderful opportunity, as one interviewee put it, to 'develop policy that is sensitive to local needs and local expectations, and an opportunity for "hands-on" government'. More practically, the realization was that the Assembly needed time to grow. This view was clearly stated in Disability Wales, an umbrella body representing disabled people's groups:

> Will there be a real change in our lives after May 6 [1999]? The short answer is no. It will take time for the Assembly to map out its agenda and to start the process of change. In the long term it could bring real changes to Wales but that will depend on disabled people engaging in the debate and communicating ideas. (Disability Wales, 1999a: 23)

Our interviews with disabled people in Wales revealed that for them the first election to the Assembly was not altogether a positive experience. The most significant disappointment was the lack of proportional descriptive representation of disabled people amongst AMs. Despite the significant numbers of disabled people in the population as whole, just two AMs declared themselves as disabled. As far as the campaign itself was concerned, the general feeling amongst disabled people was that it did not address their concerns. One noted that 'disability did not raise its head. Politicians made merely rather generalized statements about support.' As one activist put it, there are 'lots of thoughts about creating an inclusive society but the plans to achieve this are not in place'. One of the few disabled candidates spoke of the general need to understand 'what the barriers are' and, further, to fight 'the institutionalized discrimination that exists within that sort of party structure' and the 'traditionalists' who feel that disabled people 'aren't able to take up those sort of places'. He noted: 'If they really want to talk about inclusion they will have to look at positive action around race and disability as they have done around gender.' The low level of interest in the election and what was seen by some as the capriciousness of politicians led to interviewees expressing disappointment and feelings of marginalization. In the words of one activist: 'I obviously don't feel it bodes well for the future. I think a lot depends on the effort we make on the ground now. We need to make the effort to reach out to them [AMs].' Interviewees were generally dismissive of the perceived limited efforts that the political parties made to engage disabled people. A leading figure observed:

> Plaid [Cymru] were the most vociferous in their verbal support and in fact ran a number of days in their [election] campaign on disability issues, e.g. 27 April 1999, [and] concentrated specifically on that in their media campaign for whole days, which is something the other parties didn't do.

Disability organizations themselves varied in their involvement in the election. Small local support groups did not appear to know how to engage the system, nor could they react quickly enough to the campaign. Some doubted the impact of what they were doing. Organizations that gave a particular service to disabled people did not have the time or the resources to get involved. Almost all of these groups left campaigning to the regional or national groups to which they were affiliated. They in turn most frequently contacted candidates by sending them information, either leaflets or information packs outlining their organization's aims and policies.[11] Here the tradition of administrative devolution and co-working with the Welsh Office prior to 1999 meant that such groups advanced specific, well-formulated policy demands. Disability Wales[12] mounted a significant campaign. They were one of the few groups to attempt to mobilize the interest of disabled people by running articles in *Disability Wales News* which pointed out the importance of voting, how to register and what to do if the polling station was inaccessible: 'We will all face a steep learning curve, including Assembly Members. So vote, think, discuss, lobby, form alliances. It is up to us. Its scary stuff, but we can make a difference' (John, 1999a: 16). We now examine whether disability issues have impacted on the initial work of the Assembly and the issues associated with creating a dialogue between the Assembly and disabled people.

Disability issues and the Assembly

In the first few months of the Assembly's operation, disability organizations were keen to press forward on issues relating to resources and
budgeting. But these issues were submerged in the more general problem
of what the overall relationship between disability organizations in Wales
and the National Assembly could be. To date, this process has been largely
presented as one of providing solutions to a number of practical and often
physical problems relating to inclusion. For example, as a leading figure
asked:

> How can disabled people access the information systems of the Assembly, and
> the National Assembly building itself? How can the Assembly relate to north
> Wales and the rural and marginal areas? What will be the role of the Assembly
> Regional Committees? How can the AMs be monitored on their attitude and
> performance on disability issues? What is the relationship between the WCVA
> and Disability Wales? How can individual disabled people influence the
> agenda? What are the mechanisms for consultation with disabled people in
> Wales used by the National Assembly? What is the role of organizations such
> as Disability Wales in setting up information systems to ensure contact
> between the Assembly and disabled people?

While these have been the pressing questions, a less pragmatic approach
raises other themes, such as the way in which AMs must, as a prominent
figure observed, find ways of 'helping people to speak and not to not speak
on their behalf', of ensuring that 'Assembly Members do not become too
strident as champions on our behalf. We need allies not advocates.' One
campaigner asserted that the 'Equality of Opportunity Committee as an
overarching committee needs to learn a new mantra: that all Assembly
decisions and policies affect disabled people and all policies affecting
disabled people have implications for the wider community.' What these
concerns and ideas suggested was that the most important issues for
disabled people were to establish effective ways of monitoring and
lobbying the Assembly.

It is too early to say with any certainty, how the relationship between
AMs and interest groups is developing following devolution. What is clear
is that the present system is largely built on personal friendships and
shared professional interests, and if disabled people are to be fully
represented a lot needs to be done to develop appropriate structures and
networks to serve their interests. Knowing an AM is seen as being
important: a manager claimed, 'We've got an AM based here, which is
quite good really because she can help us.' Because so few AMs appear to
be positively interested in disability, the past record of a small number of

AMs who are interested and informed is seen as vital. The co-ordinator of an umbrella body said: 'It is very early days, but of course some of the Assembly people – Val Feld, Helen Mary Jones, Jane Hutt, Edwina Hart – have worked actively in equality issues and I'm sure they're going to be very good champions for equality in general within the Assembly.' Some organizations feel they have built on these relationships and have already made significant headway. One director observed:

> It's only been going five or six months . . . we seem to have been there all the time [i.e. the Assembly] . . . so we're kind of regulars – 'Oh no, not them again!' We can't really fault the level of access we've had . . . [and] the willingness of people who see us.

Not everyone is so trusting, and because of the historic importance of personal relationships in Welsh politics, some are reluctant to give up contacts that have served them well in the past, a view summed up by one activist in the field of mental health: 'My contact is with people who actually work in the Welsh Office, because the Assembly's quite a new thing really; that's the way we try to influence things.'

The establishment of effective relationships is also inhibited by the unease some feel about the understanding of disability shown by AMs and whether they really comprehend the policy and economic implications of developing a fully inclusive agenda that would embrace disabled people. A manager stated:

> From the disability point of view Disability Wales is pushing as hard as it can, working as an NGO, and they are pushing to get into that position that they never have reached before with centralized government. I am not so sure it's been pushed by the AMs, but we haven't got any representation in the Assembly, I mean there aren't any disabled people there, which would have been a real breakthrough for us.

The move from influence based on personal contact to one based on a more formal evidenced-based relationship is also confounded by the absence of additional funding to develop effective information systems. To overcome this problem some organizations felt the need to appoint an information officer. One director said:

> That's one of the things that we're trying to get funding for . . . we're on-line at least . . . but that relies on somebody, a member of staff calling up the Assembly . . . web pages . . . We don't have the resources to do that . . . we just don't have the resources.

While another, reflecting on the lack of resources, saw a role for volunteers:

> We had hoped to get a volunteer who's a retired person who's very *au fait* with everything, and that was going to be our solution to [monitoring and lobbying the Assembly], that he would read the [news] papers everyday, read the [Record of] Proceeding and so on, but that didn't actually transpire, we're very dependent on those kinds of things.

Reaching out: reaching in

In the early weeks of devolution the Assembly civil service saw the voluntary sector as the main way of reaching out to all sections of Welsh society including disabled people. When asked, a senior Assembly civil servant said: 'You look at the Government of Wales Act, section 114 and it says how we will consult . . . We meet in the first instance via the WCVA and all that we do is by the WCVA.' While the use of the WCVA may be seen by government as an attractive way of consulting the voluntary sector in Wales it may not totally fulfil the requirements of a democratic lobby in that the relationship may not be open and observable. Parallel to the concerns of women's groups, questions have been raised as to how capable the WCVA is going to be in representing disability interests. Many small organizations, particularly those that are involved in supporting or giving aid to individual disabled people, are part of the WCVA and are happy to work within its framework. Some national organizations, such as Scope, also welcome the opportunity to work with the WCVA. Others, such as Disability Wales, which promote the civil rights of disabled people, are not part of WCVA. The difference in strategy appears to be related to whether the organization sees itself primarily as a group concerned with caring for disabled people or one that is representing the rights of disabled people. For some of those who act as advocates of the rights of disabled people, the inclusion of disability as part of the voluntary-sector provision tends, in their eyes, to reinforce the medical model of disability.

The formation of an effective 'lobby' system – a way of providing a continuous consultation between the governed and the government – is very important if new ways of representing people in the political process in Wales are going to be achieved. The lobby, if it is openly constructed, embodies two basic democratic principles: the right to participate in policy-making and the right to demand redress of grievance. In a democracy the lobby is open and observable, and access is not to be dependent on wealth or social connection, or on the absolute level of group mobilization. Those who participate in the lobby should characterize the interests they claim to represent. The construction of a lobby is a two-way process, important for those on the outside who wish to influence the policy of the Assembly, and important for those on the inside as a means of obtaining advice and 'testing' out policy proposals. By the end of September 1999, the lobby in Wales was already in the process of formation. In all, twenty organizations, representing a wide range of interests, had appointed liaison officers, but only four of these represented disability interests.

The development of the lobby depends just as much on the social forces outside the Assembly as on those within. The evidence from those who have tried to reach into the Assembly over the first few months of its life has been very mixed. Inevitably there are some organizations that have had no contact at all. Some were almost defiant, such as one manager who said: 'We don't have any contact with the government. We have no support from them.' Others were just getting started; a policy officer recalled: 'There was a report. It was sort of laying the foundations of the way in which the Assembly might move forward now. Other than that, I can't say that we've had any direct contact, no.' For some organizations lobbying was a matter of resources. As one chairperson stated, 'I know you can use it as an excuse but we just can't do it, we can't keep up with what's happening tomorrow, you know; there's no money.' In contrast, other organizations had been extremely active: a director confirmed:

> Since September a couple of years ago, it was realized that there was going to be an opportunity for voices to be heard because it was going to be on such a local basis. Wales has always been regarded as an add-on bit to the UK when it comes to government listening.

Another manager recalled, '[We established] a Welsh Assembly Working Group in Scope (Wales) in April 1999 but there had been some work before that stimulated by members.'

Elsewhere the needs of disabled people were addressed in designing the Official Record of the Assembly's proceedings. A director related:

> I had a phone call from a guy that's in charge of producing the Record of Proceeding; he said 'I've been given your name, can we have a talk about producing alternative formats? So they were proactive in that. So when he came to see me it was good . . . I saw him within two days.

The main information newsletters within the disability lobby also tended to give a very positive view of such instances of lobbying and liaison on disability. Throughout the year they recorded increased contact between the Assembly and the disability lobby. Typically they reported that,

'Howard John, director of Disability Wales, gave a paper to the National Assembly Economic Development Committee' (Disability Wales, 1999b: 14). Further, that members 'met ministers and Members of all parties . . . [who they felt were] very supportive of our cause . . . [we were] thrilled with the reception' (Farmer and Farmer, 1999: 9). When invited by Jane Hutt to address the Health and Social Services Committee, the Cardiff and Vale Coalition of Disabled People felt they were 'amongst friends [and that they] . . . felt confident that the Assembly can help promote equality of opportunity for all Welsh disabled people' (Harris, 1999: 7).

However, the evidence of the interviews reveals that such high-profile contacts were important but not typical of the work of disability organizations as a whole. For the rest, their aim was to inform their own members about the new developments. This was done in a number of ways: informally in conversation and at meetings and formally, as one interviewee outlined, by preparing, 'papers for our committee on the formation of the Assembly and how the various committees were going to work . . . and generally by providing information about what sorts of things you need to lobby your MPs on and what you need to lobby your Assembly Members on'.

It is difficult to estimate the number of meetings that have taken place between AMs and individuals around the issue of disability. There have been some large and well-publicized 'events', such as a series of regional meetings organized by Disability Wales, and many informal, private and personal meetings. A prominent manager revealed, 'We have been making personal, largely informal, contact either on a social or a personal level.' These points of contact generally reflected relationships between disability organizations and political activists that had existed long before the creation of the Assembly.

It is too early to assess fully the progress that has been made by the fledgeling government body for Wales. However, the following examination of the Assembly's work during its first months suggests discontinuity with past practices and evidence of a new inclusive approach aimed at women and disabled people.

AN INCLUSIVE AGENDA

The evidence from the Assembly's work during its first year suggests that the high expectation of some interviewees may not have been ill-founded. Important and pioneering work has been undertaken by the Assembly Standing Committee on Equality of Opportunity. Notably, it has developed what it hopes will be seen as an example of best practice in implementing the mainstreaming of equality issues in Assembly business. In its first months the Assembly has prioritized a comprehensive review of the way it measures up to equality criteria. As part of its Equality Action Plan,[13] the committee's 'Equality Audit: Equal Opportunities Baseline Survey' (NAW, 2000c) concluded that: 'the key message . . . [is] the very low starting point that the Assembly is starting from, and the significant work that is needed to move to the position of excellence that the Assembly should aspire to' (ibid.: 3).

Mainstreaming of equality issues on a day-to-day basis has occurred in a number of ways. Women's and disabled people's groups have submitted written responses to key policy initiatives covering the breadth of the Assembly's work.[14] They have presented papers to Assembly committees[15] that have formed the basis of discussions between the group's representatives, AMs, committee advisers and officials.[16] In addition, organizations have been invited to join task groups to develop policies and implement strategies.[17] The Committee on Equality of Opportunity's annual report reveals how mainstreaming is at the heart of its work plan, and we reproduce the Assembly's position in some detail:

> The mainstreaming strategy will continue to be the Committee's main priority in the coming year and the Committee will need to closely monitor progress on implementing the action programme in each area. The Committee will need to continue to demonstrate leadership and there would be an increasing emphasis on Committee members' role in promoting consideration of equality in their Subject and other Assembly committees. However, it is also essential to ensure that responsibility for equal opportunities does not just lie on this Committee's shoulders. Equal opportunities is a corporate responsibility and a core theme which must influence policy. Applying the principle of equality of opportunity will need to become second nature to everyone in their day to day work. It should be regarded as a necessary part of a professional approach. This means that the Committee will need to redouble its efforts to raise awareness and deepen understanding throughout the National Assembly. Every part of the Assembly needs to develop a dialogue with those representing disadvantaged groups and to frame its policies on the basis of the advice and guidance they provide (NAW, 2000b: unpaginated)

Inclusiveness in the Assembly's work has also been driven by 'European' initiatives, principally through both the Amsterdam Treaty and the inter-agency working of the European Equality Partnership (EEP).[18] The EEP has developed both measurable 'targeted activities' and 'anticipated results' to improve the participation of 'minority' groups in the Welsh economy as part of the formal bid for European structural fund aid for west Wales and the Valleys (NAW, 2000f: ch. 8, Priorities 1–5). As a result of these measures, mainstreaming has promoted equality for women and disabled people (and other minority groups) in a growing number of Assembly policies[19] and in the governing administration's ten-year strategic plan, *A Better Wales*. In the latter case, equality is identified as the first of the Assembly's three 'major themes' for the decade (NAW, 2000a: 7). The level of liaison with some of the groups interviewed has triggered comments about 'consultation fatigue'. One manager observed, ' I mean in that sense they are very welcoming and very open, and it is . . . consultation fatigue, you just get – I mean – "I can't keep up", is the bottom line.'

The Assembly's first months have seen the establishment of structures and longer-term strategies and procedures to achieve inclusive governance, aspects not immediately visible to the majority of the members of 'minority' groups or the electorate as a whole. A leading figure reflected on the first year of the Assembly's existence and observed:

> Yes, we do have a better perspective of what's going on, there's a lot of preparation, there's a lot of work going on around policy formulation, none of which is apparent to the outside world at the moment. I mean I can think of a number of initiatives that are under discussion in the Assembly or in consultation groups but they're not evident to the outside world, and certainly not to people with learning disabilities. There's a housing strategy which is under consideration, there's a carers' strategy, there's a children's strategy, there's a review of learning disabilities services, the formulation of a new national service framework for learning disability services, I can think of a number of other things around policy that probably run into double figures easily. But not much in terms of product yet.

DISCUSSION AND CONCLUSION

In the early days of the Assembly the evidence suggests that expectations were high among women's groups and organizations. There was a belief that at last women's voices would be heard and women's issues would come to the fore. There were variations in the grounds upon which such optimism was based, but nevertheless there was evidence of good will and high hopes. Disabled people's expectations of what could be achieved were more varied. Some were optimistic, others negative, the majority appeared uncertain as to what to expect and appeared to share the apathy of many in the Welsh electorate. They were realistic enough to recognize the gap between aspiration and achievement; they recognized that the mere formation of the Assembly would not solve problems and that the significant representation of disabled people in the political structures of Wales lay in the future. Nor did they feel that representation would be achieved without a struggle; they were wary of politicians and of the public's attitude to disability.

In terms of participation and representation, our interviews revealed that devolution is beginning to make a difference to some of the women and disabled people to whom we spoke. However, there is an evident disparity between the two groupings. The increased participation of women in the formal political process is one of the major achievements of the National Assembly and, together with the Assembly's commitment to equal opportunities, indicates how far women have come and suggests hope for the future. There is, however, no cause for complacency. As Jane Hutt told the delegates at Chwarae Teg's annual conference in November 1999, 'Success in implementing these themes requires not only the full commitment of the Assembly as a whole but also a real and continuing dialogue with those whose needs and aspirations we are seeking to meet.' Her colleague Val Feld, chair of the Assembly's Economic Development Committee, concluded that 'despite the very considerable progress made in the early days of our new Assembly, this is a fragile achievement . . . gender equality remains, and will be for the foreseeable future, fundamentally about power relations' (Feld, 2000: 80). The comments of our respondents support this analysis, for, despite determination amongst both women AMs and women's groups to seize the opportunity presented by devolution to advance gender equality, this in itself does not amount to all that was promised by the earlier rhetoric of inclusiveness. Whilst the new structures of devolved governance are promoting equality in both the policy process and the gender balance of elected representatives, similar progress has yet to be made in fostering greater participation by women across Wales.

Our findings reveal major differences in the readiness and ability of women's groups to work with the new legislature. For some, devolution has delivered much greater engagement in the process of government, an advantage derived from personal contacts with AMs and greater levels of resources. In contrast, other groups are not so fortunate and have yet to acquire the necessary skills and resources to achieve a similar level of participation in the Assembly's activities. This contrast might be a product of the developing, and therefore transitional, nature of the new structures of governance. There is strong evidence that the formal mechanisms for pursuing equality of opportunity are one of the Assembly's greatest achievements. As Rees observed, 'I think that we are very well placed in Wales, almost to be at the vanguard in the UK for mainstreaming and integrating equality' (Rees, 2000). However, there are dangers attached to over-reliance on such formal structures to foster the promised 'inclusive and participatory democracy' (Welsh Office, 1997: 13, para. 3.1; Hain, 1999: 14). Failure to achieve wider citizen involvement would serve only to reinforce the existing exclusion and marginalization of some women from the formal decision-making process and arrest the pace of progress towards achieving inclusive government.

In contrast to the progress made by women, disabled people have failed to achieve anything like proportional descriptive representation in the Assembly. As a result they lack a comparable basis for optimism that the legislature will be able to deliver a form of government attuned to their needs. Partly in consequence of this, the construction of the disability lobby in Wales is likely to be a long, complex and dynamic process, one that has only just begun. However, a significant minority of our interviewees had very positive views of the new structures of governance based on their initial contact with the Assembly. They felt that the institution is open, approachable and friendly. The key challenge for the new government body will be to foster this feeling amongst the majority of disabled people in Wales.

As the First Minister Rhodri Morgan observed when outlining a review of the Assembly's procedures, 'it would be nothing short of a constitutional miracle if we had achieved perfection as a devolutionary body within 12 months and a few weeks of transfer of powers' (R. Morgan, 2000b). However, it is sufficient time for a large number of issues to be highlighted, ones that have a general applicability for all groups that have been largely excluded from the mainstream of politics. In the specific case of disability these are: the political potential of disability issues; the nature of disability organizations and their effectiveness as political organizations; the leadership of the disability organizations and their ability to mobilize disabled people; the availability of effective financial, human and social resources to mobilize the disability lobby; and the responsiveness of the political system to disability issues.

Fundamental to the development of an effective disability lobby in Wales is the extent to which the concerns and grievances held by disabled people are deeply held and widespread amongst disabled people themselves. If they are peripheral to their day-to-day lives and fragmented across many different types of impairment, it is unlikely that the necessary energy will be produced to mount successful campaigns or establish an effective disability movement. Effectiveness will also be increased if there is a conviction that the government can make a difference. The success or otherwise of the lobby will also be influenced by the nature of disability organizations themselves and their effectiveness in politicizing disabled people's concerns. Their initial problem must be one of mobilization, of getting and retaining the political interests of disabled people across Wales. Associated with mobilization is the question of strategy, as to what the balance should be between campaigns on the everyday issues of care, education and work, and on the more abstract concerns of civil rights and social justice. Which will be more effective in mobilizing disabled people and gaining public and political support? Is either of these strategies capable of developing a disability movement that unifies the interests and concerns of all disabled people irrespective of impairment?

Crucial to the meaning of organization is the function of leadership. A key question therefore is whether it is possible to transfer the leadership of disability organizations (the majority of whom are not disabled) to the disabled themselves. The nature of leadership is bound up with the issue of resources.[20] At the simplest level, greater resources will result in more disabled people being involved in the political system. Disabled people live in a physical, social and educational environment which is not well suited to their needs or which gives them the skills or opportunities to learn how to participate in the political system. To redress this disadvantage and develop the leadership of disabled people requires a high level of investment that neither disabled people, nor volunteers nor disability organizations are able to provide.

For adequate representation of disabled people to be achieved within Wales there must first be an acknowledgement that they are worthy, that disability is an identity that should be included in the polity of Wales, that they have a right to be represented and that they can speak for themselves. For a few disabled people, who fight for their right to be included with such force that they cannot be ignored, crossing into the mainstream may be possible, but it is not a viable option for the many. It has been argued elsewhere (Ramcharan et al., 1997) that what is required is a particular concept of citizenship that is based upon entitlement, in which all members of society will have sufficient resources to enjoy a minimum level of well-being which allows them to be included in the family, community and civil structures. There should also be sufficient leeway for them to be able to choose and determine their identity without unnecessary encumbrance from the state or its functionaries.

As Squires (1999: 185) puts it, 'Rethinking the boundaries of political representation might well allow for a more inclusive politics, but it will also generate a new set of criteria as to what is to be deemed politically pertinent, and which identities and interests are perceived as authentic.' Here the key issues are the representativeness of those that the Assembly chooses to consult and the level of access afforded to all groups.[21] It is essential that the AMs remain in touch with grass-roots movements and 'ordinary people'. For both groups 'being in touch' will necessitate 'reaching out' and not just relying on the voices of those with the skills and resources to 'reach in'. As far as women and disabled people are concerned, the present findings suggest that two types of organization are emerging. At national level some organizations have been heavily engaged. Certainly Disability Wales, Cardiff and Vale Coalition of Disabled People, Chwarae Teg and the Wales Women's National Coalition have been fully engrossed in the new systems of consultation, but the vast majority of organizations in Wales have been less involved. Many smaller representative groups, and women and disabled people as individuals, have yet to engage with the new political structures, raising fears about their exclusion from the decision-making of the devolved government. As Bryson observes when referring to the case of women: 'There is a danger that an élite minority could become assimilated into existing power structures and that such will represent the interests of middle class, mainly white women and have no more understanding than many men of the needs of less privileged groups' (1999: 122).

According to Ron Davies, 'It is only by devising new ways of incorporating people into the political process and in turn affording them a sense of ownership that we can create a genuinely inclusive Wales' (1999a: 8). The present evidence shows that this process has begun. The test of whether the Assembly ultimately produces new gender and disability settlements that adequately meet the needs of women and disabled people and facilitate their contributions will be the extent to which, in the coming months and years, it creates the opportunity to open up new dialogue with groups and individuals by building ownership at key junctures of the political process. Time and further research will be needed to assess whether or not that opportunity is grasped.

Notes

[1] Or the synonymous variant, inclusivity.
[2] Welsh-language equivalent.
[3] Ron Davies interviewed by one of the authors, 4 November 1999.
[4] The word 'disability' encompasses a great variety of conditions, relating to restricted mobility, sensory impairment and learning difficulties. In some cases these problems will be openly acknowledged, in some cases hidden. A more formal definition is presented in the Disability Discrimination Act (1995): 'Disability' applies when 'a person has a disability for the purposes of this Act if he [*sic*] has a physical or mental impairment which has a substantial and long-term adverse effect on his [*sic*] ability to carry out normal day to day activities'. See also O'Dempsey and Short (1996).
[5] See NAW (1999–2000) *passim*, for e.g. the discussion of discrimination based on sexuality, 29 June 2000.
[6] In addition advisers from CRE Wales, Equal Opportunities Commission Wales and the Disability Rights Commission in Wales attend meetings of this standing committee in accordance with Standing Order 14.4.
[7] Commission for Racial Equality Wales, Equal Opportunities Commission Wales and the Disability Rights Commission in Wales.

8   University of Wales Board of Celtic Studies-funded project entitled 'The
    Effectiveness of Inclusive Government: A Study of the Participation and Rep-
    resentation of Minority Groups in the First Two Years of the National
    Assembly' – Ralph Fevre, Paul Chaney (School of Social Sciences, Cardiff
    University), Sandra Betts, John Borland and Charlotte Williams (School of
    Sociology and Social Policy, University of Wales, Bangor).
9   Second to Sweden. See classification produced by the International
    Parliamentary Union, *http://www.ipu.org/wmn-e/classif.htm*. However NAW
    would technically be regarded as a regional assembly as opposed to a national
    parliament under this listing. Women comprise twenty-five of the sixty AMs
    and five of the nine Assembly ministers.
10 'This category includes those with a disability which has a substantial adverse
    impact on their day-to-day activities (i.e. the [definition given in the] Disability
    Discrimination Act 1995) or limits kind or amount of work and those known to
    have a progressive condition. It may exclude some people with progressive
    conditions and severe disfigurements who feel that these do not limit their
    work or have an adverse effect on their day-to-day activities' (DRC, 2000).
    Figures relate to men aged 16–64 years and women 16–59 years.
11 Examples include: MENCAP in Wales and SCOVO (1999); Wales Council for
    the Blind (1999); MIND Cymru (1999); RNIB Cymru (1999).
12 Disability Wales is an umbrella body representing approximately 370 disabled
    people's organizations in Wales.
13 It involves a four-stage programme: 'baseline interviews with policy divisions'
    . . . to establish to what extent race, gender and disability are taken into account
    in current policy'; 'each Assembly Secretary will . . . receive . . . a report on
    equal opportunities and present it to the relevant subject committee . . . [this
    will] set out the baseline position and proposed priorities for action. The action
    might include . . . improved arrangements for involving minority ethnic
    organisations, disability groups and women in discussion of policy issues . . . ';
    the Committee on Equality of Opportunity will itself consider these reports
    and 'offer comment and advice on the proposed actions, objectives and targets
    based on the overall picture and priorities identified by outside organisations';
    and lastly, 'Assembly Secretaries will approve firm action plans for their area
    of responsibility. These will together comprise the Assembly's first annual
    report and programme of action on equal opportunities' (NAW, 1999a).
14 For example, the responses of groups to the *A Better Wales* Consultation
    Document (NAW, 2000a, see *http://www.betterwales.com/responses*) such as those
    given by the Royal National Institute for Deaf People Cymru (RNIB Cymru),
    and Standing Conference of Voluntary Organizations for people with Learning
    Disability in Wales (SCOVO).
15 Including the regional committees.
16 See, for example, papers presented to the NAW Economic Development
    Committee: Disability Wales (*http:www.wales.gov.uk./Assemblydata/381B53E0009
    C2B8000012610000000.html*), September 1999: or Chwarae Teg (1999)
    http://www.wales.gov.uk/Assemblydata/3815B5CE000C83670000127E0000000.html.
17 For example, the membership of Welsh Woman's Aid, SCOVO and Disability
    Wales to the *National Housing Strategy Task Group 4 – Ensuring Decent Housing*

for All – Meeting the Needs of Vulnerable Households: Final Report to the National Assembly for Wales (2000k: 42, Appendix 1).

[18] EEP, a working group composed of Disability Wales, the Equal Opportunities Commission Wales, Commission for Racial Equality Wales, the Welsh Development Agency, the Wales Council for Voluntary Action and the civil service.

[19] Examples include: NAW (1999d) (*http://www.wales.gov.uk/polinfo/Yame_ housing _strateg/*) and: NAW (1999b), 3, para. 15, 'Cross-cutting themes': the Strategy '[should] have due regard to the principles of equal opportunities (there are issues relevant to gender, race equality, disabilities and age discrimination in relation to carers)'.

[20] For example, the modest level of funding allocated under the Promoting Equality in Wales: Project Development Fund (NAW, 2000m), and the struggle to expand the (civil service) Equality Unit within the Assembly from just two part-time posts to the equivalent of 9.5 full-time posts (NAW, 2000p).

[21] The danger is that the Assembly puts over-reliance on umbrella bodies instead of conducting wide-ranging consultation exercises. A recent directive highlights this danger: 'As an example in the first instance, dialogue with ethnic minority communities can be established through the All Wales Ethnic Minority Association; for gender groups discussions have started with the Welsh Women's National Coalition and for Disability discussions are taking place with Disability Wales' (NAW, 2000c, section 5, 'Consultation').

4

Inclusive Government for Excluded Groups: Ethnic Minorities

CHARLOTTE WILLIAMS and PAUL CHANEY

INTRODUCTION – PANDORA'S BOX?

To the majority of people from ethnic minority communities the official opening of the National Assembly for Wales (NAW) on 26 May 1999 was likely to have been perceived as something of a damp squib. Yet this great change in the political landscape of Wales undoubtedly has profound implications for the minority population, not least because of the Assembly's forthright agenda on equal opportunities. But what does the advent of this national government body for Wales mean to ethnic minorities? How well can it deliver on its promises of inclusiveness? How can the new governance be shaped to embrace diversity in Wales? Pandora may have released the potential for progress but under what conditions will it be realized?

Here we continue to draw upon the research findings outlined in the previous chapter. First we engage contemporary debates about identity, nation and belonging, and relate theoretical aspects of the participation and representation of ethnic minorities in systems of governance to the contemporary Welsh context. Subsequently, against the backdrop of limited self-government, we examine the attempts to develop the concept of 'inclusiveness' into something meaningful to people from an ethnic minority background. We explore in turn their expectations of the new constitutional 'settlement', the factors that mediated their involvement in the first Welsh general election, and their thoughts on the nature and challenges of the emerging new structures of governance. Our discussion examines the opportunity that devolution presents for improving on the pre-existing mode of governance for those from an ethnic minority background in Wales.

In addition to the Assembly's statutory duties to promote the principle of equality (Wooding, 1998; Clements and Thomas, 1999) there are a number of significant external push-factors that should give rise to a climate of optimism for ethnic minorities: the New Labour agenda with its focus on communitarianism, inclusive relationships and deepened democracy, together with the 'third way' value of 'equal worth' (Blair, 1998: 3); the MacPherson inquiry recommendations; the recent public debate on 'institutional racism'; the proposals by the home secretary, Jack Straw, on setting 'ethnic' recruitment targets for some public bodies and extending the Race Relations Act to include 'indirect discrimination' in all public services; the European Commission directives on 'mainstreaming' equal opportunities; the new policy discourse of 'social exclusion', 'social capital' and a renewed focus on civic forms of nationalism (Putnam, 1993; Delanty, 1996; Fevre et al., 1997); and growing public concern about economic and social inequalities in which immigrants and ethnic minorities have suffered disproportionately. As a result of these factors, significant political capital has been invested in 'tackling the democratic deficit', fostering 'inclusiveness' and engaging minorities more effectively in the policy process.

These agendas can be expected to shape the new devolved governance of Wales, but the potential benefits for society go beyond the interface of public policy into the realm of notions such as 'constitutional patriotism' (Habermas, 1994), claims of civic pride and belonging, and the development of civic nationalism. It is these latter aspirations that have been most forcibly expressed both by the architects of devolved government and by key commentators on the potential of the National Assembly. Ron Davies, former secretary of state for Wales, has said:

> Once the Assembly is established it must reflect the diversity and plurality of Welsh social, political and cultural life. By doing that we will have a greater status for the Assembly as a national institution; we can give a clearer focus for the development of our Welsh sense of identity. (Davies, 1995: 14).

Lord Elis Thomas observed that 'the Assembly is about creating a notion of citizenship of Wales. That citizenship is open to everybody who chooses to be here. It doesn't matter where you come from. It doesn't matter what languages you speak' (Elis Thomas, 1999). The secretary of state for Wales, Paul Murphy, has spoken of

> a new sense of citizenship – where the Bangladeshi community in Swansea and the Somali community in Cardiff have the same stake in our new democratic Wales as it has for me, the great grandson of Irish immigrants . . . who crossed the Irish sea 130 years ago, looking for a better life in Wales. (Murphy, 1999)

There exists, therefore, not only an instrumental service-orientated rationale, but also a powerful ideological ambition for the Assembly, namely that it may serve to redefine citizenship and forge a new common identity.

AND . . . ETHNIC MINORITIES

'Ethnic minorities' comprise 1.5 per cent of the population of Wales, a higher proportion than in Scotland (1.3 per cent) and Ireland (0.5 per cent). The uneven spatial distribution of ethnic minority settlement in Wales reflects the country's economic history (Fryer, 1984; Evans, 1991). Whilst the last census revealed that South Glamorgan the (former) county closest to the great industrial anchorages in south Wales was in the top ten British counties with the highest non-white population, in many rural Welsh counties the ethnic minority population totalled less than 2 per cent of the total (OPCS, 1992). As Nyoni (2000) notes, it is likely that the last census underestimated the numbers of people from an ethnic minority back-ground in Wales. However, the census did reveal its general characteristics:

> Gwent has a relatively high proportion of Pakistani people, concentrated in Newport. West Glamorgan has the highest number of Bangladeshi people, concentrated in Swansea. The BME [black and minority ethnic] population living in Cardiff is at least 6.3% and includes significant numbers from a very diverse range of minority ethnic groups, in particular a long-established Afro-Caribbean community in the docklands areas, an Asian community in Riverside and a growing Somali population' (Nyoni, 2000: 15, para. 5.6)

According to the methodology used by the Office for National Statistics (ONS), 'Chinese and others' comprises the largest ethnic 'grouping', one that constitutes almost 40 per cent of people from an ethnic minority in Wales (cf. ONS, 1996). As well as highlighting the inadequacy of the broadly drawn ONS schema, this figure reflects the 'high incidence of persons of mixed ethnic origin in areas of long settlement in areas such as . . . Cardiff' (Williams, 1995: 116). Other groupings also constitute the rich diversity referred to as 'ethnic minorities' in Wales, including those of Irish descent who comprise 0.73 per cent of the population of the south Wales Valleys (T. Rees, 1999: 23), as well as those of Polish and Italian back-grounds. It is pertinent to note that, although not regarded as an ethnic minority for the present purposes, huge cross-border migratory flows (Carter, 1999) have resulted in those born in England constituting one in five of those resident in Wales today (Blair, 2000a).

In order to understand the ambitious project to redress the marginal-ization experienced by ethnic minorities in Wales it is necessary to trace the development of an 'ethnic' dimension to 'inclusive' politics. This began in the latter half of the 1990s as officials, politicians and people from an ethnic minority background started to translate devolutionary rhetoric into action. Figure 4.1 outlines some of the milestones during this period and shows that the prime movers in this process were confined to a relatively narrow social stratum of policy-makers and managers. In seeking to understand why this is the case and the issues that this presents it is firstly necessary to look at the pre-devolution context.

Landmark events

Mid-1990s: Ron Davies communicates the ideas of inclusiveness.

1995: Commission for Racial Equality (CRE) sets up an office in Wales.

1997: CRE as part of the Equality Partnership in Wales lobbies for the inclusion of the equality clauses in the Government of Wales Act.

A leading figure in the Women Say Yes referendum campaign was 'delighted and stunned by the response from ethnic minority groups . . . there was a real desire to support the campaign, they understood exactly what this was about because they knew about colonialism' (Feld, quoted in Andrews, 1999: 138).

25 August: secretary of state for Wales addresses meeting of ethnic minority organizations including CRE and Race Equality Councils (RECs).

18 September: devolution referendum. *Video Nation* (BBC documentary 'vox pop' television programme) features young black Welsh-speaking woman arguing for 'Yes' vote. Party manifestos broaden the reach of their constituency by using inclusive language.

December: National Assembly Advisory Group (NAAG) established. 'We emphasized throughout the equality issues – and in very clear terms we emphasized race as a separate issue' (Ray Singh).[1] CRE Wales, Joint Committee for Ethnic Minorities in Wales and other groups involved in NAAG consultations.

1998: *16 February*: A leading campaigner writes to a Welsh newspaper: 'It is significant that while the Labour Party outside Wales has provided seven Black/Asian MPs in London and the Midlands and Scotland there is no indication that any black candidate stands any chance of being selected for any winnable or non-winnable seat in Wales' (Fahm, 1999).

24 August: NAAG Final Recommendations published. They 'require the Assembly to debate . . . equal opportunities arrangements and report including as a minimum the three strands of race, gender and disability' (NAAG, 1998b: 10).

16 September: Discussion forum hosted by the CRE. Calls for representation of race issues within the structures of the Welsh Office. In response, 'Welsh Secretary Ron Davies pledged that ethnic and other minority issues should have a high profile in the National Assembly' (Welsh Office, 1998).

1999: *January*: Race equality project leader appointed and the 'race desk' opens in the Welsh Office.

March: The Right To Vote, a Welsh Office-funded project to encourage people from an ethnic minority background to vote and engage with politics at a local and national level, appoints a full-time project officer.

April: Operation Black Vote – voter awareness-raising sessions held across Wales. Consultative meetings organized by RECs. Secretary of state for Wales announces the Assembly's Standing Orders (procedural rules): 'The Committee [on Equality of Opportunity] shall also have particular regard to the need for the Assembly to avoid discrimination against any person on grounds of race, sex or disability' (Welsh Office, 1999c).

6 May: Assembly Members elected: no direct black and ethnic minority representation.

15 June: The Equality Partnership Wales hosts an evening for Assembly Members.

June: CRE questionnaire on building effective forms of communication is circulated.

1 July: Assembly assumes statutory powers under the Government of Wales Act, including legal duty to promote equality of opportunity.

15 July: Assembly Committee on Equality of Opportunity is elected. A seat is reserved for a representative of the Commission for Racial Equality as a special adviser.

22 July: The Assembly Committee on Equality of Opportunity discusses the equality 'Work Programme and Timetable' that prioritizes 'arrangements for channelling the views of people from ethnic minorities . . . into the Assembly' (NAW, 1999a).

24 July: Launch of the All Wales Black and Ethnic Minority Assembly Consultative and Participatory Association (AWEMA) – attended by First Minister Alun Michael. Consultative groupings around subject area committees are established.

21 October: The Assembly Committee on Equality of Opportunity discusses the implications of the MacPherson report.

2–9 November: First meetings of AWEMA's subject focus groups (housing, education, economic development).

2000: *23 March*: Mainstreaming in the wake of the MacPherson report. Chair of Assembly Committee on Equality of Opportunity writes to chair of Assembly education committee asking for implementation of MacPherson Recommendations 67 and 68 – 'Prevention of racism and the role of education'.

11 April: National Assembly 'Diversity' Recruitment Fair; an event held, as the Assembly's permanent secretary stated, 'to ensure that the National Assembly's workforce . . . reflects the multi-cultural society in which we live' (NAW, 2000h).

13 April: Assembly Committee on Equality of Opportunity's 'Equal Opportunities Baseline Survey' identifies 'the significant work that is needed to move to the position of excellence that the Assembly should aspire to' (NAW, 2000c: 3). Survey addresses 'the need as a matter of urgency to review/replace the existing recruitment practices and procedures of Assembly civil service in order to increase number of staff from ethnic minorities'.

27 April: Assembly's European Objective One Plan (ESF) sets detailed targets on ethnic minority participation in the labour market (NAW, 2000l).

12 July: Assembly's Annual report and plenary debate on equality of opportunity identifies mainstreaming equality in Assembly's policies and work as the principal priority for the forthcoming year.

Figure 4.1 Early days – the mobilization of democracy?

It could be expected that racial and ethnic minorities might respond to sudden references to them in public discourse with a degree of scepticism and express no small measure of surprise at terms such as 'diversity', 'multiculturalism' and the phrase '. . . *and ethnic minorities'* entering political debates. In a country that has been unequivocally sluggish in its attention to ethnic minorities little more than cynicism could have been anticipated. The profile of 'race' on the political agenda of Wales has historically been neglected for a number of reasons and with far reaching consequences (Williams, 1995). The culture of disbelief about the facts of intolerance, racism and inappropriate services, and a patterning of apathy and organizational inertia, are evidenced by the paucity of relevant information available to public services and policy-makers. The Welsh Office has failed to keep any centralized records or offer directives on the collation of data, ethnic monitoring and the evaluation of services. A recent study commissioned by the Assembly Office for inclusion in the European Structural Fund programme (ESF) describes the available information as 'partial, unreliable or doubtful quality' (Williams et al., 1999: 5).

This official lethargy is well illustrated by the comments of an executive officer with the Commission for Racial Equality in Wales (CRE), who said, 'We have always struggled in Wales to get organizations to work with race equality because they see it as not being a problem here.' Until 1995 there was no statutory body in Wales to police these concerns, with the CRE in Birmingham operating a 'long-arm' responsibility for Wales. Therefore a dialogue between the main office responsible for policy development in Wales and the ethnic minority communities did not exist. 'The Welsh Office was seen as some ivory tower that wasn't welcoming to ethnic minorities . . . It wasn't a place we had access to . . . the CRE were never invited to sit at the tables where the decisions were being made', the executive officer continued, and a director of one Race Equality Council (REC) in Wales commented: 'Black and ethnic minorities in Wales had no access to the Welsh Office at all . . . and therefore there were no points of contact; understanding of race equality and multiculturalism was absent within the Welsh Office.'

The political profile of ethnic minorities in Wales has been extremely weak. There are no black MPs representing Welsh constituencies. Moreover, at the onset of political change in Wales just 1.4 per cent of local authority councillors were from black or ethnic minority backgrounds (Brown, Jones and Mackay, 1999: 5) and none of the 452 appointees of the secretary of state for Wales were 'non-white' (Hanson, 1995: 4). Compared with other UK nations and regions, black voluntary-sector activity in Wales is sparse, comprises just 1.1 per cent of the total (WCVA, 1999: 5) and operates from a very low base both financially and politically. This may be a reflection of the geographical dispersal of Wales's 41,000 ethnic minority population. Elsewhere spatial patterns and processes have been identified as central to an understanding of territorial collectivities and political power (cf. Anwar, 1986). In the case of Scotland, for example, Dunlop (1993) has argued that an absence of black political mobilization is the result of the spatial structures of ethnic communities. Similarly, Kearns (1995) suggests that active citizenship has geographical dimensions, with the nature of place and belonging being both mediator and outcome of active citizenship. In Wales the 'ethnic' population is relatively dispersed so that 'community' – a concept dear to the heart of policy-makers – as a locus of intervention may be difficult to find. Indeed, little is known about the pattern of ethnic mobilization in Wales, about diverse identities, community politics or the politics of recognition. It is likely that the establishment of the Assembly may act to stimulate and shape this patterning, as minority groups become more self-conscious and politically active. Thus devolution might open up a new dialogue unfettered by networks of old loyalties and politicking, one that will foster new and creative participatory structures.

Alternatively, and more pessimistically, current patterns of 'ethnic' exclusion and marginalization in Wales can be attributed to a threefold failure by politicians and policy-makers to consider the contextual barriers to effective participation, understand the ways in which ethnic minority communities mobilize their interests, and develop different modes of incorporation. Collectively these shortcomings may lead to a 'top-down' agenda on the ethnic minorities.

Ron Davies has argued that inclusiveness is 'the essential foundation of the whole devolution enterprise' (1999a: 7). If the ambition was originally for *political* inclusion, that is, inclusion of all the major democratically elected parties, it has perhaps opportunistically come to mean much more (Chaney and Fevre, 2001). Indeed Day and Thompson (1999) argue that it has at least four potential meanings: political, civic, social and pluralistic. In the latter case, an inclusive process is one 'in which all the diverse voices and interests of Wales are heard through empowerment of the people *as they are actually organised in civil society*' (emphasis added). This will be the true challenge for the Assembly as it attempts to develop inclusive policies that are responsive to the needs of the multi-ethnic communities. However, inclusiveness as a concept is necessarily problematic in relation to multi-culturalism for several reasons. Critics have pointed to its tendency towards consensualism, assimilation and the muffling or suppression of diverse voices (Weinreich, 1998; Mouffe, 1998; Vertovec, 1999). There is a danger that inclusion comes to mean enforced incorporation without challenge to the accepted paradigms and existing modes of association. Through processes of 'institutional channelling' it is possible, therefore, to be included and then further marginalized. The aims of the integrationist approach may mean that it fails to take account of the structural processes of institutionalized exclusion that are based on relationships of power and inequality. It may also lead to inadequate consideration of access and barriers to full participation. Indeed, integration is not the same thing as cohesion. The very idea that 'we' can be included can operate to divert attention away from fundamental and enduring differences in power. So it is pertinent to ask: who is doing the including? How? Why? Who is to be included? And what is the ambit of inclusiveness?

Another feature which serves to frustrate the attainment of inclusiveness is the idea of 'community' itself. The arguments here are twofold. Firstly, in relation to the assumptions embedded in the notion, there can be no doubt of the appeal of the idea of community with all that it conjures in terms of tolerance, solidarity, mutuality and cohesion – notions that have deep resonance with assumptions of the national character of Wales. This ideal has been particularly attached to the rural communities of Wales and criticized from a number of perspectives, not least its failure to accommodate diversity and difference and to promulgate notions of 'spoiled' or 'deviant' identities (Day, 1998; Williams, 1999). Further, it has been forcefully argued by some that the idea of 'community' in Wales operates as a form of social closure rather than as a mechanism of social inclusion (Borland et al., 1992). Thus in this context notions of 'community' and 'community identity' must be understood in ways that are sensitive to the implicit inclusionary and exclusionary elements that such terms convey.

The second issue relates to the centrality of the concept of inclusiveness as a point of intervention for policy-making and as a locus for political mobilization. Here 'community' comes to be identified with essentialist groupings, that is social collectivities categorized according to some notion of fixed and immutable culture which binds individuals deterministically to shared and essential values and behaviours. This uncomplicated view of community assumes a type of corporate unity among ethnic groups and operates to promote stereotypical understandings of minorities. Vertovec (1996: 51) has argued against the folly of focusing on such essentialist categories that produce 'a picture of society as a "mosaic" of several bounded, nameable, individually homogeneous and unmeltable minority uni-cultures which are pinned on to the backdrop of a similarly characterised majority uni-culture'.

In reality, ethnic minority experience is characterized by multiple identifications, where political and social identities are chosen in complex ways contingent on any number of interacting factors. For example, Kearns (1995) uses concepts like 'place-based communities' as factors in political mobilization, which may transcend ethnicity. Moreover, Rex (1996) has argued that minority communities are not internally homogeneous but have a perpetual internal dynamic for change. Furthermore, Vertovec (1999) asserts that the orientation of public policy towards the 'culturalist in multiculturalism' is misguided. Thus participation may be evoked along a number of axes, potentially but not necessarily based on the politics of resistance to racism. Participatory structures that evolve based on the idea of homogeneous ethnic categories, or worse still, some homogenized notion of '. . . and ethnic minorities' will only serve to contain and marginalize minority views.

ON NATION AND BELONGING – 'NOT JUST VISITORS HERE'

One of the most fundamental questions raised by the establishment of the 'Welsh Assembly' must be the relationship between this *national* institution and prominent ideas of nation and national identity. These concepts are salient to understanding the ongoing attempts to achieve the participation and inclusion of people from an ethnic minority background and in explaining the associated failures, setbacks and shortcomings already experienced in the short history of the devolved polity. We now explore the way that these key concepts have acted to mediate patterns of 'ethnic' participation and engagement. Our findings are based upon qualitative analysis of 100 semi-structured interviews with members of BME organiza-tions, politicians and officials, conducted by the authors between May 1999 and October 2000. These 'ethnic minority' organizations ranged from pan-Wales 'umbrella' bodies whose membership is composed of both individuals and organizations, to locally based single-issue groups focusing on matters ranging from health to environmentalism. Together, these interviewees comprise a theoretical sample of those associated with BME organizations in Wales. This was developed to reflect the diversity of this sector as defined by factors such as geographical location, membership size, type of funding and access to resources. Further original data were derived from field notes following participant observation of key meetings. Secondary data sources such as published interviews, organizations' newsletters, specialist literature, policy and consultation documents were also analysed in the course of this research in order to explore the themes and concepts discussed below.

As much of the demand for devolution originated with nationalist political thought (Fevre et al., 1997), it could be argued that the NAW's identification with the national question operates as a counter to the idea of inclusiveness. Such a conclusion is based upon the often ambiguous relationship of many from the minority communities to dominant notions of the Welsh nation and of Welshness. To what extent then do people from ethnic minority communities feel that they belong to Welsh society? In the run-up to the Assembly elections the expectations amongst ethnic minorities were running very low for a number of reasons. Some of these related to the election campaign itself, but others were founded in the uneasy relationship of minority communities to the majority Welsh society. The fact that there was a brief turnaround in this sentiment is something that can be attributed to the former secretary of state, Ron Davies. It is clear that his proclamations of inclusiveness, matched by some very forthright and deliberate actions such as the opening of a 'race desk' in the Welsh Office,[2] raised hopes to a considerable degree and gave rise to feelings of confidence that the Assembly just might turn rhetoric into reality. A director of one of the Race Equality Councils comments that only since the administration that Ron Davies headed has 'any meaningful movement been made to ensure that reasonable attention and effort was paid to understanding the needs [of ethnic minority communities] and making sure there was a channel of communication between the Welsh Office and the wider community'. Furthermore, the All-Wales Chair of MEWN Cymru, an organization aimed at supporting ethnic minority women, suggested that, 'when Ron Davies was around those words were beginning to feel meaningful and significant to the minority communities . . . the words were very emotive, words like *inclusive* and *accountable* and *open*. These are the kinds of words that give people hope and encouragement that there is a truly fair and representative process.'

One black Wales Labour Party (WLP) candidate spoke of being 'seduced' by the language of inclusiveness and multiculturalism. However, these may have been the feelings of a very small minority because there was a groundswell of opinion that the establishment of an Assembly for Wales meant very little to the majority of BME people. A prospective WLP candidate from an ethnic minority background commented:

> I think the ethnic minority communities were sort of curious about it [devolution]. They were interested in it but I don't think they were fully engaged in it . . . It sort of concerned itself with people who are normally sort of interested and articulate so I don't think that really it went to the level of the ordinary people.

There was some suggestion that this related, as one woman noted, to 'little understanding' of the Assembly by minority communities, but others saw this as the result of an overriding sense that the Assembly lacked meaning and relevance for them. The sense of disenfranchisement conveyed by interviewees was frequently linked to their loose affiliation to dominant definitions of Welshness and Welsh society, something that underpinned a deep sense of marginalization. One observed:

> It's the first time Wales has had its own government and, yes, it's a parliament of pride and this is the time perhaps to think particularly Welsh, and I'm using the word now to indicate to you that Welsh appears to mean simply middle-class white Welsh, and if you look at most of the candidates that have come through they seem to fit that bill.

And another respondent added:

> After twenty-two years I still feel excluded from the society. If somebody like myself who can articulate feels that, what do you think the person who's got housing problems, educational difficulties for children, any sort of problems – you name it [feels]? And they are unable to articulate their feelings about it because society just shuns them, marginalizes them, sidelines them . . . [also] I think Wales is a very élitist place . . . you've got to be part of the circle – or you've got to be, got to know somebody who knows somebody else . . .

The 'nationalist' appeal of the Assembly that may have served to enthuse many of the majority population clearly alienated members of the minority populace. Despite this, many interviewees expressed a sense of attachment to things Welsh and to Welsh identity. A member of MEWN Cymru said: 'It is not as though black and ethnic people are just visitors here. They've been living here with a history of almost 150 years, so I would have thought that by adoption they are Welsh and therefore should have had some sort of representation.' This was a sentiment also expressed by Cherry Short, commissioner with the CRE in Wales and a prospective candidate in the Assembly elections of May 1999: 'We've actually been here and contributed positively to this society for many, many years; it is one of the oldest black communities in the whole of Europe.'

In both minority and majority communities the dominant conceptions of Welshness are those that confirm the formula: 'Welsh equals white' and at times 'Welsh equals Welsh-speaking.' These points feature prominently in respondents' comments about attachment, ownership and identification with the Assembly. When asked why she felt that ethnic minorities were not interested in the Welsh Assembly one AM remarked:

> I wonder whether it's partly a spin-off from the frighteners that were put about at the time of the Yes/No [referendum] campaign, that people said it was going to be about the Welsh language . . . I'm sure they saw it as something for the Welsh, and although they, you know, a lot of them come from – and some of them were born in this country, people who might have been putting their name forward, they still do not entirely feel integrated into Welsh culture and I think they are happier putting their name forward for a UK government than for the Welsh Assembly . . . they don't show an interest . . . because of the way politics has been run, because it has been seen as a white male game.

The dominant discourse on nation may well evoke some suspicion and ambivalence on the part of ethnic minorities in Wales (Williams, 1999). It is well documented that minorities can operate to fracture the boundaries of place and nation through establishing networks of allegiance and association that transcend national borders (Gilroy, 1987; Anthias and Yuval-Davies, 1993; Rex, 1996). The choice for ethnic minorities is not simply between allegiance to the national polity of Wales and to an external nation. Crucially, it also relates to ideas of 'Britishness' as a generic point of identification. Significantly, recent debates on 'Britishness' highlight a certain ambivalence on the part of minorities towards this concept. The authors of *The Future of Multi-ethnic Britain* suggest that for many the term is loaded with racist connotations (cf. Parekh, 2000). In turn, a number of writers have illustrated the way in which racist elements of British or English nationalism are not replicated in the other nation states of the UK (cf. Miles and Dunlop, 1986 on Scotland; and Williams, 1995 on Wales) to the extent that these polities are seemingly more inclusive of minority communities. To a certain extent the nationalist movements in Scotland and Wales have capitalized on this point and in the 1980s basked in an aura of tolerance and communitarianism whereas, in contrast, Britain/England was formulated as racist, individualistic and Thatcherite (cf. Hassan 1999 on Scottish nationalism).

Nevertheless, it is to be expected, initially at least, that ethnic minorities will demonstrate loose affiliation and may be little inclined towards involvement in such national bodies as the Assembly. What may prove to be significant in Wales, however, is the large number of people of mixed descent and the high rate of intermarriage which denotes an area of long-established settlement for ethnic minorities (Williams, 1995). This feature alone could mean that a significant proportion of this population now strongly identify themselves as Welsh and are optimistic for more inclusionary definitions of Welshness.

ON PARTICIPATION – 'LITTLE MORE THAN A RIPPLE'

Given the foregoing conceptual barriers to 'ethnic minority' participation that related to notions of nation and identity, the role of the political parties was always going to be a pivotal factor that would determine whether inclusiveness would extend to these sections of the electorate. How then did people from an ethnic minority background respond to the candidate selection process, the actions of the political parties, the election campaigns, and the first-ever ballot to decide the composition of Wales's new government forum? And, importantly, where did this leave the concept of inclusiveness in the eyes of the 'ethnic' communities once the votes were counted on 7 May 1999?

Amidst the flurry of the election campaigns Operation Black Vote was launched with the aim of encouraging ethnic minorities to the polls. Several meetings were held across Wales to gather interest in the Assembly and to facilitate consultation between the political parties and minority communities. Despite these efforts there is a general recognition that people from ethnic minorities did not turn out to vote. One interviewee suggested that 'there was a lot of apathy generally, but amongst [ethnic minority] communities there was a full stop, you know, because they just felt that this Assembly was not going to be delivering anything for them, that those words [about inclusiveness] were empty words'. In many respects the activities around Operation Black Vote came too late to reverse the growing sense of detachment from the concerns of the Assembly. Many commented that the knowledge base amongst ethnic minorities was very low, and that those who were motivated to go to the polls did so for reasons expressed by a Cardiff outreach worker for the New Deal, namely 'to vote for Betty Campbell [black local councillor] in the local elections . . . if it was just for the Welsh Assembly I don't think many people would have voted at all.' A commonly expressed sentiment was how out of step the parties were with the concerns and needs of minority communities. Thus the campaign only served further to alienate black voters. A community worker observed that: 'there was nothing within their election campaigning that gave me the impression that they were actually looking towards listening and taking on board minority ethnic community views. It seemed like a lot of lip service was being paid.' Another suggested that the minority populations were being 'led up the garden path'.

At times the comments expressed by interviewees indicated powerfully the level of *mis*-communication between the political parties and the ethnic minority voters. Black and ethnic minority organizations were dismissive of any suggestion that the election campaign addressed issues of importance to them, a factor that had a major dampening effect on participation. Even at the meetings convened during the campaign to create links between parties and members of ethnic communities complaints were made about politicians not understanding the issues and being plainly out of their depth to the point of being, as a number of interviewees observed, 'tokenistic', 'patronizing', 'shocking', 'shallow' or just plain 'embarrassing and worrying'. Others reported that parties just did not bother to show up, and when they did they 'failed miserably'. A member of an ethnic minority youth organization suggested that 'it was so patronizing . . . almost pre-seventies in the attitudes and ignorance that were displayed towards members of ethnic communities from the parties . . . they didn't actually have anything to say about what they were going to do.'

The directors of key ethnic minority organizations in Wales endorsed these views: 'I wasn't actually aware of the parties really getting to grips with the issues and really sort of meeting with black and ethnic minority people or focusing on their agendas, you know I think it was pretty tokenistic', and

> The campaign . . . it's been poor! . . . In relation to the issues of inclusiveness, fair representation and ensuring that social inclusion was a priority – I don't think it has been addressed by any of the political parties, in fact when we have held our community meetings through the Right to Vote Campaign what has been very evident is the lack of knowledge and awareness on the part of the candidates from all parties in relation to knowledge of where the black communities are and what issues are of concern to those communities.

Some of this discontent clearly arose from the way in which candidates were selected to stand for election to the new legislature. One WLP activist, whilst defending the integrity of the selection committees in the party, pointed to flaws at the beginning and end of the selection process. She reasoned that ultimately the local party members have the power to accept or reject a candidate's nomination and that this had caused some problems in backward-looking constituencies. Crucially she observed, 'we need to get more black and ethnic groups involved at the *outset*.' The theme of machinations within the Wales Labour Party selection process (see Flynn,

1999; Jones, 2000b; Morgan and Mungham, 2000) is one that was frequently cited by interviewees, rising almost to accusations of a conspiracy to keep ethnic minority members out. One candidate reflected:

> I wanted to stand for Riverside [a district of Cardiff] which holds twenty-two and a half per cent of ethnic minority people. They chose to deselect one of the black persons and chose three white people . . . they were telling me to go and maybe stand in Carmarthen or north Wales, which represents a reference to areas where ethnic minority populations are sparse and therefore it is difficult to get votes.

Another interviewee argued that what was needed was a black forum of the Wales Labour Party to work against such marginalization. Whether the events of the election campaign amount to a deliberate strategy of exclusion cannot be evidenced from our data, but the perception is one of orchestrated sidelining with no small measure of damaging accusations of racism within the WLP. One respondent referred to it as 'institutionalized discrimination', others suggested lethargy, pointing to the fact that the parties have no policy for actively encouraging people from the black and Asian communities to come forward. 'They [all four main political parties] are not even aware whether they have people in their membership', one campaigner claimed. Some party managers have realized this and have approached one of the principal race equality bodies requesting their help in getting greater numbers of black and ethnic minority people involved in politics. The director suggested that, 'in fairness, some of them individually have been very proactive people from both Plaid Cymru, the Liberal Democrats and recently one or two individuals from the Labour Party . . . But we have had absolutely no interest from the Tories . . . none whatsoever.'

Varying explanations are offered for the low level of participation by ethnic minorities, which indicate a self-defeating tension between their being ill-equipped for active citizenship and being given little encouragement or sponsorship to undertake it by politicians. Several interviewees' comments suggested that minorities felt little motivated to get involved because the parties were not reaching out to them. One said: 'There was no impetus for them to actually go and partake in the vote', and another added that 'there was no signal given to the ethnic minority communities . . . to motivate you to go and vote'. Another key individual commented on the failure on the part of the politicians to identify the barriers to participation or to do 'anything to encourage ethnic minorities into the democratic process'.

On the other hand, there was a noted degree of apathy amongst ethnic minority voters that was related to their having little understanding of the policy process or being unable to see how it might impact on their lives. Others spoke about the lack of established networks and links with influential individuals or organizations. One community development worker offered a number of reasons for the low levels of participation: 'There's a perceived distrust of the authorities, there is a feeling of inherent racism within society which has discouraged them. [The]. . . lack of accessibility and the institutional racism and endemic racism within British society are hindrances.' The same worker suggested that there was a need to look at comparative models from areas of higher-density ethnic minority settlement in the UK and beyond. In the interviews this type of commentary was at times coupled with some clear acknowledgement of the responsibilities of active citizenship and the need for ethnic minorities to be more proactive. A leading campaigner noted: 'It's also the responsibility of black and ethnic minority communities to acknowledge that they need to do their homework . . . [and] see ways of being more effective next time.'

In the immediate aftermath of the opening of the Welsh Assembly interviewees responded to mention of 'inclusive' politics with expressions of disappointment and deep disillusionment. Almost without exception, those interviewed spoke of dashed expectations and a heartfelt lack of confidence in the new legislature. The discontent was largely focused on the lack of direct ethnic minority representation amongst the sixty-strong membership of the Assembly. This failing is not unique to Wales but also applies to the devolved governments of Scotland and Northern Ireland and to the majority of democratic government bodies across Europe (IPU, 2000).

This deficiency highlights the barriers to achieving fair representation for people from an ethnic minority background in a territorial system of electoral representation (focused on the constituency as the basic spatial unit) in a country characterized by a low-density and dispersed 'ethnic' population. Of the 415 prospective candidates, hopes came to be focused on Cherry Short, the only candidate competing for one of the first-past-the-post seats. The two other potential (WLP) candidates, an Iraqi-born academic and a former black student leader, came through the vetting procedure onto the party lists for the other twenty 'list' seats[3] but were too low down to have any chance of winning.

The questionable legitimacy of the Assembly for black and ethnic minorities is nowhere more powerfully expressed than over the issue of descriptive representation. The interviewees' discourse illustrates very clearly a number of complex issues around minority representation in the political process. At a very straightforward level a good deal of the discussion focuses on the case of Cherry Short and the high level of disappointment at her defeat. A manager with a carers' organization expressed the view that 'the whole purpose of the Assembly was to be as inclusive as possible but the very fact that they do not have a minority ethnic representation suggests that it has failed already'; whilst an activist argued that amongst the AMs there was a need for 'people who we trusted, people who we could relate to, we could go to with our problems'.

A Plaid Cymru AM acknowledged that 'it was a collective failure by *all* the political parties that we haven't got anybody from the ethnic minority communities directly elected'. Several others expressed the view that the presence of ethnic minority names and faces in the Assembly would have meant the potential to identify with the institution. One observed: 'I think our greatest frustration is that we were made promises of inclusiveness, of multiculturalism, of fair representation and really in one sense one could use an emotive term and say that in effect we were *hoodwinked*.' Interviewees were divided in their thoughts. One project worker felt that, 'one person cannot possibly represent the whole of various communities under the umbrella of "black" and that's where we go wrong each time'. Another added: 'You can't rely on one person and what we don't want is token gestures . . . the idea that because we've got one person in there we are going to be heard.' A Plaid AM said: 'It's not just enough to have more women or to have a black face or to have somebody in a wheelchair, it's having different sorts of those people as well.' And another interviewee noted: 'Although [it's] disappointing and disillusioning that Cherry Short did not get in . . . because that's happened that will raise the profile of the issue and so perhaps make progress quicker.'

Several writers have commented on barriers to effective participation faced by minority groups. These, they suggest, relate not simply to huge and enduring social biases at the interface between policy-makers and those who would seek to be involved (Sanderson, 1999), but to other factors such as the pre-existing patterning of voluntary-sector activity, a sense of belonging (Kearns, 1995) and the numerical concentration of people from an ethnic minority background amongst the population as a whole (Anwar, 1986). It is these factors that have mediated the activism of the ethnic minorities in Wales and restricted their opportunity to see themselves as a community of interest.

ON CONSULTATION – 'DIFFERENT WORLDS COMMUNICATING'

In the absence of descriptive representation in the Assembly both politicians and those from an ethnic minority background began to explore the other available mechanisms for participation in the emerging structures of devolved governance. How could these two groups rebuild mutual trust and understanding? And how would the fledgeling Assembly get inclusiveness 'back on track' in the wake of the initial failure to engage people from an ethnic minority background? How could the Assembly undo the years of exclusion and marginalization that they had experienced?

As the effective 'disenfranchisement' of the first elections to the Assembly continued to sink in, thoughts turned to the way ahead. When interviewed one campaigner spoke of 'getting our act together' and suggested that the political parties

> go back to the communities and consult them in terms of how they want it to work, who they want to be representing them . . . It's not about community representatives it's about having the skills and experience with different subject areas . . . It's about time and commitment about . . . talking and campaigning in the language that the people are going to hear, both on the ground as well as on the political level.

This was a process, she continued, of 'different worlds communicating'. Another suggested that those attempting to reconnect 'ethnic' communities to the process of devolution should think in terms of

> diversity when we're dealing with communities. We have to be a little bit more non-traditional in the way we communicate and feed back . . . It is a different world, sometimes we have public meetings, sometimes we have a one-to-one, sometimes we go in a community and just address communities as they are, we talk to community leaders, but you can't have *one* way of communicating.

This call for a multi-layered form of engagement is implicitly critical of any assumption of homogeneity within and across ethnic minorities, of the role of ethnic brokers and the search for specific formulas for communication. In short, it acknowledged the complexities involved in these 'different worlds communicating'. Other interviewees echoed these concerns and highlighted the diverse needs, different priorities and contrasting demands of the minority communities. This is important, for it indicates that consensus is not necessarily a corollary to inclusiveness.

In the wake of May 1999 an important shift occurred in the position of the ethnic minority lobby, one that might tentatively be marked out as a second phase, when the emphasis moved from descriptive representation – of 'getting our voices heard' – to how to participate in devolved policy-making in Cardiff Bay. The Assembly itself was instrumental in this change. This can be seen as part of a wider process whereby dominant

institutions operate to shape the demands, goals, strategies and functioning of minority associations so that they are able to capitalize on the
available opportunity structure. This in turn impacts upon the way that
'ethnic' organizations are organized in civil society, often leading to their
demands being mediated through an institutionalized spokesperson
(Vertovec, 1999). This can lead to a form of neo-corporatism, a mode of
governance described by Mansbridge (1992: 495) as a *laissez-faire* institutional mechanism for representing interests not easily represented in the
territorial representative process, one that attempts to look beyond traditional economic and sectoral interests for the interests in fostering wider
participation in government. She concludes: 'As a system of interest
representation becomes more directly involved with state law-making and
law-enforcing processes, it more fully deserves the name of "corporatist",
and to the degree that it recognises non-traditional interests, it more fully
deserves the prefix "-neo".' The setting up of the 'race desk' in the Welsh
office and Operation Black Vote to some extent illustrate this tendency, but
the most prominent attempt to connect the ethnic minorities with devolved
government has been the All Wales Ethnic Minority Association
(AWEMA).[4] Based on early ideas of Ron Davies and others, implemented
by figures in the CRE and civil service Equality Unit, shaped by the
literature on citizen juries (see Coote and Lenaghan, 1997; Barnes, 1999)
and launched in July 1999, it aims to link people from an ethnic minority
background into the subject specialisms of the Assembly's seven policy-
making subject committees.

Speaking at the launch of AWEMA, Assembly cabinet minister Jane Hutt
said: 'What you can expect and what you should expect, is real
involvement. Every part of the Assembly needs to develop a dialogue with
those from and representing disadvantaged groups and to frame its
policies on the basis of the advice.' The then First Minister, Alun Michael,
added: 'The mechanisms that this Association proposes will enable a very
loud and clear message to be consistently and coherently put forward and
acted upon' (AWEMA, 1999: 1, emphasis added). Several interviewees felt
that AWEMA has been a great success, not least for the way that it has
encouraged new groups and individuals to come forward. As one
respondent put it, they have come 'out of the woodwork. . . The word
seems to have spread . . . because it's gone beyond that old network now
. . . There is feedback coming from the people in the association as to what
they see as the priorities and mainly the priorities have been health, and
education.'

However, not all are happy; one interviewee expressed how he thought
that AWEMA was a poor substitute for descriptive representation. To him
it felt as if the politicians were saying, 'You can't get in with the top boys

but we'll feed you a bone that you can fight with amongst yourselves.' Several interviewees questioned whether this was the most effective mode of communication. One group that felt that it had been ignored cautioned against setting up a dialogue with a small group of ethnic brokers whilst the rest of the ethnic minority remain 'invisible'. Their spokesperson said: 'We are invisible. It's all about visibility and . . . they are blind to certain people from certain communities and so the people continue to lead an existence as invisible people.'

Elsewhere the views of people from an ethnic minority background have been linked into Assembly decision-making via the Standing Committee on Equality of Opportunity, where representatives from the CRE sit alongside AMs. This has been an important locus of debate where leading race equality campaigners have presented policy papers. The committee in turn has been proactive in ensuring that 'race' issues are mainstreamed into all the Assembly's work. The recruitment policies of the former quangos (ASPBs) and the MacPherson inquiry recommendations – particularly on the content of the school curriculum – have been early areas of progress.

Several stakeholders expressed some cautious optimism at this. A civil servant observed: 'I do not for one minute underestimate the difficulties that we may face . . . I do consider there is a real opportunity to make progress. An opportunity which should not be wasted.' Interviews with leading campaigners revealed that a vision was now beginning to emerge of what needed to be done and how to go about getting it done. From a very low baseline a tentative agenda has emerged that has been voiced by, amongst others, the CRE. This statutory body spoke of 'changing the "mental models" of AMs and of putting them on a "steep learning curve" . . . [and] carefully and gently encouraging them to use an equality lens in examination of policy formulation, implementation and evaluation'.

Whether these developments will lead to an open dialogue between a wider 'ethnic' constituency – something that can be seen as evidence of deepened democracy – is open to question. It is as yet early days, but there appeared to be some evidence that new and smaller groups were entering into policy debate. From a slow start therefore it seems the engine is moving. This provides a point of comparison with other 'minority' groups. As with the disabled people spoken to (see previous chapter), many BME interviewees made reference to advances in the area of gender equality. The remark of one interviewee was typical: 'They've made a lot of advances in terms of getting women represented . . . I feel they need to go a little bit further now and include other members of the community.' Another figure suggested: 'If everybody thinks of it as they think about gender . . . then we will think "Yes! We've arrived."'

DISCUSSION AND CONCLUSION

Ron Davies has argued (1999a) that the establishment of the National Assembly is not an event but an ongoing process, but what can be said about the opening phase of this process from the standpoint of ethnic minorities? The overriding sense appears to be one of deep ambivalence. In the initial stages key politicians were highly successful in 'ratcheting up' the expectations of ethnic minority groups. This was evident in the pro-devolution campaign, in the NAAG consultations and in the drafting of the paving legislation. The initial rhetoric of inclusiveness proved to be quite beguiling to some members of the ethnic minorities. However, minority groups' expectations remained rather narrowly focused on the symbolism of descriptive representation in the Assembly. The core aspiration appeared to be 'getting a voice', and beyond this there existed little coherent strategy. As a result, when no candidate from an ethnic minority background was elected hopes turned into disillusionment.

However, the fact that the Assembly has mostly failed to engage ethnic minorities lies well beyond the issue of representation. What transpires from the encounter between the political parties and the minority communities is a lack of the tools, mechanisms and commitment for a real dialogue. A profound unpreparedness on both sides meant that to a great extent all the participants were caught unawares for the responsibilities of inclusive politics. For the minority stakeholders the 'process' has been one of exacerbated disenfranchisement that emanated from an institution that for many was quickly associated with fundamentally alienating constructions of 'Welshness' and nationhood. This was compounded by the inability of the political parties to communicate any assurances that they understood or had taken on board ethnic minority concerns. This was reaffirmed by the establishment of what was seen as an 'all-white club' where AMs were drawn from a closely networked narrow stratum of Welsh society. This raises concerns that the new institution will operate to reinforce a pattern of established associations and fail to 'mainstream' inclusiveness. Despite the mechanisms for involvement that are being put into place, a lot appears to ride on the willingness, ambition and commitment of this new stratum. That there may be widespread indifference, a lack of confidence and a prevailing air of mistrust amongst the ethnic minority populace must therefore be no surprise. From Pandora's box came a stream of rhetoric that may too hastily be translated into existing and questionable paradigms of incorporation that serve only further to marginalize and disenfranchise the ethnic minority communities.

Davies points to a fundamental paradox within the inclusiveness debate: 'We have a system that is designed to be inclusive but a culture which is not . . . as a result it [the Assembly] is under-performing in developing policies which engage with the everyday needs of the people of Wales' (2000a: 27–9). Achieving an appropriate culture of inclusiveness for ethnic minorities will demand that the notion of inclusiveness itself be laid open to question. What is it we are trying to achieve, whom are we aiming to include and how? Critics of inclusiveness have pointed to neglect of deep power divisions in society so that the ambitions of political inclusiveness somehow assume social and pluralistic inclusion. Day and Thompson (1999: unpaginated) pertinently observe that some of the rhetoric conveys the impression that 'it is as if all the divisions and difficulties of Welsh society have been abolished with a stroke of the constitutional pen'. Weinreich (1998), when commenting on the European agenda on inclusion, questions the assumption that social and cultural inclusion will follow from economic inclusion. In a similar vein it could be argued that Day and Thompson's dimensions of inclusion are too readily being assumed as axiomatic. Lessons from other areas of Britain illustrate that effective models of incorporation rest on multifaceted inclusiveness, – that is, on the many fronts of public incorporation – such as representation on public bodies, involvement in local institutions, forums and umbrella organiza-tions, the emergence of key and strategically placed individuals such as head teachers, councillors and chief executives. In short, this suggests the pressing need for a renegotiation of the political culture of the public sphere in this country, one that exhibits multiple social, cultural, economic and political modes of incorporation (Vertovec, 1996). Our evidence shows that these wider dimensions of inclusiveness have yet to develop in post-devolution Wales.

Several cautionary notes resonate from our interviews. The poor quality of the dialogue between those who govern and those whom they would seek to include gives rise to fears of tokenistic consultation or the tendency towards institutional gatekeeping of minority voice. There are concerns that the process will come to sponsor, manage and 'tame' communication around 'safe' and predefined issues rather than negotiate diverse and sometimes conflicting interests. Worse still, there is a danger that a situation may emerge where the dominant discourse operates largely in isolation from an ever-increasing proliferation of culturally defined and politically mobilized groups engaging in sectionalist fighting on the sidelines. It is pertinent to ask, therefore: What form of multiculturalism is it that we are institutionalizing?

From the picture that is emerging there is some evidence that attempts are being made to eschew some of the pitfalls of following a '(neo-)-corporatist model' of association with the development of the open forum for ethnic minority consultation (AWEMA). Access to this association is open and there is reason to believe that new voices, that is, smaller previously unheard voices, have now entered the arena. The CRE, a statutory body itself, remains a key gatekeeper in this process, as do the civil servants responsible for 'race' matters. Twelve months on from the establishment of the Assembly there are some encouraging signs that ethnic minority groups are not being overlooked in the legislature's policy process. The CRE in Wales is optimistic that the new structures have 'the chance to make sure that the Assembly policies on education, health, policing and local government have been "equality proofed"' (CRE Wales, 2000: 2). Thus far, a policy of mainstreaming race equality in the Assembly's seven subject committees has ensured that the needs of ethnic minorities have been addressed. This assessment is based, *inter alia*, on the Assembly's ongoing work in raising the educational attainment level of school pupils whose first language is neither Welsh nor English (NAW, 2000d), a black and minority ethnic housing strategy (Nyoni, 2000), scrutiny of staffing structures and appointment procedures of the Assembly's sponsored bodies (formerly 'quangos' – NAW, 2000g), equality measures in the public sector (NAW, 2000e), and measures aimed at valuing cultural diversity and preventing racism in the new National Curriculum for Wales (NAW, 2000d). Several of the participants interviewed emphasized AWEMA's key role in the policy process (and were sensitive to suggestions that it is a passive administrative mechanism for ethnic minority consultation), arguing that it has a developing and overtly *pro*active policy role. However, the major challenge for AWEMA's officially sponsored bureaucratic structures will be the extent to which they can be truly proactive and articulate independent views reflecting wider opinion.

It is too early to say how the race equality agenda and dialogue will be managed and how significantly they will influence policy and practice. At the moment the agenda is relatively restricted and the *modus operandi* appears to be 'service-orientated' rather than truly 'citizen-orientated' (Kearns, 1995). We do not yet know whether it will emerge as a neo-corporatist filter for managing and containing the minority voice or a truly unique platform for negotiated diversity. As yet there is little evidence of widespread ethnic minority mobilization throughout Wales. Minority groups in the regions have found sheer geography a barrier to participation. One significant point here is that the spatial distribution of ethnic minorities in Wales acts as a strong counter-force to political mobilization. Whilst Hirst (1994) argues that 'communities of fate' – such as the nation and attendant expressions of nationalism – are counter-productive to associative democracy, their salience must not be dismissed in the rush towards the new politics. Such communities have been important loci of political activity for ethnic minorities. It could be argued that black and ethnic minority political mobilization must first rest on individuals becoming aware of themselves as a community of interest if they are to be empowered to assert their concerns onto the wider political agenda. Often for excluded groups the politics of recognition and identity develop as a precursor to wider associational politics. What should be achieved therefore is not a diminishing of the salience of racial, ethnic or such sectional ties but the creation of frameworks that allow for a rethinking of their articulation. What are needed are public space and a political culture that provides multiple forums in which ethnic diversity is given status and dignity. The argument often promulgated is that before ethnic identity can be transcended it must be asserted in order to ensure that inclusion does not come to mean 'white' or simply 'white tolerance'.

There now exists a strong legislative and policy mandate for ethnic minority participation, and arguably there are structures with the potential to engage the voices of the minority. Some cautious optimism has been expressed by members of minority communities with regard to this potential, and as the new political consciousness emerges, so does the realization that we must not squander the opportunities provided; consistent with the Greek myth, this might be characterized as the hope that remained in Pandora's box once it was opened. However, progress is unlikely to be achieved without a persistent and ongoing struggle against deep-seated ideological, cultural, political and organizational assumptions that represent very real barriers to political participation and restrict the capacities of minorities to get involved. Without significant steps being taken to bolster the inclinations and the capacity of ethnic minority communities and individuals to engage in active citizenship, without real efforts to demonstrate positive outcomes for them and without real and significant shifts in power in Wales, inclusiveness will remain an elusive goal.

Notes

1 Ray Singh, commissioner with the CRE, interview with one of the authors.
2 A senior civil servant was appointed to deal with 'race' issues at the Welsh Office.
3 Involving the use of proportional representation.
4 Originally known as the 'The All Wales Black and Ethnic Minority *National Assembly* Consultative and Participatory Association' (emphasis added).

5

The National Assembly and the Voluntary Sector: An Equal Partnership?

BELLA DICKS, TOM HALL and ANDREW PITHOUSE

INTRODUCTION

This chapter reports on research undertaken in the first year of the National Assembly's operation, exploring the notion of inclusive government through a study of the emergent partnership between the National Assembly for Wales and the voluntary sector. In mapping early preparations for partnership, the research has explored the extent to which the creation of a National Assembly for Wales might alter the nature of relations between the voluntary sector and government in Wales. Specifically, we have asked how, and to what extent, such an alteration has (thus far) constituted a democratization of relations with government. Our findings necessarily reflect the fact that post-devolution institutional relationships are still very much 'work in progress'.

There have been three strands to the research: a survey of seventy voluntary organizations across Wales; a series of 'key respondent' taped interviews with leading politicians in the Assembly, civil servants and leading figures at the Wales Council for Voluntary Action (WCVA); and a small, intensive series of case studies, tracking the particular experiences of four different types of voluntary organization over the first six months of the Assembly's existence. This material has been rounded out by attendance at a series of meetings and consultations with voluntary organizations, at the Assembly and across Wales.

INCLUSIVE GOVERNMENT AND THE VOLUNTARY SECTOR

The devolutionary process in Wales has not proved to be an easy one, thus far. The close referendum result, initial difficulties in finding a home for the Assembly, and the rerun Labour Party leadership contest all made for a somewhat uncertain inauguration; subsequent events have been no less interesting and involved. In this context, the Assembly continues to be watched closely and critically by many in Wales who remain to be convinced that it will work, and work well. One issue on which scrutiny is focused is the extent to which the Assembly will deliver on the promises of consensual and inclusive government that have been part and parcel of the devolutionary argument.

Pluralism and inclusiveness are amongst the founding aims of devolution in Wales.[1] These aims emerged from what Ron Davies (1999a: 6), in many ways the architect of Welsh devolution, has called the 'democratic deficit', or 'crisis of representation' in Wales. Inclusiveness, however, is a potentially vague and slippery term – as are the other key words, such as 'participation' and 'civil society' that have been used extensively in Wales to make the case for devolution. For Davies (1999a: 7), inclusiveness is 'a willingness to share ideas, talk to others, to include those with common objectives in the pursuit and exercise of power'. It is thus centrally concerned with communication, and the question of how these channels of communication can be established and sustained will be key to the success of the policy. It is also, however, concerned with who can communicate with whom: inclusiveness is clearly allied to an older rhetoric of equal opportunities. Inclusiveness, then, relates to the establishment of participative and accessible structures of government, as well as to the pursuance of policies dedicated to furthering equal opportunities in society at large.

Enthusiasm for the values of inclusion and participation in government has not been restricted to Wales. The fostering of an active civil society is fundamental to the Third Way agenda (see Giddens, 1998), which, in the formula of the prime minister, Tony Blair, aims at strong communities based on 'shared values, and a recognition of both the rights and responsibilities of citizenship' (Blair, 1998: 12). New Labour envisages communities in which civic activism, mutuality and social capital provide the foundations for 'social inclusion'.[2] It would be wrong to suggest, however, that Wales has merely borrowed the language of inclusiveness. In Wales, the tentative inclusiveness that emerged to underpin both the civic alliance of the 'Yes for Wales' referendum campaign and the extensive National Assembly Advisory Group consultations was a hard-won achievement. Both the 'Yes' campaign and the Advisory Group strongly influenced the final form of the Assembly prescribed in the enabling legislation of 1998. The Advisory Group specifically assessed the proposed working arrangements for the all-Wales body to see if they met the joint criteria of 'democracy and inclusiveness', defined as ensuring that 'decision making processes are open, accessible and transparent' and 'arrangements provide [for] effective scrutiny of decisions' (National Assembly Advisory Group, 1998a).

Inclusion, then, is a key term for the National Assembly for Wales, and has figured prominently in the rhetoric on which the devolutionary argument has been constructed. As a result, the Assembly can expect to be held to account, by a range of commentators as well as the general population of Wales, on the extent to which it actually delivers government that is appreciably inclusive and open. In this context, the National Assembly can be expected to work and consult closely with the voluntary sector in developing and delivering policy. Partnerships with the voluntary sector will publicly and practically demonstrate a declared commitment to inclusive and open government. And, indeed, the Assembly has been explicit about its intention to work closely with the voluntary sector. The Assembly's former First Secretary, Alun Michael, has insisted that the Assembly 'must recognize the voluntary sector as a key player and partner . . . at the heart of our work to build a better Wales'. Similarly, Jane Hutt, the National Assembly secretary for health and social services, has described the voluntary sector as having 'a strong and powerful role in supporting us in our work, in revitalizing Wales and ensuring that we have a voice that represents people who have been excluded, who have not previously been heard in government'.

Support and enthusiasm for the voluntary sector in Wales is not confined to the Labour administration.[3] There has been considerable cross-party support for partnership, inflected, inevitably by differences in ideological motivation. Thus, for example, whereas a Labour vision might be said to lean towards the community-based, co-operative elements of voluntary-sector partnerships, a Conservative stance gives greater play to the entrepreneurial, innovative, competitive potential of voluntary organiza-tions, as actors independent of government.

> The voluntary sector can probably be compared more to the inventors in enterprise. They are coming up with ideas; they are testing ideas . . . They can also act in an open market which ensures that the state services are not just simply accepted but do face, if not competition, than certainly comparison . . . Conservatives . . . do like things that are seen as distinct from the state. (David Melding AM)

The values of 'partnership' and 'active citizenship', though strongly associated with New Labour in recent years, are ones that the Conservative Party can also claim to hold dear (see Hurd, 1988). Similarly the Liberal Democrats are strongly identified with the values of voluntary association and activity, both in Wales and across the UK. Of all the political parties represented in the National Assembly it is Plaid Cymru that has been least vocal in making explicit play of its support for the voluntary sector as a partner to devolved government in Wales.

THE VOLUNTARY SECTOR IN WALES

It has been argued that civil society in Wales has historically been underdeveloped (see Paterson and Wyn Jones, 1999), and that the Welsh voluntary sector has suffered from a paucity of funding, relative to England (see Kendall and Knapp, 1996: 155). It is certainly the case that many UK voluntary organizations have not developed distinctive and substantial Welsh branches, and that locally based voluntary organizations in Wales have generally struggled for recognition from local authorities which have not viewed the third sector with any real enthusiasm until relatively recently. The Wales Council for Voluntary Action (WCVA), an umbrella body serving and representing the voluntary organizations across Wales, has, however, provided a sense of coherence to the voluntary sector in Wales that is arguably not as evident elsewhere in the UK. Prior to the arrival of the National Assembly, the WCVA worked closely with the Welsh Office in profiling and promoting the interests of voluntary organizations; it continues to do the same work now that the Welsh Office has been replaced by an elected Assembly.

Recent years have seen a significant rise in the profile of the voluntary sector across the whole of the UK; incomparably so in respect of the delivery of welfare (Johnson, 1999: 166), and the Welsh voluntary sector has benefited, to some degree, from this wider development. In this context, despite continuing resource constraints faced by many voluntary organizations in Wales, and with the new opportunities offered by the arrival of devolved government firmly in its sights, the WCVA is prepared to be optimistic about the health of the voluntary sector in Wales. The recently published *Wales Voluntary Sector Almanac* (WCVA, 1999) gives the overall impression of a burgeoning and vital sector, and helps make the case for the voluntary sector in Wales as a substantial resource that a devolved Wales would do well to call on (and a substantial constituency it should not ignore). The *Almanac* estimates that there are currently some 25,000 voluntary groups in Wales, and further to this:

> Over 80 per cent . . . of the adult population in Wales are volunteers, contributing nearly four hours per week of voluntary time. Of these, 1.1 million are formal volunteers, and 1.7 million are informal volunteers assisting neighbours and their communities outside of formal organizations. The value of this volunteering is estimated at £3.4 billion for Wales. (WCVA, 1999: 1)

These figures are impressive, and stand in contrast to the WCVA's own assessment of the sector in the 1980s (see Hunt, 1984).

THE VOLUNTARY SECTOR: READY FOR THE ASSEMBLY?

The longevity of many voluntary organizations is only partly explained by their good deeds (or at least expressed intentions) and the continued appeal of these as a 'worthy' cause to various publics. They of course have had to adjust and change with the times and relodge themselves frequently in the public imagination. We might agree therefore with Morgan (1990: 152–4) that organizational survival is not reducible to random unconscious mutation so much as to rational, if bounded, intention. Indeed, if we consider the current highly topical notion of the 'learning organization' as one that can better explore and exploit knowledge about its complex environment, then this suggests a very conscious and deliberate approach to survival and control.

Such perspectives have helped inform our study of the voluntary sector. In short, we see it as likely, at least conceptually, that agencies in the voluntary sector are as culturally competent as other modern organizations; and we would expect them to be aware of the Assembly and the need to make some adjustments internally and externally to this significant development in their environment; a development that many of our research respondents have recognized as offering the possibility, at least, of substantially expanded opportunities for organizations to bring their influence to bear on policy-making in Wales: '. . . an opportunity for us'; '. . . an opportunity for thousands of voluntary organizations'; '. . . what we've got now is an opportunity for us to have a direct involvement'; '. . . into something that directly affects Wales, where we can have a lot more say than just going to a Secretary of State'.

Thus our working hypotheses draw on a well-established literature on management in welfare and asserts that modern welfare agencies recognize the importance of systemic and critical approaches to the complex and multifaceted nature of organizational life and organizational learning (albeit that 'organizational learning' denotes no single conceptual framework, see Finger and Brand, 1999). Thus it is likely that agencies will have adjusted or developed various media and roles by which they can engage with, 'learn' about and influence the Assembly.[4]

Our research opened with a modest survey of a sample of voluntary organizations in Wales, which were asked to complete a questionnaire about their preparedness for the new Assembly. In developing this survey within the constraints of time and costs, we thought it useful to delineate our field of enquiry by imposing some working hypothesis to conceptualize the likely responsiveness of agencies to the Assembly. In order to achieve this we considered those generic features of organizational life that might obtain in the modern voluntary organization and by extension the sorts of mechanisms and measures likely to be used in relation to the new Assembly. We started from the position, as noted earlier, that the empirical complexity of the voluntary sector in Wales in respect of the purpose and structure of around 25,000 organizations with some 1.8 million adults engaged in volunteering or community activity (paid and unpaid) and with an annual turnover of £675 million resists any but the most general grasp of a continually shifting phenomenon. The voluntary sector is highly differentiated, with an unmapped ecology of new, surviving and dying agencies that continually redraw an environment which is self-evidently beyond some straightforward notion of 'involvement' with the Assembly.

Yet, the Assembly aims to set policies, influence or control public funding, and by extension the activities of agencies, as well as to provide the parameters in which a strategic approach to the sector will emerge (see Bryant and Hutt, 1999). What cannot be doubted, however, is that there will be an impact upon the sector. While the dimensions of this are yet to be discerned, the Assembly itself now exists, and relationships with it are unlikely to be ignored by those agencies for whom survival depends upon skilful negotiation of a turbulent policy and financial environment.

A complete list of voluntary organizations which were full members of Wales Council for Voluntary Action (n=162) was obtained from the 1998 *Wales Yearbook*. We attempted to sample every other voluntary organization in order to achieve a crude random sample of some eighty-one agencies. The listing in the *Yearbook* did not indicate key characteristics of agencies, and so more stratified sampling techniques were not available without considerable expense and time engaged in further inquiries. However, a careful and oft-repeated telephone trawl through the listing revealed that several agencies no longer existed; one did not consider itself a voluntary organization but a business; the telephone number was not listed for some, and proved unavailable on further inquiry; calls leaving messages were not returned. From this universe of registered voluntaries something of an opportunity sample of seventy contacts was made. Five of the organizations requested that they be given the opportunity to complete the questionnaire themselves as well as to complete the questionnaire by telephone interview. In all, telephone interviews were carried out with sixty-eight organizations; one questionnaire was completed and returned by post, and one interview was carried out by text phone. Data were analysed using SPSS, and associations between key variables were sought, particularly in relation to organizational type and size.

The interview/questionnaire gathered material on core topics in relation to the above themes, which, simply put, assumed that many agencies were likely to appoint/allocate senior staff specifically to Assembly-related matters; have knowledge of new Assembly structures; create promotional materials for Assembly readerships; attend meetings within their own organization(s) and with other agencies about engaging with the Assembly; set relevant policy and have developed some notion of benefits and disadvantages of the new Assembly arrangements. Our preamble to these topics requested information about the agency function and its geographical location as UK/Wales/regional/local body. We requested information about number of volunteers, paid staff and their status as full- or part-time, and approximate annual gross income. We also recorded the length of interview and the position within the organization of the respondent. The key findings are as follows.

Agency purpose

Of the respondents from seventy voluntary organizations, all apart from one were either in middle or senior management positions and could speak with some authority on their preparations for the new Assembly. Most interviews lasted between fifteen and thirty minutes. The majority of respondents (66 per cent, n=46) were from agencies that were social welfare- and/or health-related; there were eight from organizations that had an 'umbrella' function in that these represented various voluntary groups at some district or county level. Five (7 per cent) respondents represented organizations with a cultural interest; five respondents represented social housing organizations; there were four (6 per cent) respondents from environmental agencies and two (3 per cent) from organizations with interests in promoting international relations.

Location, staff and income

Eighty per cent of the organizations contacted were based in south Wales, seven (10 per cent) in mid Wales, six (9 per cent) in north Wales (that is, north of Aberystwyth). One agency was based in Bristol. Around forty-nine (70 per cent) agencies had less than twenty paid staff (thirty-seven had less than ten paid staff) and some 11 per cent had over seventy-five paid staff. Seventeen (24 per cent) organizations had an approximate annual income of over £500,000 with thirty (57 per cent) having an income of £250,000 or more. Eight (11 per cent) organizations had an income of under £100,000. In twelve (17 per cent) cases respondents were either not prepared or were unable to provide information on the annual funding.

Dedicated staff member(s)

Over a half (n=43, 63 per cent) of the organizations had a single person designated to take sole or major responsibility for Assembly dealings; ten (14 per cent) agencies had no dedicated person, instead, existing staff responded as required; five (7 per cent) said that this was planned for the future. A minority (n=12, 17 per cent) of agencies said that they had no person in post responsible for dealing with the Assembly. Thirty-four (74 per cent) of social welfare or health organizations had a single person designated to sole or major responsibility for Assembly dealings. Five of the eight umbrella organizations had similar designated staff, as did all four of the organizations concerned with environmental issues. None of the five cultural organizations contacted had a specific person to take responsibility, but in two a range of people fulfilled the role. Proportionately, those with more paid staff were more likely to have a single member of staff dedicated to deal with Assembly matters.

Material produced

Most (n=45, 64 per cent) organizations had assembled briefing literature or documentation on the Assembly while twenty-five (36 per cent) had not. Thirty-one (67 per cent) of the social welfare/health organizations, three of the five environmental organizations, five of the eight umbrella organizations and both international relations organizations had assembled relevant literature on the Assembly. None of the cultural agencies had done so. As a proportion of organizations in relation to number of paid staff, 85 per cent of organizations which had between ten and nineteen members of staff had assembled documentation on the Assembly, whilst just 43 per cent of organizations which had between fifty to seventy-four paid staff had done so. A smaller overall proportion of respondents (39 per cent) indicated that briefing material on their agency had been sent to Assembly members and/or officers.

Meetings

Overall, a strong majority (n=59, 84 per cent) of respondents said their organization had held or attended formal meetings to discuss relations between their organization and the Assembly. Multiple responses revealed that 40 per cent had been invited to or had attended meetings as members of an umbrella group; 30 per cent had been invited to or had attended a multi-agency regional or all-Wales meeting organized via the WCVA; 19 per cent had attended internal meetings or internal training days which included discussion of the Assembly; 6 per cent of organizations had attended political party conferences. Meetings with other agencies were held or attended by over 80 per cent of all agencies apart from housing organizations, of which around a half stated they attended such events.

Internal policy and knowledge of Assembly structures

Twenty-one (30 per cent) organizations had initiated internal policy or a clear action plan to respond to the new Assembly, and forty-eight (69 per cent) had not, but most of these were in the process of developing policy. Their policy formulations were informed in part by knowledge of the new Assembly structures, and 86 per cent of respondents claimed familiarity with the Assembly's proposals for engaging with the sector. Some three-quarters of respondents mentioned the WCVA and/or the voluntary-sector compact as the key mechanisms by which the Assembly and sector would connect.

Advantages and disadvantages

This area of questioning did not elicit strong majority responses in either direction; and most respondents were circumspect about the likely benefits of the Assembly for their organization. Just under a half (thirty-four) of respondents felt that the Welsh identity/prioritization of Welsh issues by the Assembly may prove to be an advantage for their organization, and a similar proportion felt that closer relations with policy-makers were an advantage for their organization. Fourteen respondents could identify no disadvantages for their organization with the arrival of the Assembly. Twelve respondents felt that it was early days and that the Assembly remained an unknown quantity. Eleven respondents felt that the increased volume of people in influential positions within the Assembly could be a disadvantage in that it might result in more bureaucracy, more people to lobby and possible confusion over whom to approach.

Given the uneven nature of the sample and small numbers in some categories it would be unwise to offer any bold generalizations about the population as a whole. What might be suggested tentatively is that while there were notable proportional (but not statistical) differences in relation to cultural and housing organizations compared with other groupings, overall there appeared to be strong evidence of response across the sector as defined by this sample. Staff had been designated clear responsibilities, materials had been produced, policy formulated, contacts had been made with the Assembly and a variety of meetings attended. In short, many in the sector had been galvanized by the new Assembly and its proposals. It cannot be inferred that similar actions have been taken elsewhere across the sector amongst those organizations not entered on the lists used for this survey. Equally, it would be unwise to assume they have not. What does seem evident is that those agencies responding to this survey were able, in different ways, to orientate themselves to an anticipated new environment promised by the Assembly. Our contact with various voluntary organizations over the course of our research, additional to the survey reported on here, confirms this general impression, and this bodes well for the ambitions of the Assembly. Whether these ambitions come to fruition is yet unknown.

THE ASSEMBLY: READY FOR THE VOLUNTARY SECTOR?

The voluntary sector is not only valued by the National Assembly as a potential democratic resource, but successful relations with the voluntary sector are also a legal requirement. Under the terms of the Government of Wales Act the Assembly is required to establish a Voluntary Sector Scheme, setting out how it proposes, in the exercise of its functions, to provide assistance to and consult with the voluntary sector. No comparable statutory scheme exists in England or Scotland at the present time, and so devolution in Wales presents the Welsh voluntary sector with something of a unique opportunity. Accordingly, our research followed the early development of the scheme as a key mechanism by which a new partnership between the Assembly and the voluntary sector will be translated into practice.

Thus far, the Assembly has moved steadily towards putting the scheme in place. Progress has been somewhat slower than many of our research respondents originally anticipated, but not so as to cause significant disenchantment. As on a great many issues, it has been difficult to gauge from the outset what was reasonable to expect of the Assembly as a new institution. In any event, hopes expressed by some of our research respondents that the scheme might be in place before the first recess have proved to be overly optimistic. The final plenary session before the summer recess of 1999 did see Assembly Members vote both to endorse the existing compact between the Government and the Voluntary Sector in Wales[5] and to agree the values and principles of the compact as the basis for the scheme.

After the recess, an ad hoc meeting between voluntary-sector representatives and Assembly Members was held to discuss, among other items, the development of the scheme. This meeting was attended by a cross-party representation of eleven Assembly Members and by twenty representatives from across the voluntary sector. This was the first meeting of the Shadow Voluntary Sector Partnership Council (see below). The meeting was chaired by the then First Secretary, Alun Michael, who had taken lead responsibility for the development of the scheme. This significant first meeting saw voluntary-sector representatives urge the Assembly to move quickly on the scheme and to insist that, once in place, the scheme should provide 'machinery that the whole voluntary sector can use in equitable fashion'.

During the course of our research, a draft of the scheme was produced and made available for consultation. The draft restated the principles enshrined in the compact – notably to encourage and support the activities of the voluntary sector and to ensure that relations between it and the Assembly are 'inclusive', 'participatory' and 'democratic', based on 'partnership' and 'equality of opportunity'. It also began to link these broad statements of principle to practical arrangements (for example, Assembly Secretaries are to meet with relevant voluntary-sector networks at least twice in any one calendar year), but overall the language remained one of general intention; practical arrangements for dialogue and co-operation at the operational level were not codified but were to be agreed with relevant networks. Although the Assembly has been working with voluntary-sector networks since its inception (the WCVA in particular) the real test for the scheme is only just beginning (the scheme was launched late in 2000).

If the scheme is to provide a successful framework for an ongoing partnership, the proposed annual review of its performance will be an important process. However, we anticipate that a familiar difficulty will present itself here: the tension between auditability and accountability. We have found that voluntary-sector organizations are primarily concerned with the quality of partnership and dialogue between the voluntary sector and the Assembly, whereas performance of the scheme will almost certainly be measured against quantitative indicators.

New relations: lobbying and access

Many voluntary organizations, and certainly the WCVA, are hoping for a mature democratic relationship with the National Assembly, in which the voluntary sector's 'partnership' is a full and meaningful one (despite any tensions that this might entail). Such a partnership is not imagined as restricted only to the receipt of briefings and presentations, or to *post facto* consultation exercises, but as entailing substantial inclusion – in the development of policy, for example. Our research suggests that routine public access, formal meetings by invitation and arrangement, and the emergent mechanisms for partnership that the scheme will outline may provide the grounding for (but not the meat of) 'opening up' Assembly practices and policy formation that many of those in the voluntary sector hope to see. The underlying question here is that of how the National Assembly's rhetoric of partnership is to be realized in practice.

It is certainly not the case that relations between the voluntary sector and the National Assembly have been at a standstill until such time as the Voluntary Sector Scheme is in place. Many organizations, as we have shown above, are already mobilizing themselves to get their voice heard in the Assembly. A significant development in this context has been the creation of new posts within a limited number of the better-resourced voluntary organizations, specifically given over to Assembly liaison. These new posts – what we shall term here as 'assembly workers' – provide organizations with a more sophisticated means of liaising with the Assembly (informing decision-making, contributing to policy debate, cultivating contacts) than is made possible by briefings and presentations. We have seen the number of such posts grow during our investigation, with two of our case-study sites proposing to recruit on this basis by the close of the research. In addition to contacting some of these assembly workers individually, the research has had access (in the context of ongoing contact with the National Assembly Voluntary Sector Centre) to the assembly workers' group. This ad hoc grouping was convened as a forum for exchange and mutual support and has been meeting for over six months. Observing meetings held by this group allowed us to chart their access to, and inclusion within, the new political machinery, and the relevance of this for the wider sector.

A persistent anxiety for assembly workers in the wake of devolution has been that of the Assembly's perception of their role and function. In this context the assembly workers' group has been concerned about the levels of support and access made available to its membership by the National Assembly. There have been clear signals from the National Assembly that lobbying organizations are not to be welcomed into the business of government in Wales. However, a general distaste for 'lobbying' of any kind has created some difficulties for those voluntary organizations (and their assembly workers) who would see lobbying, by any other name, as one important aspect of what they do – profiling a particular agenda and seeking to influence policy. Assembly workers have been at pains to distinguish their work in this respect from that of other potential 'lobbyists', although the boundaries here are not always entirely clear.

A practical issue on which this debate has turned has been the issue of passes to the Assembly. At present, 'assembly workers' from voluntary organizations can routinely gain access only to those parts of the Assembly buildings open to the general public (the public milling area and the public gallery). Many would have preferred to see passes issued granting access to other parts of the building, enabling assembly workers to meet with and contact AMs and civil servants other than by invitation and formal appointment. The assembly workers' group has not met with the co-operation for which it wished on this issue; early requests for passes were resisted by the Assembly Presiding Officer. The main argument against the issuing of passes has been presented as one of democratic principle – that the Assembly will not grant privileged access, of any kind, to any particular interest group or network; doubtless there are practical objections too. Nevertheless, the withholding of passes has disappointed many assembly workers and has been construed by some as challenging the Assembly's promissory statements about partnership and inclusion.

> When the Assembly first came into being we imagined that it was going to be this open and inclusive thing and that we would all get passes because they would recognize that they wanted to work with us . . . the reality has been different to how we thought it would be.

Given the restraints of proximity and opportunity, this is an issue that has directly affected relatively few organizations; yet the wider symbolism of social and political distance may, regrettably, resonate more widely in the sector.

Information

Access to the Assembly is not just a question of physical ingress to those parts of the building that remain 'off-limits' to lobbyists and others except by invitation. The intention has always been that the windows, if not the doors, of the Assembly should (metaphorically) be open to all, and that the business of the Assembly should be transparent and open to public scrutiny. Thus, for example, the Assembly's Code of Practice on Public Access to Information makes a commitment to publish routinely a range of documents, including a verbatim record of plenary sessions (available within twenty-four hours) and minutes of certain committee meetings; these documents are made publicly available on the Assembly's website.

Internet technology has been heralded for its potential to deliver 'virtual' access and participation from across Wales. Such technology has the capacity to reduce familiar (for example, geographic) obstacles to participation, enabling individuals and groups to 'access' Assembly proceedings remotely and voice opinions and participate 'instantaneously' by e-mail.

However, so far as those voluntary organizations looking to involve themselves closely in the emergent business of the Assembly have been concerned, the Assembly has not yet delivered sufficient and satisfactory information about its practices. In its early months, the Assembly Information Service was described to us as unhelpful and 'a disaster', an inadequate source of material about Assembly structures and procedures.

> They have an 'Assembly this Week' page on the internet that's not updated until Tuesday lunchtime. So when you log on on Monday or Tuesday morning you get last week's [information]. This week there was an Audit Committee meeting [timetabled] for tomorrow, and I know that that has been cancelled for a fortnight. So it's just a mess.

There is no doubt that this situation has since improved, but problems persist.[6] Poor advance warning of Assembly business and delays in publication of some committee meeting minutes continue to make it difficult for voluntary organizations to mobilize and contribute as effectively as they would wish on a range of issues; the assembly workers' group has met to discuss these difficulties with the Deputy Presiding Officer.

PROBLEMS ON THE HORIZON

Voluntary organizations – large and small

The voluntary sector is often spoken of as if it were a homogeneous whole – its own constituents describe it as such sometimes; those looking from the outside in are still more ready to do so. Any such unity very quickly fragments under close inspection. Organizations grouped under the umbrella of 'the voluntary sector' are likely to be engaged in a range of different activities and to vary considerably in their size, organizational structure and resource base. Variation along this latter axis – size, structure, resources – is considerable and highly significant in the context of a partnership between the sector as a whole and the new National Assembly.

How then to make sense of this profusion? Is it meaningful to talk of a single, unified voluntary sector in Wales? Or are there *sectors*, in the plural? The most cursory study of the varied resource base of voluntary organizations in Wales invites the suggestion that the National Assembly is faced with not one but effectively two voluntary sectors – a small élite of 'professional' organizations and a much wider swathe of organizations belonging to what research respondents have referred to as 'the *voluntary,*

voluntary sector'. This is a crude bifurcation but it is not made arbitrarily, and is recognized by many who work and volunteer within voluntary organizations throughout Wales. To flesh out the distinction a little further, the voluntary sector élite comprise those better-established, larger and well-resourced voluntary organizations, many of which are based in and around Cardiff and most of which operate with a Wales-wide remit. This leaves a significantly larger number of what can be characterized as small-scale voluntary and community organizations with a local remit and often minimal resources, many of them exclusively reliant on voluntary contributions and volunteers. This distinction is significant for a host of reasons. In the context of a partnership between the National Assembly and the voluntary sector in Wales, the significance lies with the differential ability of organizations within the sector to *realize* partnership, and the possible skewing of relations as a result.

Voluntary organizations seeking to make their voice heard in the National Assembly vary considerably in their ability to do so. Some are in the relatively fortunate position of being able to build on pre-existing links with the civil service in Wales, and have the resources with which to develop these (through the appointment of designated Assembly Officers, for example). Others lack experience and contacts and the capacity with which to take advantage of new opportunities for dialogue. A recurrent theme in feedback to the WCVA in the course of its regional consultation with County Voluntary Councils and smaller voluntary organizations in 1999 was the need for capacity building to enable meaningful partnership between the Assembly (and its varied committees) and voluntary organizations. This has been matched in our own dialogue with research respondents:

> They [the Assembly] are expecting us to participate and to do more work, to be involved in more consultations. But unless that is backed up with the resources and funding then it is very meaningless . . . It is one thing to say that you have partnership and links, all these things that sound very good, but unless you are offering additional help for people to become involved and participate it is certainly not what I would call equal partnership.

Capacity-building is, of course, an issue for all voluntary organizations, large and small. Each and every new and expanded opportunity made available by the arrival of the Assembly invokes new and expanded workloads, and many organizations are already struggling to measure up to and make the most of these. But some will struggle more than others. And in the absence of significant and innovative steps to enable a wide-ranging and inclusive dialogue, it seems likely that the Assembly will hear most from and work more closely with the already established and better-resourced organizations in the voluntary sector.

There is a dilemma in the making here. The rhetoric of partnership and devolution draws heavily on the public perception of the voluntary sector as a store of the normative values associated with small-scale and 'community' organizations (see Tonkiss and Passey, 1999); political enthusiasm for the voluntary sector as a source of democratic renewal builds on this perception. However, the potential difficulty here is that, claiming partnership with 'the voluntary sector' as a whole, and drawing on values associated with community voluntary activity, the Assembly may find it all too easy in fact to cherry-pick a (relatively) small number of organizations with which to work closely. Such organizations could be expected to be among the more established, politically articulate and well-resourced organizations in the voluntary sector (very probably with existing relationships with the civil service in Wales). Should opportunities for meaningful 'partnership' prove to be limited to a select group of larger and established organizations in this way, this would fall short of the promissory statements made about a new and genuinely inclusive style of government for Wales, and could be taken as a sign that little has changed since the days of the Welsh Office.

This is not just a question of resources. Many 'smaller' voluntary organizations simply do not work to an agenda that would make close contact with the Assembly an obvious priority. None the less, it is important that AMs be cognizant of the general interests of these organizations as they constitute the majority membership of a sector with which the Assembly has declared a partnership. This would be to break with the perception that, under previous arrangements, a small 'clique' of larger voluntary organizations enjoyed something of a privileged relationship with the Welsh Office to the exclusion of a range of other voluntary agencies (see Kendall and Knapp, 1996: 156). Our research neither confirms nor refutes this perception, but there is no doubt that the perception persists and is recognized as having at least some residual validity (and not only by those organizations that see themselves as losing out in the process): 'Once you manage to get to the funding circles, you're there forever . . . I don't think that's healthy; I think that should be challenged.'

Representation – the Wales Council for Voluntary Action

Smaller voluntary organizations working to a local remit may not be looking for close, continued relations with the new Assembly, but they may, from time to time, wish to make representations to the Assembly and, in aggregate, may share sectoral interests of which they will wish the Assembly to be cognizant (given that they constitute the majority membership of a sector with which the Assembly has declared a partnership). This raises the issue of representation; the WCVA has a key role to play here as 'the voice of the voluntary sector in Wales' (see WCVA, 1998).

There can be no doubt that as the voluntary sector has moved centre stage in national politics in Wales, so has the Wales Council for Voluntary Action. The WCVA has been centrally involved in the process of drawing up devolution legislation and preparing Assembly procedures. As a result, the WCVA has entered the era of devolution with expectations of being a significant and key player in the Assembly and its development. Such expectations have been nurtured through the ability of the WCVA to 'win' key demands and guarantees for the voluntary sector during the drafting of the compact and scheme. The director of the WCVA outlined in interview how the 'four pillars' of the scheme that the WCVA considered crucial to its success did, duly, become reflected in the Labour administration's plans for bringing the scheme into operation. The four pillars identified were: absorbing the compact, creating the Partnership Council, instituting a working relationship between each Assembly subject committee and its relevant counterparts in the voluntary sector, and finally the incorporation into government of voluntary-sector advisers.

In interview for this study, the then First Secretary, Alun Michael, identified these same provisions as key elements of his thinking on the conduct of the scheme; his symmetry reflecting the ongoing dialogue in which these two individuals and their respective organizations had been engaged during the drafting of the scheme. This close relationship between the WCVA and the Labour administration does not, however, mean that WCVA demands are unquestioningly and obligingly absorbed into government strategy; on the contrary, there is an ongoing effort on the WCVA's part to get its 'four pillars' translated into clear policy documents.

The WCVA had early on identified in the preparations for the Assembly an opportunity to prise open channels of communication with government which were previously closed or unavailable under the Welsh Office/ Westminster regime:

> What has happened in the past has been a slightly artificial relationship between voluntary organizations in Wales who have tried to influence Welsh Office officials . . . on policies that have been set in London. We have either big charities influencing London, but from a London or English perspective, or other organizations, including us . . . not really having seen it as a good return on time and effort trying to influence Westminster. The Assembly changes all that and has made the politics real here, which in turn has meant that . . . the policies have got to get real and the lobbying has got to get real. (WCVA director)

Another senior officer from the WCVA agreed that there had been several problems in the voluntary sector's interface with the Welsh Office in the past. There was, for instance, a lack of 'joined-up working' with 'one bit of the civil service not knowing what the other bit is doing with the voluntary sector'. The respondent noted that 'a lack of consultation for key policy issues has been a common feature in the past', as well as a 'lack of inflationary uplift to grants'. Also voiced were concerns that, with the much more central and prominent role now occupied by the WCVA, relations with civil servants could become somewhat strained, in that it was not evident 'how delighted they are that AMs are having all this direct contact with – not just us, but a whole range of voluntary organizations'. Thus, one of the key shifts in voluntary-sector–government relations after devolution centres on the reconfigured role of civil servants, who no longer act as a filter between voluntary-sector demands and politicians. As an example, the senior officer described how the draft scheme was passed directly from the WCVA to the Assembly debating session, without first having been 'fiddled about with' by civil servants.

The WCVA thus see themselves as able to fulfil a powerful lobbying function – a term that their senior staff were not afraid to use – in their role as representatives of a more coherent and unified voluntary-sector structure than in England or Scotland. In the WCVA's view, it is this coherence that has enabled key voluntary-sector demands to find their way onto the Labour government's policy agenda.

It is logical that the Assembly should turn to the WCVA as a single, easily identifiable representative of the voluntary sector in Wales (and also a broker of sorts, capable of directing Assembly committees to relevant individual voluntary organizations). The WCVA can claim, with some legitimacy, to be the voice of the voluntary sector in Wales; its position as such is undisputed (whereas, in England, its sister organization, the NCVO is only one of a number of umbrella organizations):

> We have reached a stage in development here in Wales in my view, where the WCVA provides more in terms of that sort of standard and a good, inclusive underpinning of the voluntary sector than is the case anywhere else in the UK . . . In the case of Wales we have just got one level [of representation] . . . It means, therefore, that we have got a situation that is so much simpler, more effective and more ripe for development than anywhere else in the UK. (Alun Michael, AM)

However, whilst the WCVA works for and with voluntary organizations across Wales, its representative role is not without ambiguities. To begin with, the WCVA's coverage is far from exhaustive; its core membership is only a fraction of the estimated 25,000 voluntary organizations operating in Wales. In addition, Kendall and Knapp (1996) include the WCVA among those voluntary organizations described as having enjoyed a 'cosy' relationship with the Welsh Office prior to the arrival of the Assembly. Whatever the accuracy of this description, it remains the case that the perception among some voluntary organizations is that the WCVA's agenda is somewhat distant from their own concerns.[7] Representing the interests of the voluntary sector as a whole is, of course, a gargantuan and unenviable task. Inevitably the WCVA finds itself attempting a difficult balancing act. Eager to involve itself closely in the work of the Assembly so as to maximize its ability to influence emergent policy agendas and protect the interests of its membership and constituency (as it sees these), it must also endeavour to keep the trust of a range of disparate organizations whose aggregate notional existence as a 'sector' representing civil and community values figures so prominently in the Assembly's plans for inclusive democracy.

Those we interviewed at the WCVA recognize these difficulties only too well, conceding that the diversity of the sector can make it 'very difficult to speak with one voice' and that the WCVA is caught in something of a double bind in terms of its close working relations with the new Assembly. On the one hand, the WCVA has to try and create links with the Assembly, 'otherwise, what is our purpose; why do we exist?' On the other hand, the more successful these efforts are in forging close relations and channels of communication with the Assembly, the more the WCVA becomes open to the charge that they lack the distance necessary to represent the sector's interests independently.

> The problem is . . . the perception that WCVA is gatekeeping the Assembly, and wants to sew up all the influence – to be seen to be the golden child of the voluntary sector. That is not the case . . . We are just trying to provide pathways for communication, not gatekeeping. (WCVA policy officer)

This is an inevitable problem of being an umbrella body, but one which, according to its director, does not prevent the WCVA being critical of government where necessary:

> People want it both ways. They want us to be a powerful, critical mass so that we can be considered a serious player with the usual suspects . . . But they also then criticize us for being too well in . . . It is something that you have to balance all the time. What we have here are two very distinct constituencies. We have our members and what they want, and at the end of the day that is what is most important. That is what we are here for. To get what they want we have to use whatever tactics we need to use. Clearly, those will range from the best tactics – which are those which never surface in public – and if that doesn't work for whatever reason, we need to move up the scale – the last scale

of which is a public campaign. We'd do that as a last resort because it is resource-intensive . . . The Assembly makes all that much more complicated as well because we have a lot more actors to keep playing or juggling with . . . It is the dynamic and natural tension of an umbrella body.

This interview extract reveals the challenges involved in ensuring that the voluntary sector can maintain its independent, critical and campaigning voice. It suggests that, post-Assembly, there will be more need for the WCVA to evidence its independence by being ready to criticize Assembly policy, campaign for policy changes, and be seen publicly to do so.

Other routes and representation

The Voluntary Sector Scheme, however, introduces a further tier of representation. The scheme makes provision for a Partnership Council or Forum, which will advise on the implementation of the scheme and facilitate consultation with relevant voluntary organizations. Representatives to the council will be drawn from the twenty-one different categories of voluntary activity/interest identified in the WCVA's database of voluntary organizations (see WCVA, 1999). The selection of these representatives will be a potentially delicate matter; the council is already operating on an ad hoc basis as a shadow council and those voluntary-sector representatives currently serving have been selected through an informal process of identifying existing networks and 'lead' organizations in various fields (rather than by democratic election). It remains to be seen how the council will be perceived by the different organizations whose interests it is tasked to represent, once the scheme is in place, and how its role will develop alongside that of the WCVA.[8]

There are at least two further means whereby smaller, locally based voluntary organizations can hope to have their voices heard in the Assembly. The first of these is the National Assembly Voluntary Sector Centre in Cardiff Bay.[9] The centre has been operational since the arrival of the Assembly and exists to assist voluntary organizations wanting to contact and work with the Assembly, in particular those voluntary organizations with minimal resources and less experience of government liaison. In conception, the centre was envisaged as a venue for interaction between Assembly Members, functionaries and voluntary organizations, providing organizations from outside Cardiff with resources and 'hot desk' facilities when attending the Assembly (there was even talk of its being located within the new Assembly premises). However, in its first year of operation, the centre has had to adjust (and narrow) its remit much more towards the provision of information at a distance – it has been used much less than was at first anticipated as a physical locale for partnership. The modest take-up of the centre's facilities in this respect owes much to the resource implications, for any voluntary organization, of travel to Cardiff for the purposes of lobbying the Assembly; the argument could also be made that the centre has received less backing from the Assembly than it might have done – it does not, for example, feature in the provisions of the scheme. As a source of information for voluntary organizations across Wales, the centre has proved a valuable resource. The centre's weekly bulletin, including a digest of relevant Assembly business and advance notification of forthcoming committee meetings, has been welcomed by an expanding audience of networks, organizations and individuals.

The Assembly committee structure itself makes some provision for organizations and individuals wishing to participate in Assembly business but restricted from doing so by the resource implications of travel to Cardiff. The four regional committees of the Assembly meet away from Cardiff – in the south-west, south-east, mid-Wales, and north – taking the work of the Assembly out of Cardiff. However, as the regional committees are not party-balanced (proportionately equivalent to party strength in the Assembly), they operate in only a consultative capacity and have no decision-making/legislative power of their own. This has not gone without notice among research respondents in the south-west, mid- and north Wales regions: 'I think a lot of voluntary community groups expected the Regional Committees of the Assembly to be stronger – for there to be more of a regional flavour, generally. That doesn't seem to have materialized.' Anxieties of this sort are compounded by the perception, expressed to us on several occasions, that the larger voluntary and charitable organizations in Wales – those with established contacts with the civil service in Wales and sufficient resources to take advantage of the opportunities that the new Assembly brings – tend to be those that 'have been transplanted into Wales and have not grown here'.

CONCLUSION

There is no doubt that the creation of a National Assembly for Wales has already altered the relationship between the voluntary sector and government in Wales (and has the potential to do so further). Voluntary organizations were among the best-prepared and quickest off the mark of a range of organizations, interests and sectors with an eye to working with the new Assembly; at the present time, voluntary organizations are probably the most active and regular of the varied audiences, visitors and lobbyists to which the Assembly plays host. The voluntary sector, in the view of several respondents, had done much more than, for example, the business sector in Wales to make its voice heard at the Assembly. However, various developments cross-cut here, which preclude some singular statement on the question of democratization. Our study concludes, as did many respondents, with judgement reserved.

> The Assembly has yet to make hard decisions that show that it has actually made a radical shift in how things were before. One day I'll think, 'My God, they really have made a big shift', and then another day I look at it and say, 'Hang on, this is business as usual'. (senior WCVA officer)

Almost all of the organizations we have contacted during the course of the research have broadly welcomed the Voluntary Sector Scheme, but as a means to an end rather than an end in itself. Concrete, formalized arrangements for consultation and partnership to which the Assembly can be held accountable are important, but many voluntary organizations are looking beyond this and expect the Assembly to keep to both the letter and the spirit of the scheme. The proposed annual review of the scheme by the Voluntary Sector Partnership Council will be an important test, but voluntary organizations will also be making their own judgements based on the quality and character of their interactions with the National Assembly – be these direct or through sector representation.

The most significant obstacle to a full democratization of relations between the Assembly and the voluntary sector lies with the existing imbalances in the capacity of voluntary organizations to participate. While a handful of larger, established voluntary organizations are increasingly orientating their activities towards the National Assembly, many of Wales's smaller voluntary organizations remain ignorant of the detailed workings of the Assembly and lack the resources to monitor and liaise with this new tier of government. In this context, claiming partnership with the voluntary sector as a whole, the Assembly may find it all too easy to cherry-pick a relatively small number of established and 'politically articulate' organizations with which to work closely; this is to be expected, of course, and to some extent it is an unavoidable development. But it raises the possibility that existing lines of cleavage in the sector will be exacerbated as a voluntary-sector élite is established, enjoying a privileged relationship with government. The perception that the larger voluntary organizations in Wales do not always best represent the autochthonous democratic resources of the sector cuts to the heart of the rhetoric of partnership, inclusion and democratic renewal.

Sectoral imbalances may be somewhat levelled through the efforts of the WCVA as an all-Wales network representative and co-ordinator. It is already clear that the Assembly sees the WCVA as a key partner and as a representative of the voluntary sector. If the WCVA is to act successfully in this capacity, however, it will need to ensure that its own reach extends as far as possible into the sector and that it is working with the confidence of a whole range of voluntary organizations in Wales, large and small, established and non-traditional. It will need to overcome some diffuse suspicions that, whilst being a powerful advocate for the sector, it may become distanced from the concerns of its grass-roots constituencies.

The Assembly's distaste for being 'lobbied' needs to be considered alongside its promise of inclusive government, as there are potential ambiguities here. It is at present unclear whether the Assembly's unfolding vision of partnership will recognize the voluntary sector as a source of challenge and dissent, as well as representing a source of support and collaboration. The WCVA, in particular, faces the difficult task of working closely with the Assembly to achieve a shared agenda whilst simultaneously maintaining a sufficient critical distance from government to permit of genuine challenge and argument. These dilemmas are familiar to the voluntary sector and are to be lived with and worked at, rarely overcome or avoided.

Future research attempting an assessment of the partnership arrangements between the Assembly and the voluntary sector will need to recall the considerable optimism and sense of potential voiced at the outset, by the WCVA and key politicians of varied political hues, committed to ensuring that the voluntary sector should contribute significantly to (and enhance) the democratic process in post-devolution Wales.

Acknowledgements

The research on which this chapter is based was funded by the Economic and Social Research Council (Grant L327253033).

Notes

[1] The previous regional administrative body, the Welsh Office, historically played a very directive and arguably hierarchical role in Welsh affairs (see Osmond, 1998; 1999; Hutt and Bryant, 1998; Morgan and Rees, 1999; Day et al., 1999).

[2] It should also be noted that the current vogue for these terms in the political arena has been accompanied by a growing academic interest in notions of social capital (see, for example, Granovetter, 1985; Coleman, 1988; 1990; Hall, 1999), 'trust' and civil society (see, for example, Tester, 1992; Gellner, 1994; Fukuyama, 1996; Seligman, 1992; 1997; Hann and Dunn, 1996; Keane, 1998).

[3] Nor is it entirely guaranteed within the Labour Party in Wales.

[4] Should such agencies wish to deploy public relations practices in the way they manage their various publics there is a large, mainly US, literature on PR with a rich diversity of conceptual schemes in which to grasp the mechanisms and arts of persuasion. These essential elements of public relations are succinctly summarized by Wilcox, Ault and Agee (1997: 6–8) by reference to key words. These suggest that PR is deliberate, planned, performance-orientated, responsive to the environment, beneficial to the organization and its publics, behoves two-way communication, is a management function and part of decision-making of top management. The normative dimensions of these themes is not disguised in the literature, and modern PR claims that it fosters open communication and mutual understanding with the idea that the organization also changes its own attitudes and behaviours in the process (see also, Grunig and Hunt 1984: 8; Spicer 1997; Lesly 1998). Some of these key words informed the design of our survey of the sector in Wales, particularly in relation to the appointment of dedicated staff to Assembly relations and to the production of specific (internal and external) material by which to engage with the new Assembly in its various institutional contexts.

[5] The compact between the Government and the voluntary sector in Wales was developed by the Welsh Office and the WCVA, in consultation with the voluntary sector in Wales, as *Command Paper 4107*, presented to Parliament by the secretary of state for Wales in November 1998.

[6] A new 'improved' multi-media Assembly website was launched in February 2001.

[7] Furthermore, it should be noted that the WCVA has been used to operating as a conduit for Welsh Office funding to the voluntary sector, administering and allocating grants to individual voluntary organizations. This role, which continues with the National Assembly now in place, would seem to sit a little awkwardly with any representative function.

[8] Complications may arise from the fact that the WCVA executive similarly comprises twenty-one sector representatives. There is some potential for confusion and overlap here.

[9] Funded through the National Lottery and managed by the WCVA.

6

Learning by Doing: Devolution and the Governance of Economic Development in Wales

KEVIN MORGAN and GARETH REES

INTRODUCTION

The creation of the National Assembly for Wales on 1 July 1999 marked a sea change in a process of Welsh devolution which extends back at least to the latter part of the nineteenth century. What was crucial here, of course, was the shift from administrative devolution to more democratic forms. The growth of the Welsh Office since its creation in 1964 and its progressive acquisition of increased powers, as well as the establishment of a wide range of Non-Departmental Public Bodies (NDPBs; popularly known as 'quangos') (most notably, the Welsh Development Agency (WDA)) were widely recognized as having contributed significantly to the 'modernization' of the Welsh economy and society more generally. However, these devolved institutions were also widely criticized for their lack of accountability to the people of Wales through directly democratic mechanisms (Morgan, 1994; Council of Welsh Districts, 1995; see also Ashworth et al., this volume). In this regard, therefore, the establishment of the National Assembly was justified in terms of introducing an electoral mandate; it was a means of *democratizing* the governance of Wales.

Equally, however, constitutional reform was justified – officially and otherwise – in terms of the capacity of the Assembly to produce effective policies, more closely attuned than hitherto to the particular 'needs' of Wales. More specifically, it was the Assembly's performance with respect to the Welsh economy on which it would ultimately be judged. As the then secretary of state for Wales (1997) put it, ' . . . one of the Assembly's most important tasks will be to provide clear leadership and strategic direction to boost the Welsh economy.' Given the limited – albeit still significant – secondary legislative powers available to the Assembly, a key element here was its ability to bring about a wider transformation of governance structures, thereby creating the conditions through which more effective policies would be delivered.

Viewed in this light, then, what was important was the extent to which the Assembly would foster changes in the nature and interrelationships of a range of organizations concerned with the formulation and delivery of economic development policies. Clearly, employers (and their representative bodies) and, to a lesser extent, the trade unions were crucial; as well as the WDA; the Training and Enterprise Councils (TECs); the local authorities; and voluntary-sector organizations. Moreover, it was not only the character of the emergent relationships between these latter organizations and the Assembly which were important here, but also of those between these organizations themselves. Hence, it is striking that the emphasis upon 'inclusivity' in the politics of the Assembly was paralleled by that on 'partnership' and effective 'organizational networks' at the level of policy development and implementation. The Assembly was expected not only to provide a strong lead in establishing a framework of priorities for economic development, but also to foster effective collaboration with and between the organizations responsible for its implementation.

As its proponents constantly remind us, the National Assembly remains in its infancy. Nevertheless, sufficient time has passed since its inception to permit at least a preliminary evaluation of how far the Assembly has succeeded in instigating new forms of governance of economic development in Wales. This is what we attempt in what follows. Our conclusions remain tentative and may clearly need amending in the light of future developments. Nevertheless, what this initial analysis suggests is that there is no *simple* relationship between, on the one hand, the greater openness and transparency of governmental decision-making that democratic devolution brings, and, on the other, the development of more collaborative and inclusive forms of economic strategy, let alone actual improvements in economic well-being. Rather, the latter have to be worked for and constructed in a complex and demanding process of 'learning by doing'.

DEVOLUTION AND THE GOVERNANCE OF ECONOMIC DEVELOPMENT

With the advent of the National Assembly, Wales provides an important 'laboratory' for testing some of the analytical claims – both academic and 'political' – made about the impacts of devolution on the UK's system of governance. The traditional view, of course, has been that the British system remains highly centralized, especially when compared with federal systems such as that in Germany. However, it has been recognized for some time that this form of centralized government is better understood as one part of a more complex 'differentiated polity' (Rhodes, 1997). In this

conception, centralization coexists with fragmentation and interdepend-
ence; and policy intentions – especially as envisaged at the 'centre' – are
often swamped by their unintended consequences. Certainly, there is not
one, but multiple decision-making centres, linking many levels of
government: local, regional, national and supranational. Hence, it is the
relationships between these levels which become crucial in shaping such
multi-level governance systems.

More specifically, within the British–European Union system, the
concept of subsidiarity has come to play a critical role, emphasizing that
decision-making should be devolved to the lowest level at which it can be
effectively executed. In practice, of course, subsidiarity is contingent on
two very important conditions: firstly, that the centre assents to devolving
(that is, giving up) power; and, secondly, that the local or regional level is
competent to absorb additional powers. Where, in effect, a level of
governance is being substantially reconstituted (as has happened in
Wales), the question of whether these conditions are fulfilled in reality is
posed especially acutely.

'New governance' theory also highlights the phenomenon of what may
be termed 'governing without government'. Services are delivered not by
government directly, but by a set of self-constituted, organizational
networks over which, it is claimed, central government has only loose
regulatory leverage. Hence, for example, economic development strategy
in Wales is not implemented simply through the actions of central
government, but rather depends on the activities of interlocking networks
or partnerships of organizations, in which no single body can accomplish
its goals without the active collaboration of a host of others. What are most
significant on this view, therefore, are the nature of the organizational
networks through which strategy is developed and implemented; and the
quality of the interaction between the organizations within a network
(Morgan, Rees and Garmise, 1999).

These arguments resonate strongly with recent thinking about normative models of regional economic development. Here, there has been
growing dissatisfaction with *dirigisme* and neo-liberalism, the classical
economic development repertoires, which sought to privilege either state-
led or market-driven processes regardless of time, space and milieu.
Hence, for the new approaches, the key issue in achieving effective economic development strategy is not the boundary between state and
market, but rather the framework for effective interaction between organizations. More specifically, it is argued that the capacity of organizational
networks to mediate information exchange is crucial, as effective interactive learning within and between organizations provides the key to
knowledge creation and innovation, and hence to regional economic

growth (Lundvall and Johnson, 1994; Sabel, 1994; Cooke and Morgan, 1998).

The interaction between the organizations comprising a network reflects not only market relationships, but also the wider social and cultural context. In particular, the quality of relations between organizations is profoundly shaped by the 'institutional regime' of social rules, cultural norms, routines and conventions (what some commentators call 'social capital') through which interaction between organizations is regulated. For example, where the interrelationships between organizations are character-ized by high levels of trust – that is, expectations of honest, non-oppor-tunistic behaviour – then uncertainty in relation to knowledge exchange is reduced, stable and reciprocal interactions are developed and consequently innovative capacity is greatly enhanced. Where such trust is absent, then organizational learning through interaction is correspondingly much more difficult and may be absent altogether (Maskell et al., 1998). Accordingly, where the institutional regime provides the basis for trustful relationships between organizations, the latter co-operate through interactive learning and lower the cost of doing so (OECD, 2001).

But why should devolved governance structures make for a more effective system of regional policy-making? In theoretical terms, there are at least two answers to this question. Firstly, devolution potentially empowers *local knowledge*, part of which is tacit, and this can never be properly accessed by decision-making centres which are external to the region. This, in turn, allows regions to design and deliver policies which are attuned to local circumstances instead of being a product of some centralized template (Morgan and Nauwelaers, 1999). Secondly, the regional level is perhaps the most appropriate for building *social capital* because this is the level at which regular face-to-face interactions – one of the necessary conditions for trust-building, for example – can be sustained over time. The literature on trust and co-operation suggests that these are more likely to occur where there is a strong possibility that the actors will meet again, in other words where the shadow of the future looms large over the present (Luhmann, 1979; Axelrod, 1984).

In this chapter, we are concerned to explore the changing governance structures of economic development in Wales in the context of the transition from administrative to more democratic devolution. More specifically, we shall argue that this transition has involved a shift in the structure of network relations between organizations. Administrative devolution had produced a strongly hierarchical organizational network in economic development, focused vertically on the dominating Welsh Office (and WDA). This has shifted to a somewhat less hierarchical, but as yet still indeterminate pattern of network relationships. There is less evidence, however, that there has been an equivalent change in the institutional regime of social rules, norms and conventions; indeed, it is arguable that the persistence of an institutional regime from the era of administrative devolution constitutes the greatest obstacle to fulfilling the potential which more democratic forms of devolution offer.

Nevertheless, even establishing the character of these shifts in network structure is very important because, in terms of the normative models sketched earlier, hierarchical, vertical networks are less helpful than horizontal ones in solving the dilemmas of collective action and facilitating localized learning. As Putnam (1993) puts it,

> A vertical network, no matter how dense and no matter how important to its participants, cannot sustain social trust and cooperation. Vertical flows of information are often less reliable than horizontal flows, in part because the subordinate husbands information as a hedge against exploitation. More important, sanctions that support norms of reciprocity against the threat of opportunism are less likely to be imposed upwards . . . In the vertical patron–client relationship, characterized by dependence instead of mutuality, opportunism is more likely on the part of both patron (exploitation) and client (shirking). (p.174)

The creation of the National Assembly certainly raised expectations in Wales that network relations would become less vertical and more horizontal in character, more open and transparent and more conducive to participation. It was widely assumed, too, that these changes would in turn make for a more innovative and effective regional policy-making process. But this assumption – that a more open and democratic process would necessarily be a more innovative and effective process too – is clearly something that needs to be scrutinized rather than accepted at face value.

THE WELSH OFFICE ERA: A 'RAJ' STYLE OF GOVERNANCE

The Welsh Office and multi-level governance

The principal element in the system of governance in Wales during the period of administrative devolution was the Welsh Office. Following its creation as a territorial department of government in 1964, the Welsh Office had to fulfil the somewhat schizophrenic role of being the 'voice of Wales' in Whitehall and the 'eyes and ears of Whitehall' in Wales. Its development therefore illustrates with some clarity the complexities of establishing the relationships between levels of government within multi-level governance systems. The product of a long campaign for administrative devolution, the creation of the Welsh Office was bitterly resented by centralist politicians and civil servants in Whitehall, most notably Richard Crossman, who notoriously referred to it as an 'idiotic creation' (Crossman, 1976). Despite opposition from Whitehall, however, the Welsh Office created a new momentum for more functions to be devolved from London to Cardiff, to the point where it was employing some 2,400 staff by the mid-1990s. In fact, the real historical significance of the Welsh Office was that it furnished an institutional framework within which a Welsh system of governance could develop.

Comparisons with the Scottish Office invariably leave the Welsh Office looking second-best. Having been established as early as 1885, the Scottish Office had evolved into a robust department by the time its counterpart in Wales appeared. Indeed, a senior civil servant in the Welsh Office spoke of a very different 'mindset' in the two territorial departments: where the Scottish Office tended to be proactive and developmental in its thinking, the Welsh Office was inclined to be reactive and more dependent on Whitehall. These differences can be explained by the fact that the Scottish Office was always far better resourced, with respect to both budgets and staffing levels; and geographical distance meant that the Scottish Office was not so integrated, either culturally or professionally, with Whitehall as the Welsh Office. More generally, of course, Wales had been assimilated into England earlier and far more deeply than Scotland, where elements of independent statehood continued to exist in the form of the Kirk, the legal order and the educational system. For all these reasons, the Welsh Office rarely if ever departed from the Whitehall script, except when it was required to give a minor Welsh gloss to policy designed in London (Rhodes, 1988).

A former under-secretary of state at the Welsh Office confirmed this interpretation and drew a link between what he identified as a 'risk-averse culture' in the department and the problem of chronic under-resourcing. Speaking of the Welsh Office he said:

> There's a lack of dynamism and a very traditional way of working . . . that can often just be fossilized and lack creativity, with a tendency to look for problems and reasons not to do something, rather than solutions . . . It's terribly important that people understand how hugely under-resourced it is. So when a regulation comes through . . . that applies to England and Wales, yes, you might tweak it a bit, but the immediate inclination will be, well, let's see how we can make this work. How do we implement this, because there's just not the resources to be able to do much else . . . we are under-resourced and . . . the culture has been that the Welsh Office is a rather conscientious but sleepy backwater.

These twin problems of a risk-averse culture and chronic under-resourcing were enduring elements of the institutional regime associated with administrative devolution. They clearly posed more difficulties for Labour than Conservative administrations. The former have tended to enter the Welsh Office with a transformative agenda, most notably in 1997. That this risk-averse culture did not change with the new administration in 1997 was perfectly illustrated in the response to post-election proposals for educational reform in Wales. Responding to the Institute of Welsh Affairs, which had sponsored the radical idea of a Welsh Baccalaureate, a senior civil servant explained his lack of enthusiasm by saying that 'the Welsh Office is not in the business of transformation'. This conservatism in the institutional regime would become an even more pressing problem for the National Assembly, which came into being with high expectations of transforming the Welsh economy and society more generally (an issue to which we return later).

Conservative administrations, on the other hand, have for the most part been content with a less demanding, managerialist agenda. Certainly, for a time, it seemed that there was an unwritten political convention that the Welsh Office was a sanctuary for 'one nation' Conservatives in the tradition of Disraeli, Macmillan and Heath, who believed that government has a moral obligation to play an active role in promoting economic renewal and social justice (a tradition very close to the *practice* of Labourism). In actual fact, this tradition at the Welsh Office was most marked during the years 1987 until 1992, when Peter Walker and David Hunt were successive secretaries of state. Both men made a great deal of partnerships between the public and private sectors, contrary to much of the Thatcherite mainstream. However, as their Programme for the Valleys, designed to regenerate the former coalfield region, illustrated, many of their policies amounted to a triumph of style over substance (Rees, 1997).

The appointment of John Redwood in 1992 shattered this 'one nation' tradition. The Redwood era demonstrated that the post of Welsh Secretary could vary enormously, depending on the ideological position of the incumbent. For example, as a leading Eurosceptic, he reversed the pro-European message which his predecessors had given to Welsh organizations to help them engage more productively with the European Union. Amongst other things, this meant that the WDA, the first UK agency to secure EU assistance under the Regional Technology Plan programme, almost lost it because the secretary of state was reluctant to give his approval. Even more seriously, John Redwood was also reported to have 'returned' some £112 million from the Welsh Office budget to the Treasury, enabling him to champion cuts in public expenditure, not only in Wales, but also in government and the Conservative Party more generally. It was widely perceived in Wales that here was a secretary of state using the Welsh Office to champion a political creed which was demonstrably unpopular in Wales. This politically perverse, but, at the time, constitutionally legitimate, result of the system of administrative devolution ultimately proved to be a powerful stimulus to the cause of democratic devolution (Morgan and Mungham, 2000).

Administrative devolution and the building of organizational networks

There were, however, other elements in the institutional regime associated with administrative devolution that were also significant in shaping the pattern of organizational networks for the promotion of economic development. Certainly, critics of the Welsh Office tend to forget that its partners in these ventures, such as the business community and local government, for example, were themselves often committed to limited and rather conservative agendas. It has been argued, for instance, that – perhaps inevitably – local authorities in Wales have been reluctant to extend their vision beyond their own 'turf', making collaboration for more strategic objectives in economic development difficult. Equally, however, these shortcomings were exacerbated by what was seen as the sustained offensive which successive Conservative administrations waged against local government, cutting powers and resources, and making for extremely difficult relationships between local and central government.

For its part, the business community has played a very limited role in Welsh civic life, especially since the inter-war depression. Such was the curmudgeonly civic behaviour of the coal-owners, the dominant employers in Wales historically, that one historian was forced to conclude that, when they disappeared with nationalization in 1947, it was 'as if they had never existed' (Williams, 1980). Of course, the diversification of the Welsh economy spawned new employers, the most prominent of which have been branch plants with their headquarters, and thus their centre of gravity, far removed from Wales. More concerned to make a name for themselves inside the enterprise than the local or regional community, branch-plant managers are naturally keen to move up the corporate ladder as quickly as possible, an aspiration which invariably means moving out of Wales. In contrast to *Mittelstand* firms in Germany, where owner-managers have set a high premium on local civic engagement, Wales has an under-developed medium-sized corporate sector (Cooke and Morgan, 1998). This leaves small and micro-sized firms, locally owned perhaps, but hardly locally engaged in any meaningful way. This relative absence of civic commitment is compounded by the fact that, on the whole, the corporate sector in Wales consists of low-skill and low value-added activities, which helps to explain why 'Corporate Wales' is not an innovative interlocutor which makes exacting demands on business support agencies and politicians to innovate in economic development strategy (Morgan and Rees, 1994). In Wales, then, the involvement of the 'business community' actually means the activities of the peak associations of business, namely the Welsh branches of the Confederation of British Industry (CBI), the Institute of Directors (IoD) and the Federation of Small Businesses (FSB). It goes without saying, perhaps, that while these associations may speak in the name of the 'business community', they are not identical with it and, therefore, they are not necessarily always at one with it.

In the absence of a strongly developed organizational presence for business within the governance system of administrative devolution, the WDA came to play an important role, almost as a surrogate for business interests. Formed in 1976 to promote economic and environmental renewal, the WDA quickly established itself as the flagship NDPB in Wales. Although there was always much more to the Agency than inward investment, the latter became virtually synonymous with its economic renewal strategy in the minds of politicians and the public. Despite the fact that foreign investors directly account for less than 10 per cent of total employment in Wales, inward investment was accorded a status wholly disproportionate to its real significance. The reasons for this are not difficult to fathom: indigenous job creation is a diffuse and largely imperceptible activity compared with the highly visible impact of a large inward investment project, such as the major investments by Ford, Bosch, Sony or Toyota, the high-profile projects where politicians like to cut the ribbon or unveil the plaque for posterity.

The process of attracting foreign inward investment became progressively more competitive in the 1990s, and the WDA, having won as much as 20 per cent of all inward investment projects in the UK at the start of the decade, found it ever more difficult to sustain this level of activity. Close collaboration between the WDA and the Welsh Office was essential to success in the inward investment stakes, not least because inward investors appreciated the low transaction costs associated with a 'one-stop shop' to answer all their inquiries, a task which the WDA had honed to an art form. Apart from this task, the WDA was responsible for assembling the whole package of incentives, which could include land, site development, premises, training support and supply chain support. But the key part of the incentive package, Regional Selective Assistance grants, always needed to come from the Welsh Office and the latter had to approve the whole package to ensure it did not exceed certain cost-per-job ceilings set by the UK and EU authorities.

More generally too, given the institutional context, the bulk of economic development initiatives in pre-Assembly Wales originated from the Welsh Office. Paradoxically, despite its rather weak and reactive stance towards levels of government *outside* Wales, *inside* the country – and almost by default – the Welsh Office became the prime instigator of economic development strategy, with other organizations, such as the local authorities, the TECs and training bodies, for example, brought on board as and when required. The pressures to involve other bodies grew progressively stronger through the 1980s and 1990s because, to access EU or UK regeneration funds, applicants were obliged to form 'partnerships' between public, private and voluntary-sector bodies. If the Welsh Office became relatively adept at forging partnerships, the top-down manner in which it did so provoked suspicion and hostility from below, not least because other organizations felt themselves to be decidedly the junior partners. This situation is well illustrated by the activities of the Monitoring Committee for Industrial South Wales, the regional partnership which managed EU Structural Funds. Chaired and serviced by civil servants, the Monitoring Committee was dominated by the Welsh Office, and the latter had a conception of partnership which was totally at variance with that of its partners. Hence, a European Commission review of the partnership arrangements was driven to conclude that

> Many of the partners see partnership in a horizontal sense in which equal partners move towards common ends. Central government has tended to see partnership in vertical terms in which the Welsh Office plays the decisive role with any alternative model viewed as unacceptable . . . Working relationships in industrial South Wales, although reasonably good, are limited in scope. (European Commission, 1991)

This verdict could actually summarize the entire structure of organizational networks for economic development in Wales during the period of administrative devolution. Whilst there was the potential for close working relations between the Welsh Office and local authorities, for example, the latter felt that the Welsh Office had neither the will nor the resources to initiate its own policies effectively, and that it was loath to delegate responsibilities because it did not trust its partners (Welsh Local Government Association (WLGA), 1996). The point was made very clearly by a senior official in the WLGA:

> There was a feeling of mutual hostility, certainly a lack of understanding, and a feeling in the Welsh Office that local government ought to be their agent . . . The political values [of the Conservative government] had almost become absorbed at official level. There were a few areas of working together, but they were the exception rather than the rule.

This interpretation was reinforced by an inquiry by the Welsh Affairs Select Committee, which said it was 'disappointed to discover that so much mistrust exists between the regional partners, especially local authorities and the Welsh Office' (Welsh Affairs Select Committee, 1995). Equally, it is instructive that there was not a single representative from local government on the WDA's board until 1997.

Even where partnership was thought to be strongest – in the relationship between the Welsh Office and the WDA – there were manifest problems. In the fast and furious inward investment stakes, where time and teamwork were of the essence, the partnership between the WDA and the Welsh Office was most pronounced and most successful, no doubt driven by a 'needs must' mindset in exceptional circumstances. By contrast, the more prosaic realm of indigenous investment – new start-ups, micro- and small-firm assistance and support for existing companies and so forth – could never command the same level of political attention, hence its Cinderella-like status until 1997, when the incoming Labour administration sought to give foreign and indigenous investment parity of esteem in its new economic renewal strategy. Aside from exceptional moments, therefore, when a foreign investment deal had to be 'closed', the relationship between the Welsh Office and the WDA could best be described as low-trust and arm's length; again, not so much a horizontal network of equal partners, more a hierarchical network of regulator and regulated (albeit not very effectively, as we shall see below). Though the temperature of this relationship could vary, depending on the rapport between the secretary of state and the chairman of the WDA, this rarely affected the day-to-day interactions between officers 'below deck', as it were, where each side divulged information on a 'need-to-know' basis, a hallmark of a low-trust relationship. This low-trust and mutually suspicious culture became more pronounced in the wake of the governance crisis of the WDA in the early 1990s, a crisis precipitated by a fatal combination of overtly political appointments on the one hand, and a weak regulatory regime on the other (Morgan, 1997).

More generally too, these well-publicized 'scandals' within the WDA served to focus the widespread discontent in Wales with what was seen as the *undemocratic* character of the governance system of administrative devolution. There was a 'democratic deficit' associated with the proliferation of NDPBs, which were unelected and therefore not accountable to the communities in which they operated. Moreover, what the WDA experiences exposed was that – what had long been suspected – this lack of accountability provided the opportunity for a series of highly irregular activities, which the government, through the Welsh Office, was manifestly unable to prevent. Despite the public funds which were spent by the WDA, regulation was clearly very weak. Not surprisingly, therefore, the reform of 'quangoland' became a major objective of the democratic devolution programme (Morgan and Roberts, 1993). However, what was not clearly thought through was how a more democratic and more effective system of governance of economic development was to be achieved; the creation of the National Assembly was seen as a panacea in itself (an issue to which we shall return later).

In summary, therefore, the organizational networks during the period of administrative devolution developed a markedly hierarchical structure, with the Welsh Office (and, to a lesser extent, the WDA) the dominating influence. This reflected the asymmetrical power relations between the Welsh Office, with its command of resources and decision-making, and the other organizational actors, which were thus encouraged to be dependent rather than self-reliant. The linkages within networks therefore tended to be formalized and restricted in scope, focused on the achievement of closely defined goals. Whilst these arrangements were often successful in delivering concrete programmes of development, they appeared to constrain the establishment of trust and partnership-building among the various players because relations assumed a dependent rather than inter-dependent flavour (Garmise and Rees, 1997; Morgan, Rees and Garmise, 1999).

Compared with the English regions, where there was very little institutional capacity to co-ordinate governance functions, Wales had the capacity for many years to practise what is today called 'joined-up government'. To some degree the most damning criticisms of the Welsh Office are motivated not by the modesty of its achievements, but rather by the disjunction between its potential and its practice. Although the limitations of its sphere of action were all too real, particularly as regards powers, resources and personnel, the governance style which it practised for most of the time bred mistrust and suspicion among its partners, so much so that the latter actually felt disempowered by the hierarchical networks which the Welsh Office designed and managed (Morgan, Rees and Garmise, 1999). Not surprisingly, perhaps, the hierarchical and imperious attitude of the Welsh Office was acidly described as a 'Raj style of management' by officers in local government (Morgan and Mungham, 2000). The remedy to the discontents with this system, moreover, was seen to lie largely in improved accountability and openness in the organizations involved in economic development; and this was what democratic devolution was expected to deliver (Huggins, Morgan and Rees, 2000) .

The transition to democratic devolution: the Welsh Office after 1997

The election of the New Labour administration in 1997 itself marked a significant departure from the governance system which had developed previously under administrative devolution. Certainly, it is difficult to imagine a greater contrast in governance styles than that between the Ron Davies period at the Welsh Office and that of, say, John Redwood. It is clear that the new administration set out to redefine the relationships between the Welsh Office and Whitehall. As a former under-secretary of state at the Welsh Office put it,

> . . . there was a very noticeable sea-change very quickly . . . when people, and I think that they responded to it, mostly, with great enthusiasm, had a set of ministers who were giving them a different agenda and were saying . . . 'Well actually, we want to do this in Wales.' I really think that . . . this . . . had an enormous impact on morale and on . . . the priorities that officials here saw for themselves . . . there was almost a revolutionary change – that's a big word – a radical change in the relationship between Cardiff and Whitehall . . .

Establishing this more assertive relationship with the British level of government can be seen as an important development, preparatory to taking the greater step of establishing democratic devolution.

Moreover, across a wide range of policy fields – not only economic development, but the environment, health, and education and training too – the policy-making process became more inclusive and more interactive, as Welsh Office civil servants were actively encouraged to engage with external interlocutors. As a senior civil servant put it,

> There's been a strengthening of the 'Team Wales' approach . . . We have done all we could to prepare the [National Strategy] proposals in as open and inclusive a way as possible. If it had just been a few Welsh Office officials going into a huddle and producing a strategy and saying 'Oh, you know, we've consulted and here it is. Now you can sign it off', that wouldn't have been in keeping with the principles under which the Assembly was being established.

This shift also registered with the other members of 'Team Wales'. According to the WLGA, for example, the Ron Davies administration created a totally different atmosphere, 'as if someone had attached a "welcome" sign to the Welsh Office' (Morgan and Mungham, 2000). As a senior local government official put it, 'my experience since the election has been pretty much a transformation in the relationships. Partly, I think, there is now recognition that local authorities are important. In a very real sense we've started to feel that we're coming in out of the cold.'

This is not to suggest, of course, that even this partial transition was unproblematic. The New Labour administration also faced the seemingly intractable problem of what to do about the NDPBs, a problem which resonated especially deeply in Labour Party circles. In opposition, as we have seen, there had been a good deal of loose talk about 'a bonfire of the quangos' and of a 'quango-free zone', in which the Assembly would 'take over most of the work being done by the 1400 appointees now running unelected bodies, with the rest of their duties going to local councils' (Sparrow, 1995). Much of this was ill-informed and ill-considered because, even in opposition, the Ron Davies team had never intended to abolish NDPBs across the board; rather the aim was to render them more accountable and, wherever possible, to reduce their number through merger.

Labour's promise of a new era of open and meritocratic appointments to NDPBs bore fruit when Elan Closs Stephens, the newly appointed chair of S4C, became the first person (and, indeed, the first woman) to head an NDPB by virtue of replying to a public advertisement. What spoiled the new era (at least for 'quango' critics such as Rhodri Morgan, who had personally played a prominent role in exposing malpractices in the WDA), however, was the revelation that the chairman and chief executive of the WDA had both been reappointed without recourse to such public advertisements. The decision to reappoint was defended on the grounds that it provided some continuity amidst so much flux, a reference to the impending merger of three NDPBs, the existing WDA, the Development Board for Rural Wales and the Land Authority for Wales, into what Ron Davies called the 'economic powerhouse' of the reconstituted WDA.

These reassurances from Ron Davies and Peter Hain, the under-secretary of state, did not entirely satisfy their own Labour Party critics, a portent of the problems to emerge later between the Assembly and the WDA. However, what the critics in the Labour Party and elsewhere arguably failed to recognize was that a robust regulatory regime has to strike a judicious balance between controlling the NDPBs and encouraging them to innovate. There appeared to be little understanding of this issue. Regulation was seen solely in terms of its control functions, and relatively little attention was devoted to thinking through the mechanisms for achieving innovative economic development strategies.

More generally, as we have seen, whatever the politicians' agenda and irrespective of the undoubted enthusiasm for change of the then permanent secretary at the Welsh Office, Rachel Lomax, there are indications that the civil service was ill-equipped to deal with the new demands which were placed upon it and, therefore, clung to the more conservative habits associated with previous administrations. Indeed, one of the main criticisms that was levelled at this Labour-led Welsh Office was that it was rather *too* open. That is to say, it launched too many new initiatives and consultation exercises, with the result that civil servants were too overstretched to follow through properly.

Moreover, outside parties too were overburdened by the demands of constant consultation. In other words, this more open and interactive governance style exposed the limited capacity not only of the civil service in Wales, but also of the partners necessary to effective economic development: business, the trade unions and the local authorities. These potential partners in organizational networks simply did not have the resources to cope with the intense interaction which new initiatives demanded. Moreover, the fragility of the efforts to open up the policy-making processes within administrative devolution were clearly exposed when Ron Davies was replaced as secretary of state by Alun Michael, who was certainly personally less comfortable with the new approaches. Even before the Assembly came into being, therefore, there was a partial retreat from the innovative practices which had been introduced after the 1997 general election.

THE NATIONAL ASSEMBLY: MAKING DEMOCRACY WORK?

Civil society and the creation of the Assembly

Not surprisingly, much of the previous discussion about the impacts of democratic devolution have focused on the novelties of the mechanisms of the National Assembly itself. However, it is important to understand that the capacity of the Assembly to deliver effective policies is shaped not only by these mechanisms, but also by the character of Welsh civil society, as reflected in the patterns of voting in the 1997 Referendum on the establishment of the Assembly and the 1999 election of Assembly Members.

In contrast to Scotland, where the demand for a Parliament was justified as an expression of national rights, the campaign for the National Assembly was prosecuted in far more utilitarian terms: principally as a step towards a more democratic system of governance, on the one hand, and a means to a more robust economy, on the other (Welsh Office, 1997). The rather low-key debate around devolution in Wales was perhaps reflected in the result of the 1997 referendum itself: a wafer-thin majority in favour of establishing the National Assembly: 50.3 per cent against 49.7 per cent on a turnout of just 50.1 per cent. Certainly, it was clear that the Welsh electorate was far from strongly persuaded of the virtues of democratic devolution, no matter what the anticipated benefits. Given the fragility of the vote, together with the low turnout, it is not surprising that the Assembly has appeared to feel that its legitimacy is vulnerable; it has had to prove that it is a valuable investment and not just an unnecessary cost. For example, the continuing debate about the costs of a new Assembly building underlines the uncertainties about its role in Welsh society.

It is also clear that, at the design stage, when the powers, structures and procedures of the Assembly were being defined, few people really supposed that the new governance system would be launched into the maelstrom of a minority administration. On the contrary, during the Assembly elections, for instance, the mainstream political debate centred on the size of the Labour majority, with most polls predicting a haul of between thirty-four and thirty-six seats out of the total of sixty, giving Labour a comfortable working majority. In the event, Labour won just twenty-eight seats. The fact that it emerged as the largest single party was small compensation for what was arguably its worst-ever election result in Wales. Most notable were the massive swings from Labour to Plaid Cymru, resulting in the loss of 'safe' Labour seats such as Rhondda, Islwyn and Llanelli, as well as the very narrow retention of a number of other seats in Labour's erstwhile rock-solid heartland, such as Cynon Valley, Neath, Merthyr and Pontypridd (Wyn Jones and Trystan, 1999b). At the time, it was frequently argued that these results reflected essentially short-term considerations, most obviously dissatisfaction with the manner in which Alun Michael had become Ron Davies's successor as leader of the Labour Party in Wales. It remains to be seen, however, how far more fundamental factors were at play as well, whether dissatisfaction with New Labour's seeming abandonment of traditional Labourist policies or, alternatively, with the very outcomes of those traditional Labourist policies themselves (as encapsulated, for instance, in the chaos of Labour's local government performance in Rhondda Cynon Taff).

Whatever the explanations, these very poor results for Labour meant that the new administration, having initially ruled out a coalition with the Liberal Democrats, found itself in the highly precarious position of having to negotiate with the opposition on a seemingly daily basis to ensure the passage of its business agenda. This fragile political equilibrium, a totally novel situation in Welsh politics, provides one of the keys to understanding the trials and tribulations of the Assembly's first year, not least the dramatic removal of Alun Michael, the first First Secretary, in February 2000. Again, it remains to be seen the extent to which the decision of his successor, Rhodri Morgan, to form a 'Partnership Agreement' with the Liberal Democrats (in October 2000) will provide the basis for the more effective delivery of policies, on the basis of an agreed programme. Certainly, this is widely understood to be necessary to improving the way in which the Assembly is perceived. As Rhodri Morgan himself recently put it in a plenary debate on the new Cabinet (which includes two Liberal Democrat ministers),

> When you have a minority government – as we have had since the May 1999 elections – you inevitably struggle, and the public sees a lot of shenanigans on the Assembly floor, without good delivery of policy. We are setting out on a

new adventure of majoritarian government, without having to strike a deal over every vote with Plaid Cymru, the Liberals or occasionally with the Tories . . . We will not have to do that on a daily basis.

Apart from these basic constraints on the operations of the Assembly during its early months, it is also important to remember that the social composition of the Assembly Members themselves reflects the contours of Welsh civil society. If we focus on the largest single party, an analysis of Labour's forty constituency candidates reveals some interesting results. The average age of Assembly candidates was forty-six, compared with an average age of fifty-four for Welsh Labour MPs; and there was a fifty–fifty gender balance, on account of the party's 'twinning' policy, whereas women were thin on the ground among the MPs. Moreover, of Labour's Assembly candidates, almost 50 per cent were councillors or former councillors and, if lawyers and public relations consultants are excluded, *none* came from employment in the private sector. In short, whilst Labour Assembly candidates scored well on age and gender, the bias towards local government and public-sector employment meant that it had failed to attract candidates from a wide range of professional backgrounds (Morgan, 1999). Moreover, a very similar pattern emerges for the minority parties too, with only the Conservatives having a significant proportion of candidates with experience of private-sector employment (and, of course, only nine of these were elected, mostly from the regional lists).

It is difficult to be categorical about the impacts of this restricted social background on the policy-making process. However, it is not unreasonable to suggest that Assembly Members drawn from this type of background have approached policy formulation and development with particular mindsets: what McPherson and Raab (1988) have termed the 'assumptive worlds' of policy-makers. Given their social backgrounds, then, they may have defined problems in particular ways and reviewed policy alternatives within the limits set by their previous experience. In ways which are not dissimilar to members of the civil service, therefore, the Assembly politicians too may have defined their agendas in ways which reflect the assumptions of *past* political circumstances as much as the new ones created by democratic devolution. In these ways, therefore, the effects of the institutional regime associated with administrative devolution may have extended into the new post-Assembly era (and we return to these points later).

Powers and structures: the new governance system

The powers which the National Assembly assumed on 1 July 1999 are modest. Most notably, of course, there are no tax-varying powers and no primary legislative powers, which means that the Assembly is much more dependent on Westminster than the Scottish Parliament. Nevertheless, devolving even modest powers to the National Assembly has produced a significant restructuring of the governance system. Hence, the Assembly now has responsibility for the following activities, each of which has a clear impact on economic development:

- *Budget decisions*: the Assembly has full discretion to allocate its annual budget of some £8 billion between its devolved responsibilities (which include health, education, agriculture, economic development and the environment).
- *Secondary legislation*: it is able to make regulations which interpret the nature and implementation of primary legislation (passed at Westminster) and to make inputs into the development of primary legislation in the light of the specific needs of Wales.
- *Policy development*: the Assembly identifies problem areas for policy intervention, decides on the priorities for action and devises policy interventions to meet designated objectives.
- *Public bodies*: the Assembly regulates the structure and activities of public bodies in Wales through, for example, the process of appointments and the setting of targets and monitoring of performance (Welsh Office, 1999b).

Although the scope and limits of these powers will have to be tested in practice, it was clear after even its first year that the Assembly did not have some of the powers it believed it had, as in agriculture, for example, where its efforts to launch its own initiatives (such as a Welsh calf-processing scheme) were deemed to be illegal, as the requisite powers remained in London. These experiences seem likely to fuel demands for more formal powers to be transferred to the Assembly in the fullness of time (perhaps as a consequence of the review of the Assembly's operations which is currently being conducted).

In addition to the devolution of formal powers to the Assembly, the nature of the governance system has been transformed by the creation of a wholly new organizational structure. Most significantly, the Government of Wales Act specified that political leadership in the sixty-member Assembly was to be provided by the First Secretary; and the provision for a motion of 'no confidence' in the First Secretary underlined the fact that he or she is accountable to the Assembly as a whole. The First Secretary chairs a Cabinet-style Executive Committee. This Cabinet-style system eventually won out over the alternative of a local government committee system because the former was deemed to be better attuned to rapid and accountable decision-making. Moreover, the dangers of concentrating political power in the hands of the First Secretary were offset, in theory at least, by the creation of six subject committees, of which economic development is one, with members drawn from all the political parties according to the balance of Members in the Assembly.

These subject committees were expected to have a policy-making, as well as a scrutiny function, creating a diffused system of policy development. In reality, however, the former has as yet proved far more difficult to realize (although see our discussion of the development of policy for post-sixteen education and training below). In part, this is because the first First Secretary, Alun Michael, did not encourage such devolved policy-making. Equally, however, the committees have been overburdened and under-resourced – frequently reflected in the last-minute arrival of committee papers – leaving little or no scope for substantive debate. Certainly, the subject committees, like the Assembly as a whole, have precious little time to consider their own briefs, let alone consider how their work connects with that of other committees, with the result that 'joined-up' government has proved elusive (as, of course, it had done during the Welsh Office era).

A further element in the diffusion of policy-making was the creation of four regional committees, which, whilst only advisory in function, were designed to provide 'voice' for the populations of regions which are co-terminous with the bureaucratically designated WDA areas and the regional economic forums of north, mid, south-west and south-east Wales. The regional committees were meant to signal that the Assembly, though physically based in Cardiff, had some presence in every corner of Wales; that it was a *National* Assembly in more than just words. As a senior civil servant in the Assembly commented,

> The Assembly's been established in such a way as to try and ensure that the different interests and views in Wales are properly reflected and, at the one level, you've got that through the forty constituency members. But then, superimposed on that, you've got the regional committees and, I think, those were deliberately established in order to ensure that the various geographical voices within Wales could be reasonably represented.

The reality, however, has been disappointing. Of all the new governance structures, the regional committees have achieved the least to date, with very poor attendances suggesting that they have a low priority among politicians and have failed to capture the interest and engagement of the public.

However, despite the difficulties experienced by the regional committees and, to a lesser extent, the subject committees, it nevertheless remains clear that the new governance structures – the Assembly itself, the office of First Secretary, the Cabinet, the subject committees and the regional committees – have created *multiple* points of entry to the policy-making system. In sharp contrast, during the Welsh Office era, when political access – principally to the secretary of state and his two junior ministers – was highly restricted, it was the civil servants who were the key to influencing the bulk of decisions about policy development. Quite simply, the Welsh governance system now enables much greater accessibility, at least to those with the organizational capacity to capitalize on the opportunities which are newly available. The point is made rather graphically by a senior local government official:

> . . . in the last system, that was it. If you didn't influence officials, your chances of influencing a minister were virtually zero, unless it was on some huge issue. I mean, you know, you could only go to the minister on a big issue. You didn't bother them with all the little stuff. However, I think what you see with the committees and the Assembly is that we've got lots more bites at the cherry . . . we can have a go at influencing civil servants . . . [but] if we don't get what we want, we can have a go at influencing . . . the [Cabinet] secretaries and the committees and not only committee chairs, but committee members . . .

Whether this was what was intended by the designers of the new governance system of *democratic* devolution remains, of course, a moot point.

The new partnerships: consultation or participation?

It also remains to be seen how far the National Assembly has assumed the role of what Piore (1995) refers to as the 'orchestrator of dialogue' between the other organizations involved in initiating policy with respect to economic development. Certainly, under the terms of the Government of Wales Act, the Assembly has a duty to forge partnerships with its three principal interlocutors: the business community; local government; and the voluntary sector. According to Alun Michael, these were 'the three golden threads that run through the work of the Assembly' (National Assembly for Wales, 1999e). Such statutory obligations are unprecedented, certainly within the UK; the National Assembly is thus the first administration to have a statutory duty to consult and co-operate with its key partners. This was to be achieved primarily through the formal mechanisms of the Partnership Council and the Business Partnership. The former was intended to promote collaborative relationships between the Assembly and local government. The latter stemmed originally from section 115 of the Government of Wales Act, which CBI Wales had forcefully campaigned to have included in the legislation because of its fears that the Assembly might seek to marginalize Welsh business interests. Whatever the novelty of these organizational relationships, however, the question remains of how these partnerships have functioned in practice. To what extent have they fostered genuine dialogue and active participation, as opposed to scripted exchanges and passive consultation?

The Partnership Council comprises members of each political group represented in the Assembly (including the First Secretary), together with local authority members nominated by the WLGA, as well as representatives of the community councils, National Parks and the fire and police authorities. The crucial difficulty which it has faced is that of fostering inclusivity despite the inevitable tension between the body responsible for funding local government in Wales – the Assembly – and those spending the money – the local authorities (Gallent, Jones and Allen, 1998). As one member of the Welsh Cabinet put it, 'If things are going really badly, if we had to cut local authority spending, there's no amount of Partnership Councils that will put that right . . .' Indeed, the original terms of reference for the council were rejected by the WLGA precisely on the grounds that they were a means by which the Assembly could call local authorities to account. Even when they had been revised, the early Partnership Council meetings developed into 'uproarious and shambolic' affairs, degenerating into age-old battles of political in-fighting. As one experienced commentator put it,

> . . . the idea that the Partnership Council should be a vehicle for consultation seems to be going the same way as the idea that a sensible minority government is obliged to consult the other three parties . . . When devolution enthusiasts boasted the Assembly would be inclusive and open, no one imagined that meant a trifle better than Whitehall but far worse than any local council. (Betts, 1999)

However, the significance of these difficult experiences for the Partnership Council is limited because local government has, on the whole, succeeded in establishing other avenues through which its voice can be injected into the policy-making process. As we have seen earlier, the WLGA, in particular, has developed a significant lobbying capacity directly with the administration and, more widely, through the subject committees. As a senior WLGA official remarked,

> We very much see ourselves as an association which engages regularly and frequently and substantially with the Assembly. Much, much more so than we did with ministers, because we could never get to meet them. I mean they were just so inaccessible. You got replies, you know, that were very much 'civil servant speak' . . . I see us having much more access and influence with the secretaries.

In this context, it is significant that a number of these Cabinet secretaries, as well as the chairs and members of the subject committees, share backgrounds of prominent service in local government.

The Business Partnership too has experienced difficulties. As we saw earlier, the question as to who or what constitutes 'the business community' in Wales is somewhat more complicated than it might appear. For the business associations to speak with a unified voice is no easy task, not least because they represent very different constituencies. For example, CBI Wales is like the diplomatic elder statesman, being the most established of all the associations, and its membership includes the large, 'blue-chip' companies. In stark contrast, the FSB prides itself on being the strident voice of small business, the association which says things in public which the CBI might say only in private. However, with all these associations, it is never clear how accurately their public positions reflect their members' views.

This issue became a bone of contention between the first First Secretary, Alun Michael, and the principal business associations. In an attempt to find a unified business voice in Wales, these associations created Business Wales, an umbrella body initially encompassing the CBI, the Institute of Directors, the FSB and the chambers of commerce. However, remarkably, the First Secretary pressed them to include voluntary-sector representatives in the new body, despite the fact that it was intended to be self-organized and 'owned' by business interests themselves. To overcome these problems, and to create a direct link to the business community, Alun Michael also appointed Roger Thomas (a personal friend and a partner in the law firm, Eversheds) to be his 'business partnership adviser'. However, it is clear that Thomas was appointed not as a lobbyist for business in the Assembly, but rather as the First Secretary's ambassador to the business community, a 'trouble-shooter' whose services were constantly in demand to placate increasingly unhappy business interests.

The inaugural meeting of the Business Partnership offered business representatives an opportunity to vent their grievances directly to Alun Michael, who chaired the event, and, indeed, to the public generally. For the business community, the most contentious issue was the reform of post-sixteen education and training in Wales (an issue we address in more detail later), but other aspects of the meeting caused some concern too. For example, the business representatives had wanted the inaugural meeting scheduled in November, but instead it was held just before the Christmas vacation, at four o'clock on 16 December. Furthermore, the agenda was unilaterally drawn up by Alun Michael, with little or no input from Business Wales, and no papers were tabled until the very last minute. All of this suggested to Welsh business that the Business Partnership was a low priority for the First Secretary and his administration. In the event, the business representatives did not vent their grievances, partly because they did not want the inaugural meeting to end in an unseemly row, as the Assembly's first meeting with local government in the Partnership Council had done. More fundamentally, however, as a participant put it, 'it is not the business way to bang the drum in public'. However, he was also forced to acknowledge that it was more difficult to find 'more discreet channels' in the new era of democratic devolution.

These differences finally surfaced when Dr Elizabeth Haywood, the director of CBI Wales, did speak out publicly about the misgivings of the business community, a move which provoked an angry response from Alun Michael, who suggested that she was not reflecting the views of CBI members. In an effort to undermine her authority, moreover, the First Secretary's business partnership adviser, Roger Thomas, went over her head to try to win over the chairs of CBI Wales and the Institute of Directors. The assistant director of CBI Wales, Ashley Drake, was also told to 'stop rocking the boat'. Perhaps coincidentally, shortly afterwards, these two most robust critics of the Assembly in CBI Wales, Haywood and Drake, left for pastures new. As one business leader put it later, 'Alun Michael wanted a lapdog in the CBI.' In short, therefore, Alun Michael had tried to persuade business leaders, but it was clear that he was unable or unwilling to deliver on the undertaking which he had given to them at an Institute of Directors lunch (on 25 June 1999) when he explicitly said, 'Business will have a strong voice in the national and the regional bodies and will be paramount in respect of workplace training.'

It is true that subsequent meetings of the Business Partnership have become progressively more open, especially after Rhodri Morgan assumed the post of First Secretary and took the chair. Nevertheless, they are still perceived as stage-managed occasions in which business leaders are less than forthright. A senior member of Business Wales reflected on the operation of the Business Partnership and concluded by saying:

> The Business Partnership is too big, too stage-managed and too public. A meeting behind closed doors is the best to get real business done and to solicit people's real views, as opposed to their scripted public views. The chairs of the business community were speaking in a public venue and they wanted to maintain a polite atmosphere. But basically they were done over.

Clearly, it is one thing to have public debating forums, but it has to be asked how effective these are if one side of the partnership – namely the business representatives – is unable or unwilling to articulate its views in a forthright manner.

Whether because of these organizational difficulties or for more fundamental reasons, there have thus remained considerable doubts and confusions over the effectiveness of the Business Partnership as a means of ensuring high-quality network relationships between the business sector and the government in Wales. For example, one senior Assembly Member clearly expressed the continuing reservations about the 'voice' of the business world:

> . . . there's a huge problem, at the moment, in terms of consultation with business organizations, because you don't know who to consult. We've got Business Wales to try and solve this problem. Traditionally, people have tended to go to the CBI and TUC. That's it, bang. You've done the job. But from the early eighties onwards gradually the Institute of Directors has forced its way onto the scene. Then you've got the Federation of Small Businesses. Then you've got the chambers movement and Chamber Wales being set up . . . and I'm not sure yet we have cracked this problem of formalizing relationships with the business world.

Equally, for some of its members Business Wales has been diplomatic, while for others it has been simply pusillanimous in its dealings with the Assembly. On a whole series of issues – the level of business rates, the reform of post-sixteen education and training, the process of appointing a chief executive to the National Council for Education and Training in Wales (CETW) and the lack of business involvement in determining EU Objective One funding – the business community seems to have become progressively more alienated from the Assembly. The experience of the Business Partnership appears to have done little to raise the quality of economic partnerships in Wales, at least in the eyes of some of the partners themselves, as we can see from the following reflections:

> There are so many talking-shops around at the moment. They are rife and it is becoming a real problem . . . The biggest con with these forums is that they have to invite everyone and, as soon as you invite everyone, you get a room full of fifty or sixty people and absolutely nothing can conceivably be done. They are self-defeating. (FSB Wales)

> What we don't want is just 'ticked boxes' saying that consultation papers were sent out to the respective business organizations. We need positive and genuine responses where business forms a full part of the policy formulation process. (WDA, 1999)

It may be argued, of course, that whatever its shortcomings, the Business Partnership at least ensures that the civil service is no longer the sole source of information on economic development available to the Cabinet and the Assembly more widely. Even here, however, considerable reservations are expressed about the mediating role which the civil servants play. For example:

> Partnerships that have been set up and started out well, and are genuinely perceived as partnerships by those taking part, are actually stymied by the way the civil servants work. (CBI Wales)

> Economic development partnerships in Wales have not become more trustworthy and are unlikely to . . . given the over-dominance of the civil service within the development of strategies and policies. (Wales TUC)

It is surely no coincidence that of all the regional partnerships that have emerged in the EU Objective One funding programme perhaps the most effective is the Agri-Food Partnership. Unlike most of the other partnerships, this actually pre-dated the Objective One process and sprang up from within the agri-food sector to pursue a commonly agreed strategy, in which all the actors are able and willing to participate. In contrast, the Business Partnership is a much more bureaucratic forum for consulting the business community, as required by the legislation. It has not as yet developed into a real partnership in which both sides participate in the policy-shaping process. Of course, these are early days for the Assembly and its partners, all of whom find themselves on a steep learning curve in a process without precedents. Nevertheless, it is perhaps instructive that business interests have increasingly sought to bypass the formal mechanisms of the Business Partnership in favour of more discreet, private meetings between the Cabinet and Business Wales.

More generally, therefore, these early experiences with the Partnership Council and the Business Partnership suggest that the received image of Wales, that it is 'culturally' inclined to collaborate through partnerships, needs to be substantially revised. This image has been projected so successfully, by both Conservative and Labour politicians, that it has begun to assume a life of its own. For example, a former Labour under-secretary at the Welsh Office made the following claim:

> The thing about Wales, for which there is quiet envy by my Whitehall colleagues, is that the culture is much more partnership-based. It is actually possible to operate on a level where there is a real sense of community . . . even in the business community. It's possible to get people to work together much more easily than it is in England and, simply, the smaller scale makes that easier.

From the evidence we have presented here, however, it is time that this image was probed more critically. It may be that people 'work together' more easily in Wales, but this may reflect nothing more than the fact that Wales is so much poorer than England, and that partnerships are the only way to secure funds for regeneration. Furthermore, the received image tells us nothing about the *quality* of the partnerships or their efficacy in producing tangible results. All the evidence suggests that real partnerships, in the sense defined earlier, are more likely to spring from bottom-up civic forces rather than top-down political interventions (OECD, 2001). Certainly, as yet in Wales, the formal mechanisms within the governance system of democratic devolution for promoting partnership and networking between organizations have had limited impacts. Moreover, there is every indication that both local government and business interests have sought alternative and less transparent channels through which their voices can be heard in the policy-making process.

New governance, old dilemmas: the Assembly and the WDA

The novelty of the governance system of democratic devolution lies not simply in the new organizational elements which it introduced (and on which we have focused hitherto), but also in its capacity to innovate with respect to established aspects of the governance system of economic development. Of crucial importance to the latter has been the Assembly's relationships with the NDPBs or, as they have become, the Assembly Sponsored Public Bodies. Certainly, considerable disquiet was expressed when Edwina Hart, the finance secretary, announced not the expected 'bonfire of the quangos', but a review to decide if they were still necessary (Betts, 2000a). In reality, this simply brought forward the Quinquennial Review process, which had occurred during the Welsh Office era under the name of the Financial Management and Performance Review. Quite simply, each Assembly Sponsored Public Body has to demonstrate that it is the most cost-effective and appropriate means of executing its function, otherwise it is liable to be abolished (NAW, 2000n).

As we saw earlier, however, there is a large and vociferous anti-'quango' group within the Labour Party (and in the other political parties too). These critics were displeased that there was to be no 'bonfire of the quangos', which they (wrongly) supposed was Labour Party policy. The existence of this vocal faction, coupled with the fact that 'quango' is a dirty word for many Labour Party members, especially those wedded to the Labourist traditions of local government, meant that senior Labour politicians in the Assembly were wont to pander to the anti-'quango' lobby, and liked to be seen to be 'tough' on them. This was despite the fact that the Assembly Sponsored Public Bodies are no longer the unaccountable organizations that were so reviled in the past, but executive arms of the Assembly itself.

In other words, political attitudes towards the Assembly Sponsored Public Bodies were shaped as much by the 'assumptive worlds' of the past as by the realities of the present. This certainly seems to have been the case with respect to the most significant of these Public Bodies, the WDA.

As we have seen, the WDA had been a particular target of the critics because of both the significance of its role in Welsh economic development, and also well-publicized malpractices. Although these irregularities spanned a number of years, they had only been exposed to the light of day in 1993, following a highly embarrassing parliamentary inquiry. Most of the irregularities – which included inappropriate payments, conflicts of interest, attempts to silence former employees and the failure to identify certain financial transactions – had occurred under the chairmanship of Dr Gwyn Jones, who was appointed to his post in 1988 by Peter Walker, the then secretary of state for Wales. Perhaps the most astonishing thing about this appointment was that neither the secretary of state nor the Welsh Office officials had thought it necessary to seek a single character reference, for a post which was arguably the most influential in Wales after the secretary of state himself. Along with other failures to observe proper procedures, this had forced the Public Accounts Committee to the damning conclusion that '. . . the standards of the Agency have been well below what this Committee and Parliament have a right to expect' (Public Accounts Committee, 1993).

Although the Welsh Office had tried to avoid any culpability, blaming it all on the agency, it had itself been criticized for running a lax regulatory regime, reinforcing the general perception at the time that the 'quangos' in Wales were 'out of control' (Morgan, 1997). In the wake of the crisis, the WDA had commissioned an independent inquiry, chaired by Sir John Caines, into corporate governance in the agency and this had offered a sober and long-overdue review of the conflicting pressures under which the WDA was obliged to operate. In particular, the Caines report highlighted the difficult balance which needed to be drawn by the agency between proper accountability to the government and, ultimately, Parliament, on the one hand, and the need to be responsive to market signals and pressures, on the other. Certainly, the latter could not be an excuse for the agency's board failing to ensure internal compliance. As Caines (1993) himself put it,

> We have formed the impression that the Agency, as it grapples with the situation brought to light by these inquiries, risks an overkill reaction – copying everything to the Welsh Office, even though it may not be necessary, so that it cannot be accused of failure to inform . . . The Welsh Office also has a part to play. The Agency has to operate to the timetable of a commercial world. If the Agency is to succeed in its tasks, Government must deliver its responses at a speed commensurate with that timetable . . . It is clear that a non-

departmental public body should have its priorities set by its political masters who are its paymasters. The important thing is that in the process the value of the independent minds and talents of those appointed to the WDA Board is not diminished, that there is agreement between the Board and the Secretary of State about priorities and objectives and that the programmes which the Board is expected to deliver can be carried out within the funds available . . . The downside of this era of success, with its pressures to achieve results, has been inadequate attention to the requirements for compliance, for sound internal management and for staff capable of combining entrepreneurial vigour with attention to the details of proper administration. When the top leadership is not perceived to attach importance to enforcing sound management, good practices are allowed to slip. Corners are cut and bad decisions are taken . . . Any organisation in the public sector has to reckon with the fact that it is in the political arena and that its activities are capable of being used in party political battles. The more a Government takes credit for the success of its agencies' achievements as part of its political record, then the more likely an Opposition is going to find it difficult to resist making political capital out of any signs of management failure or other shortcomings in those agencies. (Caines, 1993)

The immediate outcome of this furore had been that, having been under-regulated until then, the WDA had suddenly found itself over-regulated by a heavy-handed compliance regime. The agency had become more publicly accountable, but at the expense of making it more risk-averse. The fact that this new compliance regime stymied innovative behaviour in the WDA had seemingly been of little or no concern to the then secretary of state, John Redwood, a devoted Thatcherite who had a deep ideological aversion to the public sector in general and to 'quangos' in particular. However, the consequences were to be much more significant after the election of the Labour administration in 1997 and even more so after the advent of the National Assembly.

In particular, despite the wholesale restructuring of the old WDA (along with the Development Board for Rural Wales and the Land Authority for Wales) into the 'economic powerhouse' of the new WDA, it remained vulnerable to external criticism, as was reflected in the disquiet over the reappointment of the chairman and the then chief executive without public advertisement. Moreover, more than a year after the Assembly had been created, the WDA continued to find itself mired in uncertainty. Having been reviewed in 1997, the summer of 2000 saw it subjected to a new Quinquennial Review, the final results of which would not be available until the early part of 2001. Other factors compounded the uncertainty, such as the Assembly's business services review, the appointment of a new chief executive and the formation of a new board.

However, far and away the most unnerving thing of all was the paradox of the agency's relationships with the Assembly. Outwardly, the WDA's

pre-eminent position within the governance system of economic development had been confirmed by the restructuring into the new 'super-
quango'. However, this was belied by the inner reality of an agency which
felt marginalized and undervalued by the Assembly. A whole series of
setbacks had persuaded the WDA board that their new political masters
neither understood nor respected the agency, culminating in the loss of the
international trade support function. This was transferred from the WDA
to the Assembly's civil service, despite the fact that it was located in a
development agency in every other nation and region of the UK. In the
wake of this particular setback, a bewildered WDA board member felt
compelled to say:

> The Agency's relationship with the Assembly is bad. Communication is poor
> and a big vacuum is developing. The National Assembly has no sense of
> ownership of the WDA and no apparent commitment to the WDA. The rules
> have changed and nobody here understands the new rules of the economic
> development game. The WDA is not consulted now. Officials are putting stuff
> on paper and just passing it over to the agency. Under the National Assembly
> the civil servants are running everything and filtering everything. Are we
> expected to market ourselves to the Assembly? The agency is not in that game.

If this account of the WDA's exclusion is taken at face value, it is
certainly consistent with what we have seen to be a widespread view of the
agency amongst Assembly Members, especially those from the Labour
Party. Within this particular 'assumptive world', the WDA is seen to have
enjoyed – and, indeed, abused – a position of unrivalled privilege under
successive governments, but now needs to be brought firmly under the
control of its political masters. This is compounded by the fact that the
Assembly's dominating figure, Rhodri Morgan, was second to none in
exposing malpractice in the WDA in the early 1990s and, as a result, earned
a formidable (and popular) reputation as a 'quango-basher'. When he
assumed formal responsibility for the WDA, on becoming economic
development secretary in the Assembly, it would be something of an
understatement to say that this was not 'a marriage made in heaven',
despite his profound knowledge of the economic development scene. What
made matters worse, however, was his decision to hold multiple posts after
he was elevated to the position of First Secretary in February 2000. The fact
that he held five posts – MP, AM, economic development secretary, First
secretary and chair of the Objective One Monitoring Committee – meant
that he could not give his undivided attention to each, a situation which
further empowered the civil service.

For their part, as we have seen, the civil servants (whether in the Welsh
Office or the National Assembly) have never had a genuinely close

relationship with the WDA. This was undoubtedly compounded by the embarrassing crisis of the early 1990s, which was an ignominious experience for them, too, because they lost face with their Whitehall colleagues over their regulatory failures. Far from being a partnership, therefore, the relationship between civil servants and WDA personnel is still very much a 'them-and-us' phenomenon on both sides of the divide. It has even been suggested that the civil service resents the credit which the WDA has earned from high-profile inward investment projects, not least because it feels that the Welsh Office's contribution, particularly in the form of Regional Selective Assistance, was always the most important element in the incentive package. If this is true, it highlights the difficulties of implementing the 'Team Wales' concept.

It is also suggested that local government regards the WDA as a rather privileged and certainly overmighty rival in the economic development governance system. As one external observer, the chief executive of a TEC, put it,

> My own view is that [organizational networking has] actually got rather weaker . . . You've got one superstar that gets all the money and all the headlines, which is the WDA, and another organization, which had been in relative disarray under the Tories, which were the local authorities. So, there's an awful undercurrent of jealousy and dislike between the two, and I think that in collapsing the number of partners down, that rivalry and antipathy has just been honed . . .

Certainly, the WLGA has argued forcefully that public bodies such as the WDA need to be more tightly controlled and made more accountable to the communities in which they operate: hence its proposal that 50 per cent of the agency's board should consist of local government representation (WLGA, 1998). On the other hand, however, the WLGA and the WDA have agreed to a 'Memorandum of Understanding' which sets out to provide a framework for co-operation and the creation of a new operational partnership. It remains to be seen how effective this will prove in practice.

The influence of these factors has gone unchallenged because the WDA has been either unable or unwilling to mobilize its own constituencies to articulate an alternative, pro-agency perspective. How is this relative silence to be explained? The answer is twofold. Firstly, having been assured of a special status in the past and despite the crisis of the early 1990s, the WDA felt that its position would be much the same with the Assembly as it had been with the secretary of state, albeit in a more open and transparent form. Secondly, Brian Willott, the former chief executive, felt strongly that the agency should eschew 'lobbying' and remain above the fray of 'party politics' in the Assembly. This was not the uniform view of the WDA board, however, where some members wanted the agency to be more robust and less deferential in its dealings with the Assembly, or at the very least to contest anti-agency messages. How this would be best achieved, however, remained unclear.

Instead, what we have here is a situation in which no one is able to address the real problem – the poor relationship between the Assembly and the agency – because no one will publicly acknowledge it. This paradoxical situation was painfully evident when, before the Assembly's Audit Committee, the then chief executive, Brian Willott, was asked about the agency's relationship with the Assembly and, in particular, with Rhodri Morgan, who was thought to have had too few meetings with the WDA since he had become economic development secretary.

> *Dafydd Wigley*: When did you, Mr Willott, or the chairman of the agency last meet the First Secretary to discuss this balance between inward investment and indigenous companies?
> *Mr Willott*: I do not think that we had it as a specific agenda item when we last met. I last saw the First Secretary at a function two evenings ago. I know that the chairman spoke to him yesterday but not necessarily on this particular issue.
> *Dafydd Wigley*: I am not asking when you met him socially. I am asking when you met him specifically on as important a consideration as the balance between these two factors.
> *Mr Willott*: I could not say when we last met concerning this.
> *Dafydd Wigley*: Have you met this year concerning this?
> *Mr Willott*: We have not met on this particular issue as an agenda item, no.
> *Dafydd Wigley*: For the clarification of the committee, how often do you meet the First Secretary?
> *Mr Willott*: Formally?
> *Dafydd Wigley*: Yes.
> *Mr Willott*: The last occasion was two months ago when he joined the board for a working dinner.
> *Dafydd Wigley*: How many times have you met this year?
> *Mr Willott*: I think that we have met on one other occasion.
> *Dafydd Wigley*: You have met twice, once over dinner?

As a former civil servant, Brian Willott was defending his minister, Rhodri Morgan, to whom he felt ultimately responsible, against Dafydd Wigley, the then leader of Plaid Cymru, the main opposition party. Critics have suggested that Willott, who was about to retire from the agency, should have been more forthright in his responses to the Audit Committee, but this ignores the habits of a lifetime in the civil service, where protocol runs deep. However, this act of loyalty produced some perverse effects because the politicians who had denied that there was a problem in the first place were able to cite Willott's testimony to the Audit Committee to support their case.

Further evidence of the poor relationship came when the Agency made a simple request for the Assembly to delay its Quinquennial Review by a couple of months, so that it could complete the process of appointing a new chief executive. A short delay would have helped remove a very difficult management problem: the agency could not appoint someone to the job until the first phase of the review had decided whether the WDA should continue to exist. In the event, the request was refused because it might look as though the Assembly was being 'soft' on the Agency. For the sake of appearances, then, the WDA was forced to postpone the appointment of a chief executive, yet another symptom of an adversarial, low-trust relationship.

Throughout this period, the WDA was especially keen to fulfil its targets, most of which seemed to have been met when it issued its results for 1999/2000, the first full year of the enlarged WDA. On the all-important jobs front, the agency had created or safeguarded some 19,989 jobs, the majority of which were in the indigenous business sector. Of the jobs created or safeguarded through inward investment, nearly 80 per cent were located in the EU Objective One region of west Wales and the Valleys. The Agency's new targets are based on the Assembly's Strategic Plan (*www.betterwales.com*), the key themes of which are sustainable development, social inclusion and equal opportunities. The WDA is thus being asked to do more with less, because its annual budget has been reduced from £138.9 million to £125.1 million. However, if the Assembly expects the agency to deliver the goods in the future, it will need to forge a much better partnership with its executive arm. This presupposes that the politicians and the WDA acquire a more knowledgeable and less adversarial attitude. As it is, the latter fears that it is losing political support at home, while in England, for example, the newly created regional development agencies are being supported with great enthusiasm.

In summary, therefore, what this saga illustrates are the ways in which the activities of organizations within the new system of governance – such as the forging of relationships between the WDA, the Assembly politicians, the civil service and local government, for example – are shaped by attitudes and perceptions which are the product of previous and, by now, historical experience. Hence, some of the failures of the new governance system of democratic devolution derive not so much from the objectives or even the organizational practices of the present, but rather the 'assumptive worlds' associated with the institutional regime of the past.

Democratic devolution in action: the reform of post-sixteen education and training

It should be remembered, of course, that the purpose of creating the new system of governance of economic development is to produce more effective policy outputs. At least in part, the latter provide a measure of the quality of the performance of the new governance system. During its first year or so, one of the principal areas of economic development policy to be processed through the new mechanisms of democratic devolution has been that of skills development and the reform of post-sixteen education and training. A brief analysis of this policy area thus provides fresh insights into how the general features of the new governance system that we have identified are actually working out in practice.

The general role of education and training in economic development had been a central issue in Welsh policy and politics at least since the 1980s and the collapse of the traditional economy based on coal, steel and agriculture. During that decade, it had become fashionable to argue that Wales's salvation lay in the creation of a 'knowledge-based economy'. Therefore, education and training had come to be seen as a central element in economic strategy. There was also a widespread recognition that the post-sixteen sector, in particular, lacked the organizational capacity to service the kind of economic trajectory which was envisaged as being the only viable one to generate a successful Welsh economy. However, at this time, there was only limited development of specifically Welsh initiatives and these were mostly associated with servicing the perceived needs of inward investors (Rees and Thomas, 1994).

These general concerns resulted in the establishment of the Education and Training Action Group for Wales (ETAG) in the immediate aftermath of the 1997 general election, charged with the task of devising a new strategy for Welsh post-sixteen education and training. It produced a consultation document the following year, which elicited a very wide range of responses – a genuine indicator of the significant position which post-sixteen education and training occupies within Welsh policy-making. In March 1999, ETAG produced an Action Plan (ETAP), which was subsequently debated in the National Assembly. In particular, it was subjected to especially close scrutiny by the Assembly's Post-sixteen Education and Training Committee.

As a result of these deliberations, a somewhat revised ETAP was produced. *Inter alia*, this provided for the establishment of a new National Council for Education and Training for Wales (CETW), with responsibilities for the development, funding and delivery of all forms of post-sixteen provision, except higher education. Beneath this national council there were to be four regional committees, whose geographical areas of responsibility were to correspond to those of the Assembly's regional committees, the regional economic forums and the divisions of the WDA. These regional committees were to act in an advisory and information-providing capacity to CETW. Finally, there was to be a local tier of Community Consortia for Education and Training (CCETs), which was to bring together the suppliers of education and training in local areas, possibly organized around the twenty-two local authority areas. These were to devise plans for the implementation of CETW's strategy, taking due regard of local circumstances. This system, in turn, was incorporated into the Learning and Skills Bill, which eventually passed into primary legislation through the Westminster Parliament.

This bland summary of events, of course, does scant justice to the intensely political processes which underpinned these policy outcomes. In particular, what was hotly contested was the role which private-sector business interests should play in shaping the agenda of post-sixteen education and training. Certainly, the representatives of business themselves felt that their contribution was undervalued right from the outset, even before the establishment of the National Assembly. As a representative of CBI Wales explained,

> CBI Wales . . . was asked to make available two prominent businessmen to work on the ETAG committee . . . Right from the word go the business community were outnumbered by educationalists and local government and in fact were shown very little respect. There were many occasions when our two nominees would have preferred to have quit, but the CBI resolved to try and help them out and persuaded them to stay on.

More concretely, business representatives believed that the restructuring of the organizational framework for post-sixteen education and training would serve to exclude their influence. Initially, this concern focused on the decision to abolish the TECs, on which majority business representation was guaranteed. Indeed, it has even been suggested that the final decision to carry through the dismantling of the TECs took place *after* the final draft of the ETAG recommendations had been agreed and only became known to business representatives at the press launch of the document. As the CBI representative again put it,

> The straw that broke the camel's back was the final draft of ETAG was agreed by everybody, including the business representatives, and at the launch done by Peter Hain, the draft had been tinkered with and in the opinion of the two CBI members of ETAG had totally disenfranchised the business community and they wished to resign.

Thereafter, the major bone of contention became the mechanisms through which business interests would be represented in the *new* post-sixteen system. At one level, business disquiet focused on the nature of its representation on the CETW. Whereas in England the broadly equivalent Learning and Skills Councils would be required to have 40 per cent of their boards representing business interests and there had been powerful ministerial encouragement to ensure its quality, the CETW was to be comprised of one-third public-sector representation, one-third community and voluntary-sector representation, leaving only a third for business representatives.

More significant, however, were the controversies over the regional tier within the new system. This regional tier was envisaged by business representatives, strongly supported by the TECs, as exercising relatively autonomous powers, based upon substantial devolved budgets (in comparable fashion to the English Learning and Skills Councils). They would thereby deliver a powerful set of strategic functions, within the national framework laid down by the CETW. Certainly, they would be functionally equivalent to, for example, the regional divisions of the WDA and could liaise directly with the Assembly's regional committees and the regional economic forums. Moreover, although business representation on the regional boards would again be only a third, it was thought that TEC personnel would transfer unproblematically into the new regional bodies, ensuring the continuation of an essentially business-orientated skills development agenda.

However, after scrutiny of the ETAP proposals by the Assembly's Post-sixteen Education and Training Committee, the recommended functions of the regional tier were actually far removed from this model. The regional committees were to be simply advisory and were to be denied devolved budgets. Hence, the principal elements within the new post-sixteen system were to be the CETW itself (on which business interests would have only one third representation) and the CCETs which were seen to comprise primarily the suppliers of education and training. Not surprisingly, perhaps, business interests regarded this as a major snub. So much so that the first meeting of the Business Partnership in December 2000 was largely devoted to debating the revised ETAP proposals. Moreover, even after this opportunity to express their concerns directly to the First Secretary, the respective chairs of CBI Wales and IoD Wales, as well as the general secretary of the Wales TUC and other representatives of the business world, wrote to Alun Michael in the following, dramatic terms:

> The recommendation for a much weakened regional dimension from that originally proposed, when considered with other recent events in the post-

sixteen arena have been the cause of some considerable concern to the business community. It seems to suggest there is a tendency amongst many members at the National Assembly to actively reduce the influence of the business sector in this critical area of economic activity . . . Without the opportunity to 'make a difference', through helping to shape the strategic and operational direction of the skills agenda, the likely outcome is that senior leaders of the business community will not wish to participate in the future. (Morris et al., 1999)

The First Secretary responded in conciliatory terms, but was unable to make significant changes. What is instructive here, however, is that the revised ETAP proposals represented a clear departure from what the First Secretary himself had earlier envisaged. For example, in a speech to an IoD lunch in June 1999, he had said:

Can I make it clear that a regional level of commissioning is implicit in the proposals and needs to be spelt out for all concerned. The likely way forward will be a regional commissioning group or board of the national council, at the level of the economic regions of Wales . . . Business will have a strong voice in the national and the regional bodies and will be paramount in respect of workplace training.

Moreover, the then post-sixteen education and training secretary, Tom Middleton, had earlier made it clear that the Cabinet's preferred option was that of a powerful regional tier, strongly expressing the voice of business representatives. Indeed, more generally, this intention to involve business closely in the formulation and implementation of education and training policy is consistent with New Labour's wider strategy of the 'Third Way'.

That these initial preferences of the First Secretary and, by extension, his Cabinet were not implemented is explicable, at least in part, in terms of the stand taken by the Post-sixteen Education and Training Committee. In rejecting the administration's preferred line and recommending a vastly reduced role for the regional tier, the committee reflected the intensive lobbying undertaken by the WLGA on behalf of the local education authorities and by the teachers' trade unions. Their interests were clearly seen to lie in defining the whole problem of post-sixteen provision in 'educational' rather than 'economic' terms and thus limiting the influence of business representatives. As a spokesperson for the WLGA put it,

. . . we have been very concerned about the proposal to create a regional tier within the new funding arrangements for post-sixteen education and training. This would have allowed for TECs to continue with only a change of name and watered down the ETAG vision. It would also have greatly reduced the influence of local authorities. We believe that the proposal came about after intense lobbying by the TECs . . . We will continue to make the case for a proper role for democratically elected councils in the new arrangements and for a funding formula which adequately reflects the needs of sixth-formers.

The influence of this lobbying was accentuated, of course, by the fact that, as we have seen, very many Assembly Members – including a substantial proportion of those on the Post-sixteen Committee – themselves had considerable experience of local government and were thus predisposed to accept the arguments being made. In addition, the public-sector employment backgrounds of the bulk of Assembly Members, and, more specifically, the fact that many had actually taught in schools and in further education, is likely to have engendered a positive view of the education sector's contribution to post-sixteen provision and, at least by implication, a jaundiced one of what employers have to offer. This is certainly how things appeared to observers from the business side of the argument. A representative of the TECs described the situation as follows:

> Too many AMs did not want to listen. The agenda was clear. The Tory TECs had to go . . . Even if we were able to display evidence of the value and success of the work of the TECs, this was either ignored completely or acknowledged with grudging praise . . . We discovered that few of the AMs had any grasp of the issues. With their predominantly local government and FE backgrounds, they had been well briefed about their 'positioning' and we were always pushing against a locked door.

In these circumstances, it is perhaps surprising that there appear to have been no very effective efforts by the administration to persuade even Assembly Members of their own party of the virtues of their preferred strategy. This left the field open for opponents both within the Labour group and in other parties to mobilize against the 'Tory TECs' and, indeed, private-sector business interests more widely. Moreover, the administration was crucially weakened by its minority status. If there had been a secure majority, it is at least possible that the First Secretary and the Cabinet could have drawn on 'party discipline' to push through their preferred option. As it was, it was relatively easy for their opponents to persuade sufficient Labour Assembly Members to reject the official line, so that in combination with members from other parties, it was clear that the administration's strategy could not secure a majority. In face of this, it appears that the First Secretary and the Cabinet opted to bow to the inevitable.

That the political influences on the policy-making process were so significant emphasizes the greater openness of the new system of governance in Wales; quite simply, things could not have happened as they have done under the Welsh Office regime of administrative devolution. More specifically, the subject committees have clearly created a new arena for influencing policy, not only by Assembly Members but also by groups within civil society through lobbying. The capacities that different lobbying groups have to affect policy, however, reflect their precise location within civil society, as well as their organizational competences. Business interests, for example, brought with them a historical baggage which reflects their particular place in the Welsh social structure and in relation to political processes. Equally, both Assembly Members and lobbying groups operate within 'assumptive worlds' which are shaped as much by the priorities of previous institutional regimes as those of the present. It remains to be seen, of course, how effective this distinctive system of Welsh post-sixteen education and training will be in operation. Indeed, it already appears that, as the new organizational machinery is being put in place, the role of the regional committees is being strengthened in order to provide a clearer strategic input below the all-Wales level. This is happening, however, largely out of sight of the Assembly politicians.

CONCLUSIONS: THE SCOPE AND LIMITS OF THE NEW GOVERNANCE

The notion of the UK as a 'differentiated polity' was originally meant to signal the transition from a centralized form of government to a more decentralized system of governance in which 'self-organised inter-organisational networks' were the defining feature (Rhodes, 1997). The latter is much broader than the former, because it embraces the non-governmental bodies which have assumed a central role in the functional decision-making process in the UK under both Conservative and Labour administrations. The advent of democratic devolution significantly enhances the notion of the 'differentiated polity' because it adds a territorial dimension to what tends to be a largely functional conception of governance. In fact, it is possible to discern the beginnings, however tentative, of a multi-level polity in the European Union which straddles local, regional, national and supranational levels of governance. In this polity, one of the key issues is the application of subsidiarity, the principle which commends the devolution of power to the lowest level that is capable of executing it effectively (Morgan, 2001a).

This is no abstract matter. It may not have been invoked by name, but subsidiarity was a common thread running through the most controversial issues which plagued the National Assembly during its first year. On each of these issues – the Welsh calf-processing scheme, the 'beef-on-the-bone' ban and the regulation of GM seeds, for example – there was genuine confusion, even at the very highest levels, as to who was responsible for what. Many policy fields (such as trade, agriculture, rural development, regional assistance, industrial aid and competition policy, for example) have to be situated in the context of a multi-level polity because the EU exerts such an important regulatory influence. The governance question of which levels are responsible for what will not be settled in Cardiff, or even in London. Indeed, such is the significance of this question that it is to be one of the main themes of the next intergovernmental conference of EU leaders in 2004.

Although democratic devolution is beginning to pose a challenge for governance outside Wales, in London and Brussels, it is within Wales that the most significant impacts have been felt (and it is on these that we have focused here). In fact, the advent of democratic devolution constitutes something of a paradox in the Welsh context. Despite the modest powers of the Assembly, its arrival has set those individuals and organizations which have to engage with it – politicians, civil servants and public, private and voluntary-sector bodies – on a very demanding learning curve. The transition from administrative to democratic devolution, from the Welsh Office to the National Assembly, may appear a limited change, but in reality it has inaugurated a new governance system, which operates in ways which are different in important respects from the era of administrative devolution.

Some critics have begun to dismiss the National Assembly as a 'toothless tiger' and an 'expensive talking shop'. However, our analysis suggests that this is at best premature. Whatever the limits of the National Assembly, and the constraints of the model of executive devolution on which it is based, the Assembly's policy-making process is more open, more transparent and more inclusive than the semi-secret world of administrative devolution which preceded it. Hence, the 'green shoots' of a new kind of policy-making are beginning to emerge, although this is admittedly most apparent to those who are actively involved in the policy-making process itself. Certainly, in the absence as yet of major policy impacts from the work of the Assembly, it is not surprising that opinion poll evidence suggests that the general electorate remains unconvinced.

The most significant difference between administrative and democratic devolution is that the latter has created multiple points of entry into the political system. This derives from the creation of wholly new organizational mechanisms: the sixty Assembly Members, the office of the First Secretary and the Cabinet, and the subject committees, in particular (as the case-study of ETAG and the restructuring of post-sixteen education and training exemplifies). Other innovations (the regional committees, the Partnership Council, the Business Partnership, for example) have undoubtedly not exerted equivalent impacts on the accessibility of policy-making. Nevertheless, the contrast with the pre-Assembly system, where entry was filtered through a limited number of access points, principally the secretary of state and his two junior ministers, remains stark.

It is, of course, clear that the capacity to take advantage of these new opportunities is not distributed equally between the different groups and constituencies in civil society. The new rules of the game have helped to institutionalize new opportunities for participation by means of the 'thirds principle', which stipulates that the membership of each partnership body must consist of a third from the public sector, a third from the private sector and a third from the voluntary sector. This new emphasis on inclusiveness has been widely welcomed by groups, especially those in the voluntary sector which felt marginalized in the pre-Assembly policy-making process. However, the 'thirds principle' has provoked severe criticism from traditionalists in the economic development world, who claim that, in practice, it tends to weaken partnerships because it extols political correctness over professional competence in the choice of personnel (Morgan, 2000).

More generally, those groups which are knowledgeable and well organized are clearly best placed to tap the potential of the new political system. For example, the voluntary sector has invested in its lobbying and policy-making functions, to ensure that it is in a position to make the most of democratic devolution. With a single peak association, the Wales Council for Voluntary Action, which has a staff of sixty, the voluntary sector has forged a more unified and more coherent sectoral voice than the business community, where several peak associations vie with one another to be the authentic 'voice of business' in Wales. Although the business community is indeed trying to forge a more coherent voice to engage with the Assembly, it readily admits that it was slow to master the new rules of the game, with the result that it has been left behind in the lobbying stakes by public- and voluntary-sector organizations which have put time and resources into their policy-shaping activities.

Equally, however, groups in civil society have differential resources on which they can draw in respect of the new governance system. Most strikingly, perhaps, the representation of business interests has been largely ineffective during the early days of the National Assembly. Business was slow to understand that, within the new governance system, political influence derived less from perceived status in a traditional hierarchy and more from organizational capacity to mobilize cross-party support in the Assembly, which was especially important in the highly fluid context of a minority administration. In the era of administrative devolution, business representatives enjoyed somewhat privileged access to the secretary of state. However, with the advent of the new governance system, even having the ear of the First Secretary may be insufficient, as the case-study of the ETAG proposals illustrates.

In fact, Assembly Members in the ruling Labour group – and of the other parties – seem to have little affinity with business interests. Given that the role of politicians has been expanded in the new governance system, this poses long-term difficulties in getting the 'voice' of business heard within the policy-making process. On the other hand, Assembly Members have much more in common with local government or the voluntary sector, where many of them have extensive previous experience. Being so much more familiar with the public sector, where their 'assumptive worlds' were shaped, and where their social and political networks continue to exist, Labour Assembly Members are much more likely to be receptive to some lobbies rather than to others. By political disposition and professional background, they were not going to be particularly receptive to the business interests. However, the corollary of this is that local government has been a major beneficiary of the new system. The WLGA, in particular, has transformed itself into a highly effective lobbying organization, well able to capitalize on networks into the Assembly via the Labour Party and the public-sector trade unions.

The politicization of the policy-making process, therefore, has been a major result of democratic devolution, albeit with highly uneven consequences for different groups within civil society. However, it is much less clear that these changes in organizational structures of policy-making have been matched by changes in the institutional regime through which the latter is regulated. Participants in the new governance system continue to function in terms of 'assumptive worlds' which reflect the priorities of the previous era of administrative devolution. Certainly, for example, there is little indication that the quality of the interaction between organizations in economic development has been transformed, as the difficulties experienced by the WDA and the very limited impacts of the Partnership Council and the Business Partnership illustrate.

A central issue here is the role played by the civil service. For all the novelties associated with the Assembly, the latter is staffed by the very same civil servants who managed the affairs of the Welsh Office. It is increasingly acknowledged that the resourcing of the civil service has not been increased in line with its new responsibilities. Perhaps in consequence, civil servants have tended to transfer their rather cautious and risk-averse approaches from the Welsh Office regime to that of the National Assembly, with adverse consequences for the latter's capacity to be transformative in policy terms. This view was expressed by a number of politicians across the party political spectrum, one of whom put it in this way: 'There is a lack of political will to get the officials to change their ways. What we lack most is innovative ideas, as we are prisoners of our officials and prisoners of time constraints in the National Assembly.' The paradox, however, is that despite this under-resourcing and risk aversion, the Assembly's civil service remains the principal repository of the bureaucratic skills and administrative procedures; it remains the custodian of 'the knowledge' of governance. This inside knowledge of the system has proved to be a remarkably powerful asset for the civil service, even though the system of governance has been in flux. Perhaps the key point is that 'the knowledge' has allowed the civil service to exercise a good deal of power and influence over its political masters in the Assembly, and this has been accentuated by the fact that many politicians, including the majority of Cabinet Secretaries, were inevitably relatively inexperienced. As one official conceded privately, 'We thought that when the Assembly got going, we would have 60 Secretaries of State instead of just one. Instead, we haven't got any at all and everything is being run by the officials. It's just like the Welsh Office' (quoted in Shipton, 1999).

Of course, this failure to adapt 'assumptive worlds' to the exigencies of the governance system of democratic devolution is not confined to the civil service. As we have seen, all of the actors in the new governance system have been confronted with a steep learning curve. Indeed, there are some indications that, for some, the effort of adjustment may be too great to make. It is striking, for example, that the business community remains unimpressed – perhaps for the reasons outlined earlier – by the organiza-tional innovations introduced in the name of democratic devolution. Its representatives maintain that the Assembly, like the public sector in general, is *process-driven*, while the business community is *results-orientated*, so much so that it avows it has neither the time nor the inclination to involve itself in ventures which are subject to stipulations like the 'thirds principle'. The demands of probity in the use of public funds, not to mention the need to respect basic democratic practices, help to explain why the public sector appears more process-driven than the private sector.

However self-serving, these business claims help to illustrate a simple but fundamental point: new structures and processes of governance do nothing, of themselves, to improve actual economic development prospects. Democratic devolution may herald a political renaissance in Wales, but this is not paralleled in the economy. On the contrary, the early days of the Assembly proved to be a baptism of fire: aside from the worst agricultural crisis in living memory, there was a raft of foreign multinationals announcing major cutbacks and Corus, formerly British Steel, was widely expected to announce the total closure of Llanwern, a plant which directly and indirectly accounts for over 6,000 jobs.

Furthermore, a survey of barriers to growth among small firms found much higher levels of dissatisfaction in Wales than in the UK as a whole, especially as regards government-funded business support services (Federation of Small Businesses, 2000). As it happens, the Assembly has undertaken a review of business support services as part of its efforts to create a new strategic framework for economic development. The review unearthed a catalogue of problems, including duplication, fragmentation and variable quality standards and, in a masterly touch of understatement, it noted that 'the lack of inter-agency agreement on roles and responsibility was greater than anticipated'. In effect, it found that the business support environment was a veritable jungle, with more than fifty-five public sector agencies vying to supply as many as 500 discrete products or services (NAW, 2000n).

The Assembly is clearly trying to forge a more strategic framework where the whole is greater than the sum of its parts, but there is a real danger that Wales may overdose on a plethora of ill-considered strategies which have little or no synergy. To date the Assembly has produced a strategic plan (*www.betterwales.com*), a National Economic Development Strategy (NEDS) and a series of strategies for the EU Objective One, Two and Three programmes in Wales. The synergies between these plans are not immediately evident and the targets, which ought to bind them all, have been argued to lack credibility. One of the key targets, for example, is to increase GDP per head in Wales to 90 per cent of the UK average by 2010, from an assumed starting-point of 82 per cent in 1997. Unfortunately, though, it seems that Welsh GDP per head is actually lower, the most recent estimate putting it at 79.4 per cent of the UK figure in 1998 (NAW, 2000q). If the 90 per cent target was regarded as 'challenging, but not impossible' in the context of the higher starting-point, one can only assume that the lower starting-point renders the target even less credible. Regardless of the starting-point, however, an economic panel has already warned that current policies and existing resources are not sufficient to break the trend rate of growth in Wales, which is precisely what is required to meet the 90 per cent target by 2010 (WDA Economic Panel, 1999).

It is becoming ever more apparent that the Assembly has neither the powers nor the resources to allow it to meet its strategic ambitions. In actual fact few people seem to realize that the Assembly devoted just 7.4 per cent of its 2000/1 budget to economic development, a surprisingly small sum when one considers that 'economic renewal' was the main reason for having an Assembly in the first place (Huggins, Morgan and Rees, 2000). Additional resources will be forthcoming from EU pro-grammes, particularly the Objective One programme for west Wales and the Valleys, a programme which runs to 2006. At some point, however, the

Assembly will need to adopt a far more strategic approach to the way it resources its ambitions and, ultimately, there is nothing more important in this respect than a new Treasury-sponsored needs assessment to allow public expenditure to be better attuned to social need.

Public expenditure in Wales is currently determined by a population-based formula, the Barnett formula, which understates spending needs because it does not take into account the above-average levels of social deprivation in Wales. It also reduces the level of EU funds in Wales because the Treasury applies the Barnett formula to these as well (Bristow and Blewitt, 2000). Far from being a mere technical matter, however, the reform of the Barnett formula could be the most incendiary question in post-devolution Britain because it goes right to the heart of the territorial distribution of public expenditure. This is an issue on which the Labour government is hopelessly divided: the Scottish Labour group wants to maintain the status quo (as well it might since Scotland does best out of the Barnett formula), while the Northern Labour group wants the formula reformed because it penalizes the north-east even more than Wales. In other words, the Barnett formula needs to be revised for many reasons, not least because democratic devolution needs an allocation system which is based on territorial justice (Morgan, 2001b).

A new trajectory of economic development requires additional re-sources, of course, but it also requires something equally important, namely the political determination to ensure that resources are being used to effect *structural* change, that they are being used to change bureaucratic habits and routines in the civil service, to raise expectations about quality among both users and providers of business services and being used to develop monitoring and evaluation procedures to ensure that recipients of public funds have met their targets. Such political determination was manifestly absent during the first year of the Objective One programme in Wales. In fact, an inquiry found a significant 'leadership gap' in the programme, a reference to the fact that politicians and civil servants were in effect managing this new and unique resource in the time-honoured ways of the past (Task and Finish Group, 2000). Financial resources, in other words, are only part of the challenge of crafting a new trajectory of development.

Aside from resources and political determination, the Assembly will also require robust and innovative partners if a new trajectory of development is to be induced in Wales, and this raises the question of civic capacity. A civil society in which citizens and organizations are well informed, where they expect high standards of behaviour of themselves and of government and where they are disposed to collaborate for mutually beneficial ends is perhaps the most important developmental resource of all. Among other things, a robust civic capacity provides government with more intelligent and more demanding interlocutors – be they businesses, community organizations or citizen groups – and these help to ensure that public policy is more creative and more accountable than it would be in their absence. Unfortunately, however, Wales is not over endowed with civic capacity, partly because of poverty and partly because the dominant political party in Wales, the Labour Party, has always recoiled from civic movements which it could not control, making independent associational action that much more difficult.

Democratic devolution, with its more open and inclusive governance structures, does not dispose of this problem of weak civic capacity. Citizens and organizations alike need to be 'tooled up' to make the most of the opportunities afforded by the Assembly: in other words, they need time, expertise and resources if they wish to be active participants. Yet, barely half way through the Assembly's first term, not a few organizations are already beginning to feel the strain of being continuously bombarded by information requests, consultation exercises, meetings, seminars, conferences and the like, all of which are part and parcel of the new policy-making process. These seemingly prosaic activities, the warp and weft of democratic devolution, may in principle be open to all, but in practice very few organizations have the wherewithal to engage with the Assembly in a sustained fashion. This underlines the need for capacity-building activities.

For its own part, the Assembly is becoming ever more conscious of its limited powers and, over time, this sense of powerlessness is likely to generate cross-party demands for a new constitutional settlement, such as parity with Scotland, for example. Even so, there is no guarantee that new powers, like new resources, will be used to effect the kind of structural change which is essential if the Assembly is ever to realize its transformative aspirations. The advocates of additional powers for the Assembly would do well to remember that there is no necessary correspondence between democratic devolution and economic development, certainly no preordained economic dividend. Indeed, the new governance structures could eventually lead to gridlock, the Basque syndrome, where there are powers aplenty, but no political consensus about what to do with them.

Returning to the question with which we began this chapter – that is, whether democratic governance structures are a necessary adjunct to regional development – we have to say that this is an open-ended question. The advent of democratic devolution in Wales may have rendered the policy-making process more transparent and more inclusive, formally at least, and these attributes may raise the quality of political debate about development. But this is not to say that a political innovation like the Assembly will, of itself, do anything positive for the economic prospects of

Wales in the twenty-first century. Democracy may be an intrinsically good thing, but its implications for economic development are more ambiguous than we may care to admit.

A note on sources

Except where specified otherwise, quotations are drawn from interviews carried out as part of the research studies on which this chapter draws.

Acknowledgements

The research on which this chapter is based was funded by the Economic and Social Research Council (Grants L311253058 and L327253029). Shari Garmise and Rob Huggins made substantial contributions to these studies and we should like to acknowledge this. We are also very grateful to the respondents who answered our questions with – for the most part – patience and good humour.

7

Devolution and Regulation: The Political Control of Public Agencies in Wales

RACHEL ASHWORTH, GEORGE BOYNE and RICHARD WALKER

INTRODUCTION

Whilst devolution has primarily been presented as a response to a growing national political identity in Scotland (McGarvey and Midwinter, 2000), in Wales it has been viewed as a solution to a perceived 'democratic deficit'. The government White Paper *A Voice for Wales* (Welsh Office, 1997) emphasized the importance of stronger public accountability as a key rationale behind the establishment of the National Assembly for Wales. Certainly UK central government has experienced difficulties holding public bodies such as quangos to account, and there is a belief that devolution provides an opportunity to resolve some of these difficulties in Wales: 'Devolution to a Welsh Assembly offers another prospect for the extension of democratic control into quangodom' (Skelcher, 1998, 45). However, whilst devolved government clearly produces a new set of politicians who are more accountable to the electorate, it is less clear whether public-sector organizations in Wales will become more accountable to politicians post-devolution. That is, devolution may have resulted in greater *political* accountability, but not necessarily in greater *organizational* accountability. This latter form of accountability is crucial to the success of devolution. Previously, monitoring, scrutinizing and regulating public-service organizations was a key responsibility of the Welsh Office. Now this responsibility rests with the National Assembly for Wales. If politicians are to be accountable to the electorate for public services in Wales, it is essential that regulatory mechanisms governing public-sector bodies operate effectively. If public organizations are not regulated appropriately by elected representatives, the chain of public accountability is broken.

In this chapter we present research findings from a recent project on the impact of devolution on the regulation of Welsh public bodies. The aims of the research project were to apply theories of public-sector regulation to the institutional arrangements for the Welsh Assembly, to analyse the regulatory mechanisms used to monitor and control public-service organizations pre-devolution, to assess the effectiveness of these mechanisms, and to evaluate the regulatory framework proposed by the National Assembly for Wales. Regulatory mechanisms were investigated in depth in a number of case-study organizations, involving the analysis of documentation and two waves of semi-structured interviews which were conducted with politicians, civil servants and regulators before and after devolution.

The format of the chapter is as follows. Firstly, we establish the framework and mechanisms for the regulation of public agencies in Wales before devolution. We present an analysis of this framework in relation to theoretical perspectives on public-service regulation. Subsequently, we detail the post-devolution regulatory arrangements for Welsh public agencies and present a preliminary assessment of the extent to which post-devolution arrangements may alleviate any regulatory problems identified pre-devolution. Finally, we conclude by determining whether our research findings confirm the claim that devolution has resulted in a new system of democracy and governance for Wales.

THEORIES OF REGULATION

Jackson (1982) argued that legal and financial regulation, combined with the doctrine of ministerial responsibility and local forms of democratic accountability, characterized the nature of accountability for public services under 'old public administration'. However, new public management (NPM) reforms have emphasized alternative forms of accountability. NPM suggests that the electorate is entitled to expect both a minimum level of service from public organizations and information on the effectiveness of expenditure allocations (Power, 1997). Consequently, it is no longer realistic that only elected politicians should be held accountable for the work of a public-service organization whilst senior public-service officials remain anonymous: 'the NPM claims to speak on behalf of taxpayers and consumers and against cosy cultures of professional self-regulation' (Power, 1997: 44). This focus on managerial accountability has led to the development of what Thomas (1998) describes as a 'counter bureaucracy', with Parliament attempting directly to scrutinize officials along with ministers. Furthermore, under NPM financial accountability could no longer realistically be achieved through an annual audit of accounts. Therefore, a new version of auditing has developed, 'performance audit', based on the value for money (VFM) provided by public-service organizations and measured in terms of economy, efficiency and effectiveness (Power, 1994; Pollitt et al., 1999). The increasing demand for information on public-service performance and the introduction of market-based provision has resulted in more complex regulatory and accountability arrangements for public-sector organizations (Hood et al., 1998). Rhodes (1999: 153) suggests that since the 1980s the British state has 'substituted *regulation* for ownership', resulting in the strengthening of audit institutions in the UK.

Our research framework draws on several theoretical perspectives on regulation in the public sector. The concept of regulation refers to an attempt by one organization to control or modify the behaviour of another (Pfeffer and Salancik, 1978). This inter-organizational dimension dist-inguishes regulation from 'management control', which refers to attempts by superiors to control subordinates within a single hierarchical organiza-tion (Hofstede, 1981). The regulation of public agencies has been defined by Hood and Scott as: 'processes by which standards are set, monitored and/or enforced in some way, by bureaucratic actors who are somewhat separate from units or bodies that have direct operational or service delivery responsibilities' (1996: 321).

This definition indicates that regulation can be undertaken by a range of agencies and units, including central government departments or organ-izations established with a regulatory task such as OFSTED. A range of regulatory 'mechanisms' is available to these regulators, which include plans, annual reports, budgetary controls, performance indicators, inspection and accounts. These mechanisms lead to processes which include the scrutiny of reports and plans and the auditing of accounts. Such regulatory activities by administrative and political bodies have grown substantially in the last twenty years. Consequently, Hoggett (1996: 23) argues that central government has spun a 'myriad of little threads' around organizations that are responsible for service delivery. Hood et al. (1998: 66) have estimated that processes of monitoring and scrutinizing public-service organizations involve 'direct costs approaching £1 billion per year and an army of regulators'. It has been argued that the growth of the 'regulatory state' reflects a wider movement towards audit and inspection in the public sector. According to Power there has been an 'audit explosion' which, in extreme cases, consists of 'checking gone wild, of ritualized practices of verification whose technical efficiency is less significant than their role in the production of organisational legitimacy' (1997: 14).

Academic perspectives on regulation include the literature on accountability in the public sector (Day and Klein, 1987; Gruber, 1988), political science research on the relationship between politicians and officials (Wood and Waterman, 1991), public choice theories of bureaucratic behaviour (Blais and Dion, 1992; Eisner, 1993) and economic models of interactions between principals and agents (Barrow, 1996). Despite their diverse disciplinary bases and methodologies, these theoretical perspectives point to a common set of five problems in the operation of regulatory regimes:

Resistance by regulatees Bodies subject to regulation may seek to undermine the process in order to maintain their autonomy. This problem may be especially severe in organizations with strong professional groups, such as doctors. Downs (1967) argues that attempts to thwart resistance are largely counter-productive, and simply result in an escalating 'arms race' between regulators and regulatees.

Ritualistic compliance Organizations that are regulated may 'go through the motions' of providing documents or data, but fail to alter their behaviour to suit the demands of the regulator. Power (1997) refers to this phenomenon as a 'de-coupling' of formal regulatory processes and substantive organizational processes.

Regulatory capture The formal balance of power in the regulatory process is reversed if the regulator 'goes native' and becomes too close to the regulatee. In these circumstances, the capacity for independent judgement is undermined or lost, and information on performance is likely to be biased. Such capture may be especially likely to occur when the staff on the two sides of the regulatory relationship are drawn from the same professional group, when 'poachers turn gamekeepers' (or vice versa), and if there is a long-term relationship between individuals in the regulatory and regulated organizations (Ayres and Braithwaite, 1992).

Performance ambiguity The meaning of organizational performance in the public sector is frequently vague and politically contested (Carter et al., 1992). Thus it is difficult for regulators to define, let alone measure, appropriate standards, behaviour and outcomes. The consequence is that public-sector regulation is inescapably messy and complex.

Data problems Even when performance can be defined clearly, regulators may find it impossible to obtain relevant information. This is a problem that has bedevilled attempts to introduce 'rational management' frameworks in the public sector for many years (Carter et al., 1992; Downs and Larkey, 1986). When hard data are lacking, regulators must rely on soft information, hunches and the opinions of regulatees (Power, 1997).

The high-profile investigation into the activities of the Welsh Development Agency by the Public Accounts Committee in 1993 highlighted problems with regulatory mechanisms applied to public-sector organizations in Wales (Law, 1999). Devolution is modifying public-sector audit and accountability arrangements in Wales, with the appointment of a separate Auditor-General for Wales and the creation of an Audit Committee within the National Assembly. Also, subject committees have been established with dual roles of policy-making and scrutiny. Before we can examine the implications of these changes for Welsh public-service organizations, it is necessary to assess the nature and effectiveness of the accountability arrangements in place before devolution.

METHODOLOGY

Our research strategy comprised the following key stages and procedures. First, we identified six case-study areas: local authority housing departments, housing associations, local authority social service departments, local authority direct-service organizations, higher education and regional economic development. We selected local government case studies as they represent a large proportion of central government expenditure in Wales. Also, local authorities at the time of the research were starting to engage with a new regime, Best Value (a duty to secure continuous improvement in performance), which provided the opportunity to compare a range of regulatory mechanisms – inspectorates, audit, performance indicators, annual reports. The remaining case studies included housing associations and the Welsh Development Agency which, as an Assembly Sponsored Public Body (ASPB), was likely to be affected by the devolution aim of 'democratizing quangos'. Finally, we included a case of 'arm's length regulation' – that of institutions of higher education by the Higher Education Funding Council for Wales.

In order to determine how devolution would impact on the regulation of public agencies in Wales it was important firstly to establish how our six case-study areas had been regulated by the Welsh Office before devolution. We conducted preliminary 'scoping' interviews with one key player in the regulatory process in each case-study area. Interviews were conducted in the following divisions of the Welsh Office: Regional Development, Social Services, Housing, Higher Education and Local Government. The purpose of these interviews was to obtain an initial understanding of regulatory instruments and problems in practice, and to identify other important actors in the regulatory process. A range of regulatory mechanisms can be identified from existing literature (Day and Klein, 1987; Power, 1997).

These include annual reports, audit, budgetary controls, inspection, performance indicators, select committees and planning documents. A major aim of the research was to determine to what extent these mechanisms were being applied to Welsh public services.

Secondly, pre-interview questionnaires were completed by six participants in the regulatory process in each case-study area (managers and politicians). The aim here was to develop a comprehensive picture of the regulatory mechanisms in use, and to identify perceptions of the extent of regulatory problems. Therefore we developed a questionnaire that contained statements corresponding with the five theoretical problems outlined above, and asked respondents to identify the extent of their agreement or disagreement with these statements on a seven-point scale (see Table 7.1 for questionnaire statements on inspection; similar statements were derived for regulatory problems associated with annual reports, audit, budgetary controls, performance indicators and plans). The questionnaire response from each key actor was then used as the basis for a structured interview with that same individual. These interviews enabled us to gain further insights into the extent and nature of regulatory problems.

We anticipated that regulators might be defensive and deny the existence of problems. As a check on this we analysed documentary evidence such as annual reports, plans and inspectors' reports, and sought to complete the process of triangulation by interviewing not only regulators but also other officials with a knowledge of regulation. For example, in the social services case study we interviewed an inspector, a senior civil servant in the Welsh Office with responsibility for social services policy, and a senior officer in the Welsh Local Government Association. Contrary to our expectations, regulators were very willing to identify regulatory problems. Furthermore, the perceptions of regulators and non-regulators were highly consistent.

Finally, interviews were conducted with three participants in each case-study area (politicians and officials from the National Assembly for Wales (NAW)) on the future direction of regulation post-devolution. For example, in the case of direct-service organizations, interviews were conducted with the Assembly Secretary responsible for local government, the chair of the local government subject committee and an official within the local government division of the NAW. These interviews provided us with the opportunity to gain an understanding of the new regulatory arrangements already put in place by the Assembly, and to elicit views on the likely developments in such arrangements.

Clearly, in order to assess the likely impact of devolution on the regulation of public agencies in Wales, we had to determine the regulatory arrangements for our six case-study areas under the former Welsh Office regime. Therefore, in this section we present empirical evidence on regulation in each of the case-study organizations. The background to each case-study organization is provided along with details of the regulatory arrangements and mechanisms in operation before devolution. Finally, a summary is presented which highlights the effectiveness of regulatory regimes for each organization.

CASE 1: LOCAL AUTHORITY SOCIAL SERVICES DEPARTMENTS (LASSDs)

Local councils, in conjunction with voluntary and private-sector providers, have responsibility for personal social services for groups such as the elderly, children, families, people with learning and mental health difficulties. Local authority social service departments must assess client need for residential, nursing and home care and are obliged to publish annual community care evaluation plans.

Regulatory arrangements

All interviewees expressed the view that the Welsh Office operated an 'arm's length' approach to the regulation of local authority social services departments (LASSDs). The Welsh Office issued guidance, and directions on the use of guidance, but had few powers of intervention. It was argued by officials we interviewed that this approach reflected the 'separate democratic legitimacy' of local authorities to make their own decisions about services. To illustrate the point, one interviewee contrasted the regulatory arrangements for LASSDs with those for the NHS. In the latter case, the interviewee suggested that a much more interventionist approach was taken with the service 'directly managed by the Welsh Office'.

Interviewees pointed to a 'regulatory gap' created by the very broad legislative framework for LASSDs. They were also concerned that this gap had widened since local government reorganization in 1996, with new structures making regulation more important (to safeguard services in small unitary councils) but also more difficult (the twenty-two new LASSDs were harder to control than the eight former counties). LASSDs were regulated by the Welsh Office in four ways: through plans, inspection, financial controls and performance indicators (PIs) (see figure 7.1). Interviewees regarded inspections as the most useful and PIs as the least useful regulatory mechanism. LASSDs had a statutory obligation to produce children's services plans and social care plans (the latter cover services for adult client groups). These were 'received' by the Welsh Office, but there

Table 7.1
Survey instrument for assessment of regulatory problems

Problem	Statement in questionnaire
Resistance	Regulatees are willing to comply with this element of regulation (e.g. they co-operate with inspectors and provide the information requested by them).
Ritual compliance	Regulatees comply with this element of regulation but simply 'go through the motions' (e.g. the regulatee pays little attention to inspectors' recommendations).
Capture	The relationship between regulators and regulatees is too close (e.g. inspectors are not sufficiently rigorous in their demands concerning access to staff and information, or are too generous in their judgements of the information provided).
Performance ambiguity	The meaning of good performance is clearly understood (e.g. inspectors' reports relate to clear service objectives, and explicit statements of the standards that have been achieved).
Data problems	Accurate data required to evaluate performance are provided to inspectors (e.g. information on the achievement of objectives, comparisons of performance over time or with other relevant organizations).

was no evidence to suggest the plans were 'monitored'. Any that were examined by the Welsh Office, seemed to be evaluated on a retrospective, ad hoc basis. For example, if a complaint was made against an SSD, this would be checked against claims about service standards in the plan. To some extent, plans also fulfilled the role of an annual report – they contained a backward as well as forward look at services. While interviewees noted that some central government money for LASSDs was 'ring-fenced' in Wales, they none the less suggested that budgetary control was not an appropriate mechanism whereby the Welsh Office could regulate LASSDs. By contrast, regulatory officials we interviewed suggested that there was a lack of control over social services spending. One stated that the Welsh Office had 'insufficient influence over total expenditure or its allocation'.

LASSDs were subjected to a twofold inspection regime consisting of five-yearly 'themed' inspections and annual 'regulatory inspections'. This regime was described by one interviewee as 'a mix of policing and consultancy'. Only one joint Audit Commission/SSI inspection had taken place in Wales at the time of the research (in Torfaen). Interviewees suggested that the judgement on Torfaen was fairly negative – the director of social services and at least one other senior member of staff had already resigned (NB: far more severe criticism awaited the Vale of Glamorgan LASSD in 2000). There was an expectation in the Welsh Office (and correctly so) that the joint inspection regime would be tougher than SSI inspections alone. Finally, in terms of performance information, in addition to Citizen's Charter indicators, LASSDs made annual statistical returns to the Welsh Office and monthly returns on politically sensitive aspects of service provision (for example, children in care).

Interviewees noted two further forms of regulation used by the Welsh Office to regulate social services. Firstly, letters from the general public alerted Welsh Office officials to local problems (some child abuse cases came to light in this way). The second concerned the vetting of staff, which has become more important as a result of the findings of inquiries, such as Waterhouse (2000), into child abuse in residential homes. One of the six strategic priorities for social services in Wales is 'to ensure that staff involved in social care are appropriately skilled, trained and qualified and that their conduct and practice are properly regulated' (Welsh Office, 1999a: 2). Following the necessary primary legislation in the Care Standards Act 2000, a new statutory body, the Care Council for Wales, an Assembly Sponsored Public Body, will now assist in the registration, regulation and training of the social care workforce.

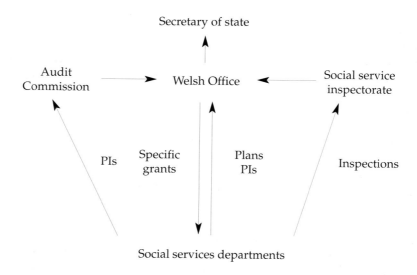

Figure 7.1
Regulatory arrangements for social services departments

Summary

The view of regulatory officials interviewed was that the pre-devolution regulatory regime for local authority social service departments was poorly directed with performance goals often unspecified. There was evidence of strength in qualitative regulation based on inspection systems, but weakness in generating reliable and comparable quantitative performance data. Overall, the regulatory system appears partially effective, particularly in relation to inspections. These were taken seriously by regulatees as was the monitoring of the implementation of recommendations. However, comprehensive inspections were irregular and any aspect of service provision not inspected was unlikely to be influenced much by other regulatory mechanisms.

CASE 2: LOCAL AUTHORITY DIRECT-SERVICE ORGANIZATIONS (DSOs)

Direct-service organizations (DSOs) were local authority agencies that won competitively tendered contracts under the 1980 and 1988 Local Government Acts. Compulsory Competitive Tendering (CCT) legislation was suspended in Wales in 1994 in order to facilitate the process of local government reorganization. In contrast to England, CCT has not been applied in Wales to 'white-collar' services such as housing management and personnel and legal services. The CCT moratorium has subsequently been extended several times, and the legislation lapsed in January 2000. During the period of our research there were some 300 DSOs in Wales.

Regulatory arrangements

These applied to two key aspects of DSO activity, the first being the tendering process. Local authorities were prohibited by the CCT legislation from engaging in 'anti-competitive' behaviour. The regulatory framework here was very mechanical and tightly prescribed by legislation: any complaint of such behaviour must be investigated by civil servants. In addition, civil servants could instigate inquiries if their suspicions were aroused by information in DSO annual reports (see below) or auditors' reports. If the complaint, or suspicion, appeared to be well founded, then the secretary of state was empowered to serve a 'notice' requiring the authority to respond formally to the allegations made against it. Examples of anti-competitive behaviour which have resulted in notices being served in Wales include occasions where work was awarded to the DSO without good reason when another bid was lower, and an instance where a council disclosed contractor information to the DSO. If the authority failed to convince the secretary of state that it was not in breach of the legislation, then a 'direction' could be issued instructing that authority to carry out a new tendering exercise from which the DSO was excluded. As a result, the DSO would cease to have the power to carry out the relevant work. The only data available from the Welsh Office demonstrate that between 1992 and 1994, eight notices and five directions were issued to authorities in Wales for anti-competitive behaviour.

The second aspect of DSO behaviour subject to regulation was financial performance. DSOs were required to break even, after taking account of capital charges, which includes a capital financing charge of 6 per cent of the value of fixed assets used in the provision of the service. This requirement continued during the period of CCT suspension. If the statutory financial target was missed, the secretary of state had regulatory sanctions he or she could apply. Firstly, the power to seek further information on a non-statutory basis (for example, a progress report on a particular DSO); if 'good reasons' for financial losses were offered, then no further action would be taken. Secondly, the power to serve a statutory notice effectively compelling the authority to explain the financial failure. In effect, around thirty notices were issued between 1990 and 1993/4. Thirdly, to issue a statutory direction if the authority appeared to be taking inadequate or

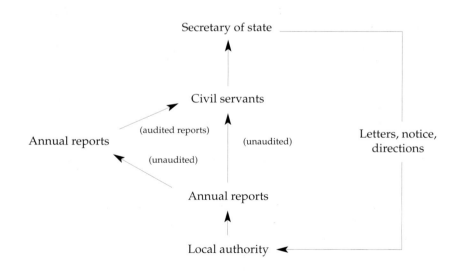

Figure 7.2
Regulatory arrangements for DSOs

ineffective steps to improve the financial performance of the DSO. In principle, the direction could require an authority to retender if the financial target was not achieved by a specified date, to retender for the work by a specified date, or prevent the authority carrying out work using its DSO. In practice, no directions have been issued to Welsh authorities in relation to financial performance.

Under the CCT legislation, local authorities had to submit an annual report to the Welsh Office for each of their DSOs. This contained the un-audited accounts of the DSOs, and was scheduled for submission six months after the end of the financial year. Simultaneously, the accounts were passed to the authority's auditors (either District Audit or a private firm appointed by the Audit Commission). The auditors in turn had a voluntary agreement to supply audited DSO accounts to the Welsh Office by the end of the following January, but had no obligation to provide any explanation of financial failure by DSOs.

Summary

Overall, Welsh Office officials we interviewed maintained that there was a clear direction for the regulatory framework for DSOs with explicit financial targets. However, they also suggested that the regulatory process was weakened by the manipulable nature of performance data and the late submission of many annual reports. Unsurprisingly, as a result, the regulatory system was viewed as largely ineffective, with regulators reluctant to take action, often resulting in vague sanctions for poor performance.

CASE 3: LOCAL AUTHORITY HOUSING DEPARTMENTS

Background

Local authority housing departments have become increasingly subject to central regulation over the past fifteen years and have been particularly affected by the 1989 Local Government and Housing Act. As a result local authorities had less discretion in relation to rent levels and rent sub-sidization, whilst housing management functions were subjected to compulsory competitive tendering, although full implementation did not occur due to the suspension of CCT legislation in Wales.

Regulatory arrangements

The Welsh Office regulation of local housing authorities contrasted strongly with its regulation of Housing for Wales and housing associations.

The secretary of state had powers to regulate local authority operations via statute and to issue guidance. Welsh Office regulation of local authority housing departments was described by the majority of officials interviewed in the Housing Division as regulation with a 'lighter touch' and an 'overview'. The view of housing officials we interviewed was that local authorities were held accountable through a combination of mechanisms: by their electorate, the Audit Commission, the Ombudsman and Welsh Office procedures. Consequently, issues came to the attention of Welsh Office officials from sources other than their formal information-gathering systems.

The Housing Strategy and Operational Plan was a critical regulatory tool for the Welsh Office. Authorities had to respond to the secretary of state's guidance, which was issued each year. In addition to addressing specific issues, authorities had to include an overall picture of their activities, policy implementation and operational performance. Visits were also made by the head of the Housing Division and other senior officers to each authority. This provided authorities with the chance for further discussion and the opportunity for authorities to raise issues of concern. However, Welsh Office officials interviewed for this research stated that their staff undertook very little analysis of the plans.

Performance information was submitted in conjunction with the Report to Tenants regime whilst other financial and statistical information was requested for subsidy payment. However, officials stated that the information was not used systematically to measure the performance of authorities. By contrast, budgetary controls were extensive and the main form of regulator control for the Welsh Office. Revenue was controlled through guidance issued on accounting practices for the housing revenue account. This regime allowed the Welsh Office to capture surpluses generated on housing revenue by setting local authority rents (a guide rent was issued) and determining management and maintenance spending. This was possible because the HRA (Housing Revenue Account) was ring-fenced and had to balance at the end of each financial year. Large elements of capital finance were also ring-fenced and issued as Supplementary but not Basic Credit Approvals. This was partly due to the large amounts of money spent on renovation grants in Wales and the need to ensure that this process continued.

In terms of audit, the Welsh Office regularly sought the views of the Audit Commission on future value-for-money studies, and also drew upon their expertise to verify information. However, the level of contact with District Audit was far greater. An example provided by several interviewees was the investigation into home renovation grant fraud in a number of authorities in the early 1990s. In cases such as this, the Welsh

Office launched an investigation which officials felt necessitated a close working relationship with District Audit, partly on the grounds that it would ensure that procedures were in place to prevent problems arising again.

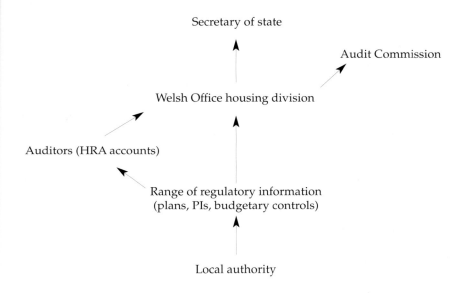

Figure 7.3
Regulatory arrangements for local authority housing departments

Summary

Overall, the view of officials in the Welsh Office Housing Division was that the regulatory system for local authority housing departments was fairly ineffective in all areas except budgetary controls. It was widely acknowledged by interviewees that plans and performance data were not systematically analysed, but they argued that the separate democratic mandate of local authorities demanded this form of 'light touch' regulation.

CASE 4: HOUSING ASSOCIATIONS

Background

Housing associations were regularly in receipt of government subsidy; those associations with over 100 homes were governed by a regime known as 'Regulatory Requirements'. These requirements set out the performance standards that associations were expected to achieve in the areas of finance, management and corporate governance. There were fifty-nine registered housing associations in Wales, of which thirty (51 per cent) met the above criteria and owned 99 per cent of association rented stock. The smaller twenty-nine associations held only 1 per cent of the stock and were deemed to be less at risk and therefore not subjected to full regulation.

Regulatory arrangements

Regulatory Requirements covered performance standards for the areas of governance, finance, housing services, development and equal opportunities. Associations were inspected and audited against these standards and additionally had to produce a range of financial and performance data and present business and financial plans. Financial and performance data were audited on a quarterly and annual basis, with each association inspected within a three-year cycle. The focus of the regulatory activity was upon (a) risk assessment to ensure associations had the capacity to meet standards, (b) validation audits, to ensure data were accurate and (c) 'topic audits' which examined specific areas of association work (recent examples include treasury management, internal controls etc.).

Housing associations had to produce annual business plans to aid Welsh Office assessment of long-term viability; it was anticipated that these would be used by Housing Division officials as day-to-day management tools. Also, associations were expected to produce annual reports giving a financial statement and some performance indicators. The view of officials we interviewed was that this helped to inform the regulatory process. Budgetary controls were maintained in relation to both revenue and capital expenditure. Revenue expenditure was controlled through a policy which influenced association rents, known as 'rent benchmarking'. Capital expenditure was controlled through the allocation of Social Housing Grant (a production subsidy). Associations increasingly raised finance without reference to government subsidy, but needed Welsh Office consent to enter into a mortgage.

The Welsh Office had a range of powers and regulatory mechanisms which could be used to alter the management of an association. These intervention powers included nominating board members to associations in difficulty (for example, over financial or governance problems) and extended to the removal of board members or officers, and statutory inquiries into an association's affairs. The Welsh Office also had a statutory relationship with the Audit Commission which to date has been limited to one small-scale value-for-money study.

Prior to November 1998, housing associations were funded and regulated by Housing for Wales, which reported to the secretary of state for Wales. Housing for Wales had its own account officer (the chief executive), it produced annual reports and strategic and operational plans containing targets. However, the secretary of state could issue directions to associations. Interviewees suggested that the Welsh Office's regulatory strength stemmed from its joint funding and regulatory functions. These were described by one interviewee as 'nuclear powers' whilst another stated that the 'best regulatory tool is the threat of withdrawal of funding'. On these grounds some referred to the regulatory regime as highly interventionist. However, the regulation of associations was complicated by their independent status. They were legally registered and therefore had relationships with their registration body (Charity Commissioners, Companies House or Industrial and Provident Society). Associations had to submit their accounts to these bodies and abide by their rules in order to maintain their registration.

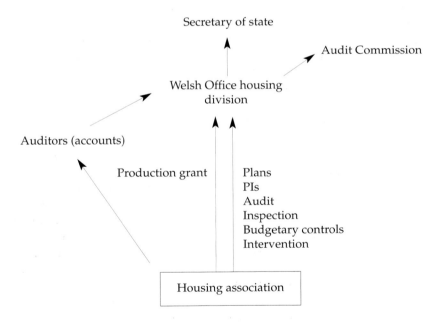

Figure 7.4
Regulatory arrangements for housing associations

Summary

The information from officials in the Welsh Office Housing Division suggested that the regulatory arrangements for housing associations were strong, interventionist and all-embracing. Interviewees identified a strong direction for the regulator, partly due to the wide range of information sources. The data provided from associations was timely and as a result facilitated the early detection of any problems. Thus, overall the regulatory system could be viewed as broadly effective although this appears due in large part to the dual role of being regulator and main funder of the regulatee organization.

CASE 5: INSTITUTIONS OF HIGHER EDUCATION

Background

This case study considers the regulation of higher education institutions (HEI) by the Higher Education Funding Council for Wales (HEFCW). HEFCW was established in 1993. The council is responsible for thirteen HEI. HEFCW reported to the Welsh Office's Further and Higher Education Division, by which it was funded. The overall framework for the sector was provided annually by the secretary of state in a detailed management statement.

Regulatory arrangements

Emphasis was placed upon the autonomous and independent nature of universities by interviewees within both the Welsh Office and HEFCW. HEFCW officials we interviewed went as far as to argue that they were not regulators but funders, and furthermore only partially funders. Officials accepted that funding provided them with a powerful lever which they could use to influence behaviour and agreed that HEI were expected to perform in return for funding. Thus, HEI are currently expected to demonstrate value for money whilst remaining accountable and adopting good governance practices. Interviewees suggested that it would be unwise for HEFCW to impose policy upon HEI. Officials feared a determined response within the sector and many objections. Consequently, one official we interviewed described HEFCW's role as consensual in terms of 'working with the grain'. This, the official maintained, would enable the agency to detect problems prior to their arising by the use of planning documents and audit. The view of the majority of officials was that HEFCW was keen to avoid being seen as running HEI as 'sub-companies' in a larger company structure.

HEFCW regulated HEI through all six previously identified regulatory mechanisms – audit, budgetary, control, inspection, performance indicators and plans. HEI have produced strategic plans (which cover a five-year period) for the last five years. The view of officials was that the capacity for planning correlated with past experience. Thus, plans from former public-sector bodies such as the 'new universities' were seen as slightly weak, reflecting a continuing learning process. Interviewees stated that there had been a shift from all-embracing plans to those focusing on particular initiatives and issues, implying a 'lighter touch' in relation to the detail of planning. One interviewee suggested this was because such plans were too time-consuming to produce. An alternative view offered by another official was that there was a lack of experience within HEFCW in relation to the evaluation of policy initiatives within plans.

Performance indicators (PIs) were set in the corporate and operational plan with most rolled over from year to year. Further PIs were being developed, focusing on, for example, wealth creation by the HE sector. These new PIs had developed in response to new policy objectives identified by government; hence wealth creation was the Labour government aim, as one respondent observed 'to turn research into a product'. Officials we interviewed within HEFCW stated that PIs for HEI were in early stages of development and consequently needed adjustment. However, the Research Assessment Exercise for universities was viewed by the majority of officials as an area where performance was clearly understood.

There was provision for the Welsh Office to revise HEFCW's financial profile, but this was normally for the agency's own expenditure and not for allocation to universities. According to HEFCW officials we interviewed there were no formal budgetary controls over HEI. Alternatively, HEFCW required financial forecasts which they used to monitor against HEI performance. Such monitoring was based on a five-year period, with HEIs reporting twice yearly (end of year and mid-point). Officials stated that HEI pay considerable attention to these forecasts, incorporating them within their operations and aiming to ensure good use of public monies and assets. Expenditure plans were detailed in the grant letter from the chief executive of the council to HEI, which very much reflected HEFCW's remit and management statement (in which the secretary of state communicated his objectives, aims and targets for the higher education sector in Wales to its chief executive).

HEI accounts were externally audited, a process which included a comparison between audited accounts and financial forecasts. According to interviewees, the internal audit of finance and process had been promoted strongly over recent years and was based on good practice issued by relevant professional bodies. HEI were also subject to a form of inspection. Officials interviewed expressed the view that the previous inspection regime (Teaching Quality Assessment) was too lax. Conversely, there was support from those interviewed for the new Quality Assessment Audit and its emphasis upon standards.

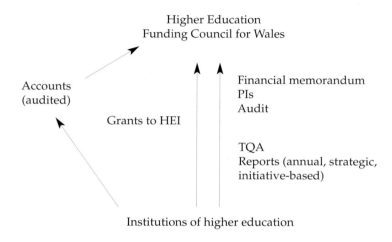

Higher Education
Funding Council for Wales

Accounts
(audited)

Grants to HEI

Financial memorandum
PIs
Audit

TQA
Reports (annual, strategic,
initiative-based)

Institutions of higher education

Figure 7.5
Regulatory arrangements for institutions of higher education

Summary

Overall, the regulatory regime for institutions of higher education appeared relatively weak, with both the Welsh Office and HEFCW placing emphasis upon their autonomous and independent status. This resulted in broad objectives for regulatees which lacked detailed performance targets. However, the detection of regulatory problems was reasonably strong, with clear financial and planning information available to the regulator, although performance data were again identified as a weakness.

CASE 6: THE WELSH DEVELOPMENT AGENCY (WDA)

Background

The Welsh Development Agency was established in 1976, assuming and expanding the role of the former Welsh Industrial Estates Corporation in relation to the development of land and the provision of premises for industry. The agency has since absorbed the former Welsh Office responsibilities of land reclamation, inward investment and Urban Investment Grants. In 1998 the agency's role was further extended to enable it to make land available for development and its functions were broadened to encompass social development. In 1999 the agency took responsibility for the services and expenditure of the Land Authority for Wales and the Development Board for Rural Wales.

Regulatory arrangements

The WDA was a Non-Departmental Public Body (NDPB) and from 1 July 1999 became an Assembly Sponsored Public Body (ASPB). The Welsh Office Regional Development Division (RDD) was the sponsor division for the WDA with the responsibilities of the agency clearly laid down in a document entitled the Management Statement. Through the RDD, the Welsh Office monitored and regulated the WDA through a combination of statutory regulation, guidance and best practice. The WDA was also regulated by the National Audit Office (NAO) and two Parliamentary Select Committees, the Public Accounts Committee (PAC) and the Welsh Affairs Committee (WAC).

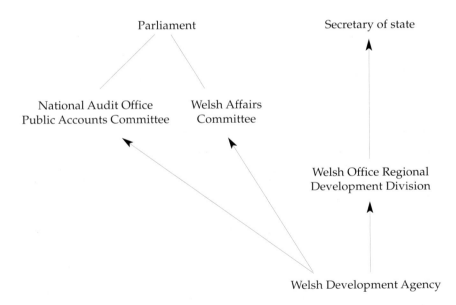

Figure 7.6
Regulatory arrangements for the Welsh Development Agency

Each year the agency developed a four-year plan within the strategic, general and specific policy framework set by the secretary of state. The plan had to be discussed with the department but did not have to be approved by the Welsh Office. The plan incorporated the agency's aims and objectives, along with its strategy for achieving them, a statement of its priorities and targets (main outputs), financial resources and priorities, performance indicators, output measures and evaluations planned. It also included implications for staffing and running costs of policies outlined. Finally, the plan contained a financial performance review based on the previous year and the approved budget for the following year.

The agency also had to submit a business plan to the secretary of state no later than the end of January each year. The plan was to be based upon an assessment of need and opportunities, judging relative priorities, taking account of the strategic guidance and targets issued by the secretary of state. The business plan formed the first year of the corporate plan and was used primarily as a management tool. Permission for any subsequent schemes/projects not detailed in the business plan had to be obtained from the secretary of state, to whom the WDA had to submit an annual report at the end of each financial year. This report was then laid before Parliament. The Welsh Office played no role in the development or content of the report which was prepared by the agency and submitted directly to politicians.

In terms of performance information, the agency had to submit monthly reports to the division concerning progress against strategic targets set notionally by the secretary of state but in practice by the Regional Development Division, and for the past few years jointly with WDA. Progress on targets outlined in the business plan was then submitted in report form on a quarterly basis, providing the year-to-date position and forecast out-turns against strategic targets. The monthly reports were linked to budgetary controls. The agency operated financial and management accounting systems, enabling management to review performance profitability, costs, cash flow and manpower against agreed budgets and targets. Monthly statements of receipts and payments were submitted and scrutinized by the Welsh Office. The director of the agency is termed the accounting officer and has several specific responsibilities, detailed in the NDPB Accounting Officer Memorandum and continually updated in 'Dear accounting officer' correspondence (these are updates on accounting officer duties which applied across the UK civil service). Consequently, the WDA had to comply with Public Accounts Committee recommendations and observe relevant guidance from the Welsh Office.

The WDA was subject to several additional regulatory processes relating to financial management and audit. Every five years, the Welsh Office conducted a financial management and policy review, examining the need for efficiency and effectiveness of WDA programmes, financial and other management systems, and of regulation of the agency. The last full FMPR was conducted in 1991/2. A decision was taken to conduct only a partial review in 1996 due to the subsequent merger and devolution.

WDA accounts were audited annually by the NAO, and the WDA had to respond to their recommendations. The NAO is totally independent of government, headed by the Comptroller and Auditor-General (C+AG) appointed by Parliament. The NAO also reported to Parliament on the economy, efficiency and effectiveness with which the Welsh Office and NDPBs in Wales expended their resources and the value for money (VFM) they provided for the taxpayer. The process entails the examination of the purpose of the agency, its statutory responsibilities and policy objectives, and involves the scrutiny of documents, plans and performance indicators, along with discussions with management on how they secure VFM.

Whilst the C+AG has complete discretion concerning subjects for investigation (White and Hollingsworth, 1999), the appointment remains at the discretion of the government. Furthermore, officials interviewed for this research on Welsh public services provided evidence of a close relationship between the NAO and Welsh Office/WDA officials. This relationship was defended by all officials interviewed on the grounds that scrutiny and oversight were impossible without the existence of a close, informal and co-operative relationship. Another serious limitation of the work of the NAO pre-devolution was that, due to its wide remit – covering all government departments and NDPBs in England, Scotland and Wales – there was simply not enough focus on Welsh public bodies. Due to this limited capacity to regulate, there were usually at most one or two VFM studies in Wales per annum. For example, of 177 reports published by the NAO between 1995/6 and 1998/9, just five focused exclusively on Wales.

The PAC has scrutinized the expenditure of public agencies on behalf of Parliament since 1861 with 90 per cent of its investigations stemming from VFM studies by the NAO. The scrutiny process involves an evidence session with up to six individuals of the relevant government department/ NDPB. The PAC has been viewed as a crucial mechanism for managerial accountability because it is the accounting officer who attends PAC sessions to answer questions rather than the minister (White and Hollingsworth, 1999). These evidence sessions were viewed by all Westminster MPs interviewed as 'the greatest weapon available to Parliament', but also recognized as an 'ordeal' which can 'make or break' the careers of senior civil servants. However, besides the short-term impact, an estimated 95 per cent of the committee's recommendations are fully implemented (Pollitt and Summa, 1997). This suggests that public-service organizations take the recommendations of the committee seriously and that investigations often result in reforms of practice and procedure.

However, the effectiveness of this form of scrutiny has long been questioned. Committee members interviewed cited examples of civil servants frustrating the scrutiny process by withholding key documents. A further problem concerned the extent to which findings were disseminated. Clearly, departments are made aware of developments through procedural updates but, as Flegmann (1986: 46) notes, publicity for PAC investigations is often lacking: 'Regrettably, inquiries which concentrate on the financial scrutiny role are seldom considered "newsworthy" and a considerable body of information revealed in the course of the inquiries goes unreported and largely unnoticed.' Nevertheless, government departments continue to view the PAC as the ultimate deterrent. Welsh officials interviewed for this research cited the lack of an appearance before the PAC as an indication of a successful regulatory regime. They assumed that as PAC investigations highlight poor performance, organizations must be performing effectively if they are not subject to a PAC inquiry. However, given that the committee can only complete thirty investigations per year, it might be naïve to assume that accountability arrangements work perfectly simply because an organization has not been called before the PAC.

The WDA was also subject to scrutiny from another parliamentary select committee: the Welsh Affairs Committee was responsible for scrutinizing the Welsh Office and associated NDPBs in terms of both finance and policy programmes. The committee had no set agenda with only a few annual investigations, including the scrutiny of the Welsh Office departmental report and financial estimates. Thus, in contrast to the PAC, members of the committee influenced the committee's programme (for example, north Wales MPs led a recent investigation into Denbighshire's inherited capital investment programme). Again, interviewees cited incidences of civil service resistance to the scrutiny process but the clerk agreed that most information was supplied to the committee 'eventually'. The Welsh Office/NDPB must respond to the committee's recommendations, but, unlike the PAC, the committee has no formal sanctions, and, as the subjects of investigation vary so widely, it is difficult to follow up prior investigations. For example, politicians interviewed pointed to repeated recommendations from the committee on the finances of health authorities and trusts in Wales which had not been acted upon by the Welsh Office. This was viewed by all Welsh MPs interviewed as the 'weak link' in the select committee system.

Summary

The regulatory arrangements for the WDA had a strong and clear direction with responsibilities explicitly enshrined within the Management Statement and financial memorandum. However, the close relationships evident between the WDA, the RDD and the NAO could lead to difficulties with the detection of regulatory problems. Welsh Office officials interviewed for the research described themselves as being 'all one team' along with the WDA and NAO, a situation which in the view of some had resulted in the establishment of weak performance targets and the production of meaningless data. Consequently, before devolution it often fell to Parliament to regulate NDPBs like the WDA. However, as the PAC rarely investigated Wales, and the WAC had no formal power to ensure the implementation of recommendations, the parliamentary system appears to have been an inadequate safety net. As Skelcher (1988: 46) states, 'Parliament lacks the capacity to gain an oversight of the appointed sector in the UK as a whole, to monitor trends and performance, or to take appropriate action.'

EVALUATION OF CASE-STUDY EVIDENCE

Use of regulatory instruments

The results of our mapping exercise of regulatory instruments are shown in Table 7.2. All six Welsh organizations were subject to budgetary controls and performance indicators before devolution. For example, some central government grants to LASSDs were ring-fenced, and all three local authority services in the sample were required to return performance data to the Audit Commission and the Welsh Office. Plans and audit were used in five of the six case-study areas (only DSOs were not required to submit plans to higher levels of government; and social service departments had no separate audit arrangements, although they were included in the general audit of local authority accounts). The regulatory instrument of annual reports was present in all cases except universities and social service departments. Finally, the least common instrument was inspection: only universities (through the current system of teaching quality assessment), housing associations and social service departments were regulated in this way. However, with future plans for both DSOs and local authority housing departments to be covered by the new system of best-value inspection, this may leave only the WDA free of this restraint.

Table 7.2
Number of regulatory mechanisms

Case studies	Annual report	Plans	Budgetary controls	Performance indicators	Audit	Inspection
Welsh Development Agency	Yes	Yes	Yes	Yes	Yes	No
Higher Education Funding Council for Wales	No	Yes	Yes	Yes	Yes	Yes
Housing Associations	Yes	Yes	Yes	Yes	Yes	Yes
Local authority housing departments	Yes	Yes	Yes	Yes	Yes	No
Local authority direct service organizations	Yes	No	Yes	Yes	Yes	No
Local authority social service departments	No	Yes	Yes	Yes	No	Yes

Table 7.3
Extent of regulatory problems

Case studies	Regulatory resistance	Ritualistic compliance	Regulatory capture	Performance ambiguity	Data problems
Welsh Development Agency	Low	Medium	Low	Medium	Medium
Universities	Low	Low	Low	Medium	Low
Housing associations	Low	Low	High	Low	Low
Local authority housing departments	Medium	Medium	High	High	Low
Local authority direct service organizations	Medium	Low	High	Low	High
Local authority social service departments	Low	Medium	Low	Medium	High

Extent of regulatory problems

The results of this element of the research are shown in Table 7.3.

Regulatee resistance   In general the interviewees identified few problems of regulatory resistance. However, some examples were evident in relation to specific cases. For example, local authority housing departments had sometimes failed to provide housing plans containing the required information. Also, some councils had not explained DSO financial losses to the Welsh Office despite requests to do so, whilst the delivery of a substantial minority of DSO annual reports was frequently late. The responsibilities of the WDA appeared clearly enshrined within the Management Statement and financial memorandum, leaving the agency little room to resist regulation. However, several officials we interviewed highlighted elements of resistance in relation to the establishment of tough performance targets. Also, politicians we interviewed from the two parliamentary select committees suggested that whilst the Welsh Office had been helpful in response to requests for information – most was provided 'eventually' – they were not as forthcoming in comparison with other government departments and their relevant select committees.

Ritualistic compliance   Evidence suggests that ritualistic compliance was slightly more widespread, although the problems do not appear to have been severe. For example, officials from the Social Services Division observed that local authority social service departments usually submitted plans on time, but that the link between the plans and social service strategies was weak. This was highlighted in the *Building for the Future* White Paper (Welsh Office, 1999a: 5): 'There is little consistency between authorities in Wales either in the range of information they produce or in the baselines and cost assumptions on which plans are built.' A National Audit Office interviewee identified ritualistic compliance in relation to the production of annual reports by NDPBs, claiming the documents were 'launched with pride' but subsequently largely ignored. Similarly, several select committee politicians we interviewed suggested that compliance with committee recommendations could be ritualistic. As a result both committees were developing and improving processes by which there is an opportunity to return to an investigation and check on the implementation of recommendations.

Regulatory capture   Regulatory capture emerged as an important problem in three of our Welsh case-study areas. Many regulatory 'watchdogs' had clearly become 'guidedogs', which may be a legitimate role, but some had come to resemble 'lapdogs', which is not. In Welsh housing in particular (both housing association and local council housing departments), interviewees provided substantial evidence of an overly close relationship between regulators and regulatees. In terms of the local authority sector, a close relationship was deemed a product of the separate accountability structure for local authorities and designed to ensure that authorities could be honest and open with the Housing Division if problems arose. There were also ongoing secondments into the Welsh Office from local authority departments to assist in the development of regulation, policies and procedures. Staff who regulated housing associations were typically drawn from regulatee organizations. As a result, housing regulators were frequently poachers turned gamekeepers (and several gamekeepers have subsequently returned to work in housing organizations). Front-line officers were frequently rotated around associations to ensure that they did not 'go native' and build up close working relationships. However, secondments from regulatee to regulator organizations also occur within social services and higher education, although it has to be stated that interviewees in these sectors perceived this arrangement as necessary rather than problematic. Close relationships were both observed by researchers and reported by interviewees between audit bodies and public-service agencies in Wales. Interviewees suggested that local authority auditors were reluctant to take strong action against local authority DSOs by 'qualifying' the accounts (that is, indicating doubts over the data) or by imposing a 'public interest notice' thereby declaring that the accounts misrepresent, wilfully or otherwise, the real financial position. It was clear that auditors felt they must co-operate closely with the authorities if their advice was to be taken seriously and improvements achieved. As one interviewee stated, 'Auditors want to be supportive – they do not want to be seen as unreasonable.' Close relationships were also identified by interviewees in relation to the regulation of the WDA, both between the NAO and the sponsor division within the Welsh Office and between the sponsor division and the agency. Again, there were suggestions that regulation and monitoring was increasingly difficult without the existence of a close, informal relationship. Politicians we interviewed from the WAC spoke of a 'cosiness' in relation to Welsh public services, which adversely affected monitoring systems. Consequently, they suggested that politicians were only alerted to problems by 'whistle-blowers' rather than official accountability mechanisms.

Performance ambiguity   Interviewees also expressed an increasing concern over the ambiguity of performance reporting in four of the six Welsh case-study areas. This has also been recognized by the C+AG, the NAO and the

Audit Commission (White and Hollingsworth, 1999). The meaning of good performance was clearest in the case of housing associations (which are judged against a comprehensive and well-established set of objectives) and DSOs (which have a single performance criterion of a centrally specified rate of return on capital). Performance criteria for the WDA, HEFCW, local social service and housing departments were less clear. The issue of performance ambiguity was quite severe in relation to the WDA, with examples of varying definitions of performance according to policy object-ives, efficiency, effectiveness and value for money. Somewhat unusually, interviewees claimed that the policy targets from the sponsor division were more easily understood than those related to financial accountability. However, even within the sponsor division there was a clear difference of opinion on the achievability of targets, with one Welsh Office official we interviewed claiming targets that should be 'stretching but achievable', contradicting his colleague who described them as 'challenging but not necessarily achievable'. There was also considerable scepticism amongst politicians and officials about the achievement and measurement of broad policy objectives such as 'securing an inclusive society'. Also evident was an inherent difficulty to control for intervening economic variables when assessing performance targets such as 'number of jobs created'.

In higher education, officials unanimously agreed that the meaning of good performance was not clearly understood and that this was further complicated as a result of an annual proliferation of new performance indicators and the changing nature of regimes such as the teaching quality assessment. However, there were suggestions that issues of performance ambiguity were likely to be resolved through the development of codes of practice establishing explicit objectives, standards and good practice.

In social services, regulators described vague and implicit perceptions of performance. Interviewees suggested that the 'arm's length' role of the Welsh Office had precluded strong prescriptions of appropriate perform-ance standards and that, as a result, social service inspectors and social service departments have a shared but often implicit understanding of good performance. This combination of 'regulatory distance' and 'profes-sional proximity' had not served to clarify the meaning of good perform-ance in social service departments.

The problem of ambiguity was greatest in the case of local authority housing departments. Performance measures were not as well developed as those of housing associations. In addition to not being particularly sophisticated, performance measures were also requested from local authorities by different bodies using different definitions. Local authorities also have responsibility for the oversight of private housing and housing management services. Consequently, the breadth of the local authority housing service served to make performance measurement more complex, particularly in relation to housing associations.

Data problems   Even when performance could be clearly defined, the data required to measure that performance were rarely available or appropriate. This was particularly so in three of our six case studies (regional economic development, DSOs and social services). Several Westminster politicians from the WAC criticized the value and measurement of data on, for example, 'the number of jobs created'. Whilst broadly supportive of performance information as an additional regulatory tool, politicians interviewed for the research suggested that 'great care' should be taken in its interpretation. Performance ambiguity in social services was compounded by incomplete and inaccurate data on service standards. All interviewees were strongly critical of Audit Commission indicators for social services. However, interviewees did place more trust in the monthly and annual returns from social service departments. There were also criticisms of the usefulness of data contained in local authority DSO annual reports. Councils have considerable discretion concerning the apportionment of costs (for example, central charges) to DSOs as a group and to individual DSOs. Thus, most DSOs could 'break even' if the local authority so desires, or an 'unpopular' but efficient DSO could find itself categorized as a financial failure. This was creative accounting rather than 'cooking the books', but several Welsh Office officials interviewed were aware that they were monitoring a *version* of financial performance as presented by the authority, rather than 'real' performance.

Problems were also identified in relation to the timeliness of the data: the social services inspectorate was often 'inspecting against out-of-date information'. This problem was also identified in terms of DSO data. DSO annual reports are scheduled to arrive at the Welsh Office around six months after the end of the financial year but, as noted above, some arrive late. The *audited* versions of all reports were then scheduled to arrive in January. However, this arrangement with auditors was voluntary, and there is frequently some slippage. By the time the small Welsh Office team (usually two people to monitor almost 300 DSOs) had the opportunity to examine the reports, yet another financial year may have started. In this circumstance, it is easy for authorities with failing DSOs to argue that they have already dealt with the problems that were occurring in the semi-distant past. A further problem arises when there are discrepancies between the unaudited and audited accounts. Several interviewees gave anecdotes suggesting that financial failure was greater in audited versions. For example, one south Wales DSO submitted accounts in October 1998 indicating a small profit of £2,500, but audited accounts received in July

1999 suggest a loss of over £500,000. One interviewee argued that the regulatory process for DSOs 'works as a warning system'. If so, the alarm bell has often been muffled and late.

Summary of pre-devolution regulatory arrangements and their effectiveness

Before devolution there is evidence to suggest that the scrutiny of public-service organizations in Wales by the Welsh Office was problematic. In principle, regulatory arrangements for most organizations had a strong and clear direction with responsibilities explicitly enshrined. However, the case-study evidence reveals a range of regulatory problems of varying severity. All five of the theoretical difficulties of regulatory regimes were present to a greater or lesser extent in our case-study organizations. The close relationships between the Welsh Office, audit bodies and public-service organizations led to difficulties with the detection of potential problems. These difficulties may have been exacerbated by ambiguity concerning organizational objectives and the lack of adequate performance data. The least serious problem was regulatee resistance. Indeed, resistance may have been low because, in some cases at least, regulatory constraints were weak, and so evasive action was unnecessary.

We also identified a further difficulty which amounted to a 'fear of regulation', not by the regulatee but by the regulator. In most instances officials did not recognize themselves as regulators and were uncomfortable with that description of their work. Also evident was a fear of the consequences of regulation, largely from central government politicians in the Welsh Office. This can be demonstrated most clearly in the case of DSO regulation, where the Welsh Office was reluctant to intervene in DSOs which were failing to meet their financial performance targets. Rather than forcing a local authority to retender services, perhaps resulting in job losses, a system of 'self-regulation' was adopted by central government.

THE IMPACT OF DEVOLUTION ON THE SCRUTINY AND REGULATION OF PUBLIC BODIES

In the White Paper *A Voice for Wales* the government stated that the National Assembly for Wales would operate under 'maximum openness and public accountability' (Welsh Office, 1997: chapter 4, p.2). The paper suggests that if Assembly audit, subject and regional committees work properly and effectively, the regulation of the executive and sponsored bodies in Wales will improve. However, there is a view that the nature of devolution in Wales is unlikely to result in improvements in the regulation of public services. This concern, emanating principally from Westminster, but also expressed within Wales, questions the extent to which an Assembly with limited powers and supported by a former Whitehall department, can provide effective regulation and scrutiny (Osmond, 1999a). In order to determine whether devolution can alleviate the regulatory problems identified above, it is important to examine the role, structure and scrutiny mechanisms of the National Assembly for Wales.

Role

Devolution in Wales is complex in comparison with the Scottish settlement: 'the national assembly will be a completely new, hybrid institution, combining a unique blend of executive and legislative functions' (Osmond, 1999a: 7). The establishment of the Welsh Assembly has been referred to as 'executive devolution', as the settlement did not include powers for the Assembly to instigate primary legislation. However, the Assembly has considerable powers in relation to 'secondary' or 'subordinate' legislation (Silk, 1998). Although primary legislation is normally required for large-scale policy changes, and courts have the power to review secondary legislation, as Silk suggests, 'it would be wrong to dismiss secondary legislation as "second class" . . . it is still "law" ' (1998: 69). Nevertheless, during the Assembly's first term there has been great debate over the so-called 'legislative deficit', although this has largely focused on the Assembly's failure to impact on the UK government's legislative agenda. However, the Assembly has been successful in amending two major UK government bills in light of Welsh circumstances: the Local Government Act (2000) and the Care Standards Act (2000) establishing a children's commissioner for Wales.

The Welsh devolution settlement for Wales has resulted in a fusion of responsibilities for the regulation of public services in Wales. The prime responsibility rests with the Assembly but is shared to some extent by the secretary of state and Wales Office, some Whitehall departments, and Westminster politicians and committees. The role of the secretary of state post-devolution is to represent Wales in the UK government, to represent the UK government in Wales and to ensure the smooth working of the devolution settlement (Wales Office Departmental Report, 2000). His responsibilities include securing the best financial settlement for Wales and representing Wales at UK Cabinet level in relation to defence, employment, fiscal, economic and monetary policy, taxation, social security and pensions. There are also several areas of policy which remain with Whitehall departments post-devolution, such as social security and Home Office affairs. Consequently, a series of concordats have been drawn up between the National Assembly and these and other Whitehall departments ensuring a process of mutual consultation. In terms of Westminster politicians, devolution means a reduced role in terms of scrutiny of public bodies, particularly in relation to the PAC. However, the WAC continues to operate and scrutinize policies on a cross-cutting basis.

Devolution has major implications for our case-study organizations. As they were previously monitored by the Welsh Office, all six public services are now the prime responsibility of the National Assembly for Wales. For the local government case studies (housing, social services and DSOs) and the fourth case study, housing associations, devolution means working to new officials, subject committees (health and social services and local government, environment and transport). The Assembly-sponsored public body (WDA) and IHE is a key focus for the Audit Committee (which is primarily responsible for scrutinizing the expenditure) and also for the relevant subject committees: the Economic Development Committee and Post-sixteen Education and Training Committee. The regular appearances officials will have to make before various committees can be highlighted as a major cultural change in the regulation of public bodies in Wales, as public service officials were very rarely forced to appear before Parliament due to the infrequency of Welsh investigations.

Structure

The complex nature of the devolution settlement holds particular challenges for former Welsh Office civil servants who have had to adjust from working under the secretary of state for Wales to working under the corporate body of the Assembly. A small group of civil servants now works in the office of the Presiding Officer, providing support for backbench Assembly Members and committees, but the main body of staff continues to operate as an executive, under a Labour/Liberal administration (at the time of the research). Osmond (1999a: 8) summarizes the situation thus:

> The assumption is that 'chinese walls' will develop between those civil servants working for the Executive and those working for the Office of Presiding Officer. However, the largest class of civil servants . . . will work for both the Executive and the Assembly more generally, drawn in by their involvement with the Subject Committees. Therein lies a potential for divided loyalties.

This situation clearly has an impact on post-devolution regulatory arrangements. Large numbers of former Welsh Office civil servants have transferred to the National Assembly, working as departmental civil servants. They are, by and large, continuing with their work as undertaken previously but it is clear that civil servants will have to adapt to new scrutiny roles, such as serving subject committees (Pyper: 1999). There have been a number of relocations within the Welsh civil service and many staff are working in different divisions post-devolution. This may have a short-term impact on accountability frameworks simply because officials are now monitoring unfamiliar organizations. Thus, previous problems of closeness and capture may be alleviated, at least temporarily. Also, whilst working under Labour cabinet secretaries, civil servants must operate in conjunction with cross-party Assembly committees. This means that the scrutiny of information such as performance indicators, plans and annual reports is now partly the responsibility of Assembly Members. In order to assess the likely impact of these changes, it is necessary to examine the early scrutiny role of the Assembly by assessing the early operations of the new subject and audit committees.

Scrutiny

Subject committees

> The Subject Committees will combine the role of Standing Committees and Select Committees of the House of Commons. That is to say they will have a policy-making function and an inquisitorial role, holding the executive to account. It is easy to foresee a clash of interest developing between these two roles, especially where confidentiality of information is concerned.
>
> (Osmond, 1999a: 24)

The *Voice for Wales* White Paper (Welsh Office, 1997: chapter 4, p.5) stipulates that a key committee duty will involve 'monitoring the performance of public bodies'. Indeed, the Economic Development Committee lists the scrutiny of the Welsh Development Agency, the Wales Tourist Board and the Cardiff Bay Development Corporation as its second priority whilst the Health and Social Services Committee cites the regulation and inspection of services for vulnerable people as one of its key priorities. Similarly, the Local Government, Environment, Planning, Housing and Transport Committee highlights as a priority the development of an inspection regime for best value.

However, there is a view that suggests the subject committees might find these objectives difficult to achieve. As Osmond (1999a) points out, information required by committee members in the National Assembly is provided by former Welsh Office civil servants, rather than by an independent support staff, as in the UK or Scottish Parliament. Clearly, this leaves elected members dependent upon officials, some of whom, when interviewed for this research, professed a desire to steer committees towards policy development and away from the scrutiny function. However, several Assembly committee chairs stated that whilst they had received support from committee staff, they experienced problems with members of the executive civil service, now instructed by a minority Labour cabinet. There was an expectation from these officials that subject committees could be directed by the executive when making decisions on subjects for investigation. One committee member went as far as to describe Assembly civil servants as 'either incompetent or deliberately obstructive'. All committee chairs and members interviewed relayed anecdotes of delayed access to crucial documentation, information and the examination of legitimate areas of focus including the corporate strategy for health care in Wales.

Despite this difficulty, there is evidence to suggest that committees are already making progress towards improving accountability. One committee chair explained that despite attempts to steer the committee, the publication of agendas on the internet resulted in members of the public e-mailing views for representation at committee meetings. Also, committee members interviewed from Health and Social Services stated that the committee had initiated a number of distinctive investigations very much against the will of the executive, refusing to operate as a 'rubber stamp'. These include the examination of the NHS resource allocation formula and the corporate strategy for NHS Wales. Politicians interviewed from this committee also questioned the value of inspection regimes within social services and expressed particular fears regarding the transfer of inspections to hospitals and GP practices. Furthermore, the Economic Development Committee has recently been scrutinizing the business plan produced by the Welsh Development Agency and is currently commenting on the terms of reference for its quinquennial review which will question the agency's purpose, key functions and effectiveness.

Therefore, information which was previously analysed by one or two officials within the Welsh Office is now subject to scrutiny by elected members, often in meetings which are open to members of the wider public, which may result in improved organizational accountability. However, the view of many politicians and officials interviewed is that public agencies in Wales are having difficulty adjusting to new scrutiny arrangements. This view is supported by Morgan (2000) who argues that the WDA must now adjust from private meetings with the secretary of state to the full exposure of public exchange with the Economic Development Committee.

Audit Committee and the Auditor-General The Welsh Assembly's Audit Committee, which is loosely modelled on the Public Accounts Committee, has the power to summon witnesses from relevant Assembly departments and sponsored bodies in order to fulfil its main objective: 'to ensure that proper and thorough scrutiny is given to the Assembly's expenditure' (NAW, 2001: 2). Chaired by a Plaid Cymru Assembly Member, the committee's main function is to analyse statements of accounts and value for money reports produced by the NAO and the Auditor-General for Wales (AGW). Before devolution the National Audit Office investigated value for money in relation to Welsh services just twice a year on average, but post-devolution audit activity has increased dramatically with the Audit Committee accepting a proposal from the Auditor-General suggesting almost forty possible investigations between 1999/2000 and 2002/3. This, the most comprehensive (and expensive) of the three options proposed by the Auditor-General, was accepted by the committee, although some members who were not yet convinced by the work of the NAO expressed a reluctance to adopt the costliest proposal. The committee has emphasized that for the first term they will be 'auditing the auditor' and closely scrutinizing the performance of his office (Record of Proceedings, 18 November 1999).

All Audit Committee members interviewed were keen to call public bodies in Wales to account but reluctant to adopt fully the 'macho' style of the PAC, aiming for a tough but constructive approach to scrutiny. Nevertheless, the Chief Executive of Cadw described his appearance before the committee during the first evidence session as 'a rather daunting experience' (NAW, 1999f). The committee has also been critical of decisions taken by public-sector organizations in its early investigations. For example, after the publication of a recent report highlighted an 'irregular payment' to a poorly performing manager at the National Museum of Wales, the chair of the committee stated: 'We expect public bodies . . . to operate to the highest possible standards. To do otherwise would bring the organization concerned into disrepute and could undermine the credibility and reputation of the entire public sector in Wales' (NAW, 2000u). There is also considerable desire within the committee to broaden its remit in relation to local and police authorities. Although constitutionally the committee has no power to summon members or officers of these authorities, it can conduct broadly themed investigations such as a study of best value in local government, planned for 2001/2 (NAO, September 1999).

The White Paper *A Voice for Wales* suggested that the National Audit Office continue with a major public-sector auditing role in Wales, creating a new post of Auditor-General for Wales (AGW). In order to preserve continuity, the first AGW is the current C+AG, Sir John Bourn. The remit of his office includes auditing twenty-seven accounts of the Assembly and sponsored bodies, along with the specific resource accounts of the Assembly and NHS Wales, VFM examinations, responding to members of the public and supporting the work of the Audit Committee. Also, despite clear distinctions between the work, methodology and remit of the Audit Commission and National Audit Office (Power: 1997), the AGW appears keen to develop an increasingly close relationship between the two audit bodies in Wales. This involves plans to undertake collaborative work on relevant subjects which will 'enable the two key public sector audit bodies in Wales to work together and share information in a productive manner' (NAO, September 1999). Therefore, whilst there has been no formal merger between audit institutions in Wales, there is evidence to suggest that the two bodies will be working more closely together. Bowerman (1994: 61) suggests that co-operation could reassure 'the general public that the auditors are making best use of their resources and are not duplicating each other's work and it could, ultimately, result in financial savings'. This situation has major implications for our local government case-study organizations and could lead to a role for the Audit Committee in respect of local authority expenditure in Wales.

EXTENT OF REGULATORY PROBLEMS POST-DEVOLUTION

It would be premature to draw firm conclusions on the likely impact of the National Assembly on the regulation and scrutiny of public bodies in Wales. Nevertheless, it is important to consider whether the emerging systems and structures of the Assembly can alleviate the regulatory problems that we identified in the pre-devolution arrangements.

Regulatee resistance

Recorded instances of regulatee resistance were rare before devolution, although there were cases of late submission of reports and performance information. However, Assembly Members interviewed all appear determined to obtain relevant information from the public-service organizations they scrutinize, although, as previously stated, all had experienced problems obtaining information and documentation from executive officials. In terms of the case-study organizations, it is likely that, if anything, levels of resistance could recede as public-service organizations become increasingly aware that late submission of information will be more visible. However, it is important to bear in mind that resistance appears more evident in local authority departments than central agencies. Therefore, whether AMs will be more successful than their Welsh Office predecessors may depend upon the relationship that develops between the new elected institutions and local authorities. Already some Assembly actions have alarmed local authorities in Wales. There have been proposals for enhanced Assembly powers in relation to children's services, whilst the local government secretary recently threatened to cap councillors' allowances in a south Wales authority. Consequently, there are likely to be growing tensions within the Partnership Council which was established to ensure consultation and co-operation between local government and the Assembly. This suggests there is a realistic prospect of enhanced local authority resistance to regulation by the National Assembly.

Ritualistic compliance

There was some evidence of organizations complying ritualistically with regulatory bodies pre-devolution. It seems likely that ritualistic compliance may lessen post-devolution, not least because information provided to Assembly committees is immediately subject to public scrutiny through the work of committees, because of its publication on the internet. This provides a stark contrast to the previous system where information was often analysed just by a single person or small group of officials in the Welsh Office. Assembly Members interviewed for the research claimed that information required from local authorities and ASPBs did arrive promptly, but many raised concerns about the availability and timeliness of documentation from executive civil servants. However, this may reflect the fact that there has been considerable movement within executive divisions during the establishment of the Assembly. Clearly, it may take some time for officials to settle down into their new roles and begin effectively to monitor public services. On a more positive note the Audit Committee annual report states that all the committee's recommendations to date have been 'endorsed' by the Assembly Cabinet but there is a specified requirement for a response within five months in respect of Audit Committee reports.

Regulatory capture

Westminster politicians representing Welsh constituencies expressed a fear that 'capture' may further develop post-devolution due to the physical proximity of organizations and a history of informal relationships between key personnel in the Welsh Office, National Audit Office, local authorities and politicians. The, at times controversial, role of the Audit Commission and constant queries over the independence of the former C+AG suggest that ensuring the true independence of new audit institutions will be difficult. White and Hollingsworth (1999) express concerns with post-devolution audit arrangements, despite the explicit nature of arrangements for audit in the Government of Wales Bill. For example, the Assembly will play a role in the appointment of the Auditor-General for Wales (AGW): 'protecting the AGW's independence . . . is tricky – it would not be good to have the Assembly responsible for appointment and dismissal given that one of the auditees of the AGW will be the Assembly itself' (1999: 207). As a result, post-devolution, the PAC retains the right to question accounting officers in Wales where it is judged that circumstances warrant further investigation. Also, the Welsh Affairs Select Committee will continue to investigate Welsh policy and public bodies within its jurisdiction. In a special report on *The Work of the Committee since Devolution*, whilst reassuring the National Assembly that its ministers and committees will not be subject to formal scrutiny by the committee, or by the UK Parliament, the committee states its preferred role thus:

> we recommended that the Committee should have a wide-ranging brief, perhaps including how the moneys allocated by Parliament are spent, examining matters within the responsibility of the Assembly in the course of scrutinising legislation made at Westminster and possible matters within the responsibility of other Government departments. In that case, it would no longer be a select committee related to a government department, but a cross-cutting committee more like the Environmental Audit Committee.
>
> (Welsh Affairs Committee, 2000: 2)

Thus, Westminster politicians are keen to retain a role in scrutinizing the performance of Welsh government, with one select committee member interviewed referring to Parliament as the 'ultimate truly independent check' on public bodies in Wales, in particular quangos. Most Assembly and committee members interviewed recognized the potential difficulties and encouraged the involvement of parliamentary colleagues and committees. However, other committee members have questioned the remit of the Welsh Affairs Committee and appear resentful of perceived parliamentary interference. They argued that the existence of the new devolved institutions may lessen the possibility of the development of close relationships between public bodies in Wales. It could be that the introduction of a set of elected politicians may help to formalize relationships between audit bodies and public-service organizations and maintain greater distance between them. Certainly, Assembly Members interviewed were keen to dispel 'cosy' images of Welsh government, in particular those on the Audit Committee who make a special effort to keep a distance between themselves and the public bodies they scrutinize. However, close relationships between Assembly officials, audit bodies and public bodies are still evident post-devolution. When giving evidence to the Audit Committee, the permanent secretary to the Assembly, Jon Shortridge, speaking of the relationship between the Assembly sponsor division and the WDA, stated: 'We do have a pretty close relationship with these people and therefore you know the nature of the people with whom you are dealing' (NAW, 2000v).

Performance ambiguity

One of the most significant problems for the National Assembly to over-come is ambiguity in performance reporting. A programme is currently under way in Wales, in conjunction with the comprehensive spending review, to reform performance objectives in order to reflect policy out-comes. For example, each local authority is developing a 'policy agree-ment' with the Assembly that covers outcomes in education, the economy, health and quality of life. Devolution may ensure that performance criteria become more explicit, with the subject committees playing a crucial role in establishing future targets. For example, the Economic Development Committee has played a major role in establishing new targets for the WDA, and the Health and Social Services Committee is developing a new performance management framework for the NHS in Wales. However, it is important to remember that performance information is only valuable if used in a positive and constructive way – as Graber suggests, politicians are sometimes 'more interested in vindicators than in indicators' (1992: 45). However, politicians we interviewed claimed that they considered performance information with a degree of care and responsibility.

Data problems

Devolution may lead to an improvement in definitions of good perform-ance but whether this emphasis on measuring policy outcomes results in the production of more accurate and meaningful performance data remains to be seen. It is important to consider the capacity of public services in delivering new performance data. For example, work on best value has revealed deficiencies in local authority management information systems, significantly reducing the capacity to produce relevant data (Boyne et al., 2000). However, the NAO is currently seeking to develop a new role in validating performance data. This is largely to maintain consistency amongst government departments and sponsored bodies throughout the move to resource accounting and budgeting, which requires a statement of finances by organizational aims and objectives and an output performance analysis. Furthermore, it is possible that closer co-operation between the

Audit Commission and the NAO may lead to a broad standardization of performance data, as both now have responsibilities for collecting and analysing data on organizational performance.

CONCLUSION

We have sought to utilize existing literature on public-sector regulation in order to develop a framework for analysing regulation pre- and post-institutional change in Wales. There is evidence that this framework is useful in analysing regulatory problems (for example, regulatory capture and data problems are evident in many of our cases). Although the framework implies that regulatory failure is due to the behaviour of the regulatee (resisting regulation, ritually complying), our data suggest that regulators are also responsible for regulatory problems. For example, there appeared to be evidence of ritualistic compliance within the Welsh Office in terms of the scrutiny of performance data and plans. Furthermore, our analysis has revealed a regulatory problem not covered by the theoretical framework: 'fear of regulation', not by the regulatee but by the regulator.

Politicians and officials interviewed for the research identified a number of key regulatory problems. The first of these was a close relationship between the Welsh Office, audit institutions and public services in Wales, with interviewees in some cases suggesting that the audit function has come to resemble consultancy. Secondly, difficulties were detected in the definition of organizational performance, although these were less evident in relation to financial performance indicators. Finally, on the rare occasions that performance targets were clearly agreed and understood, the data required to measure that performance were either missing or inappropriate.

Clearly, the regulation of public bodies in Wales is undergoing a period of transition. The Assembly will be responsible for ensuring that local authority services deliver best value. This new regime is designed to encourage all local councils to scrutinize and monitor their activities in much greater depth. Key components of the best-value framework include instruments of self-regulation such as management and financial information systems, transparent budgeting and internal audit aimed at improving the regulation and performance of local services. However, best value is widely recognized as a 'data-hungry' planning system (Boyne et al., 2000) and if the data problems identified in this research remain unchecked, best value may not deliver a more successful or comprehensive regulatory regime.

Nevertheless, there is some evidence to suggest that devolution is already making a difference to regulation in Wales. There is little evidence of a 'fear of regulation' amongst AMs in Wales as they use their committee powers to involve themselves in numerous local government issues. Also, they appear determined to intervene in public-service organizations in order to avoid any negative publicity. As one AM interviewed stated, 'I am not going to be voted out at the next election because (my) health authority cannot manage its finances.' Financial accountability is likely to be enhanced through the work of the new Audit Committee and the lengthy programme of Welsh VFM studies to be conducted by the NAO. Moreover, the subject committees' work on performance targets may result in more meaningful measures of performance. However, generating reliable and comparable performance data for public-service organizations will be a much more difficult challenge for the Assembly.

Therefore, it would seem that whilst devolution enhances political accountability, it does not automatically resolve the problems of organizational accountability identified before the creation of a Welsh Assembly. If these problems are not resolved by the newly elected politicians, political accountability itself is seriously weakened. To date, the debate on devolution has concentrated on constitutional reforms and political accountability. However, if the democratic deficit is to be reduced, more attention needs to be paid to political and managerial reforms that enhance organizational accountability. It will, therefore, be important to continue to monitor whether the regulation of public services in Wales has improved or deteriorated as a result of devolution. Only after further study will it be possible to determine whether the people of Wales are better able to hold public service organizations to account under this new system of Welsh governance.

Acknowledgements

The research on which this chapter is based was funded by the Economic and Social Research Council (Grant L327253035).

8

Reading the Runes

PAUL CHANEY, TOM HALL and ANDREW PITHOUSE

In this final chapter we draw together the key conclusions arrived at by our contributors. We consider the implications of these for the National Assembly before moving on to discuss the agenda for future research. We do so in the knowledge that events move quickly in the world of policy and politics and that the perspectives offered here date from the early months of new governance. As one pro-devolution commentator observed, 'This is the beginning, not the end. No one can pretend that a change as extensive as this can be once-and-for-all. It will have to be redesigned and rethought after it is implemented, and once people see the need for future change.'[1] We hope this book will contribute to that rethinking process. In particular, we hope that the book will provide researchers, and the users and beneficiaries of research, with a benchmark against which to appraise the nature and pace of change yet to come.

The pursuit of this 'Welsh agenda' for a new democracy has not always had the full support of the Welsh people. As we have seen from the account of political participation and legitimacy offered by Wyn Jones and Trystan in chapter 2, the birth of the Assembly could hardly be considered auspicious, given the disappointingly low turnout of the electorate. On the other hand, such low turnout is now an international phenomenon. Throughout the world it is easy to find 'dissatisfied democrats' in countries where citizens 'place a high rating on the attractiveness of democracy as a form of government but at the same time place a poor rating on the performance of their particular democratic regime' (Klingemann, 1999: 54).

The faltering start of the National Assembly must be understood in the context of wider dissatisfaction and discontent within our political system, and not primarily in terms of specific, and localized, resistance to devolution. Indeed, comparison with other UK election turnouts around the same time does not indicate a glaring disparity between elections in Wales and other parts of Britain. That young voters in Wales were less likely to vote is also clearly consistent with trends in Scotland and England (cf. Park, 2000). However, this disengagement had quite specific, and perhaps disturbing, consequences for the Wales Labour Party, which suffered a dramatic fall in its share of the vote at the first Assembly elections.

While we may assume that low turnouts are more a function of apathy than antipathy, the new government in Wales must nevertheless find ways to enhance its legitimacy, perhaps through higher participation in future elections. Yet Wyn Jones and Trystan warn that it will not be easy to address concerns about legitimacy and participation, and emphasize the need to generate more broadcasting interest in the Assembly to counter the information deficit where the dominant media appear uninterested in politics outside Westminster (cf. Wyn Jones, 2001). Wyn Jones and Trystan voice a more fundamental concern about the constitutional settlement in Wales and the belief held by some that devolution is unlikely, without increased powers, to make an impact upon daily life in Wales.

Low voter turnout is linked inevitably to this political reality, but much will depend on the way politicians campaign and exploit the media as we approach the first elections since the Assembly came to power. Politics is, after all, the art of persuasion in relation to the management of scarcity. In this sense there is no determined relationship between voter turnout, the (limited) powers of the Assembly and legitimacy. For example, much will depend on the branding and image of Assembly activities. It may be that, through time and skilful popularization of the Assembly by political leaders, the level of public approval can be raised. Leaving aside the desirability of a Welsh parliament with enhanced powers, much good will can stem from modest initiatives that enjoy high visibility.

While the active and astute campaigning of Wales's political classes could prove persuasive (about the merits of the current settlement) in the short term, there are likely to be sections of Welsh society that prove harder to influence than others. This is particularly likely to be the case amongst groups which have traditionally been less well incorporated within the political process and often marginalized in relation to economic and social opportunities. The chapter by Betts, Borland and Chaney explored the views of women's groups and organizations as well as groups representing the interests of people with disabilities. The high hopes for, and good will towards, the Assembly from women's groups were described, as was the optimism of some, but not all, disability groups. Most respondents appeared to be quite realistic about the time it would take to close the gap between aspiration and the achievement of greater participation in the political process. Indeed, in respect of gender the increased participation of women in the Assembly and its clear commitment to equal opportunities was already seen as a major advance. It would, however, be wise to remember that we are only at the beginning of the process which will foster greater participation by women in the governance of Wales, and much has yet to be done to generate the wider inclusion of women and women's groups in governance.

People with disabilities do not have a proportional presence in the Assembly. There is no well-established and broadly representative disability lobby in Wales that can voice the shared and disparate interests of disabled people. As Betts, Borland and Chaney demonstrate, the Assembly faces a formidable challenge in fostering participative democracy for disabled people. The need for people with disabilities to create an organization, a leadership and a strategy for more influential inclusion in the new political system appears to be a critical part of the process. Success or failure in achieving this goal will, in turn, have implications for citizenship, social justice and entitlement. The rights that disabled people in Wales are able to claim to mainstream opportunities will depend in some measure upon the access afforded to disability groups and the willingness of the Assembly to think of new ways to meet disabled people and agree new settlements.

While there is evidence of considerable involvement in new governance by some groups of women and disabled people, the vast majority of representative bodies have been less well engaged. The signs of widening participation are evident, but so too are the dangers that an élite minority may be incorporated instead of less privileged groups. Within such a context of broadening participation, future research can help shape the development of devolved governance by determining the success and effectiveness of Assembly strategies and structures in both tapping into pre-existing levels of social capital (cf. Putnam, 1993) and, in turn, increasing prevailing levels of social capital through innovations in government and the policy process (cf. Rico et al., 1998).

Much more ambivalence about the new Assembly can be found amongst the minority ethnic groups discussed in the chapter by Williams and Chaney. Their account shows that the early expectations of these groups were focused on the goal of achieving some direct representation in the Assembly. When no candidate from a Black or Asian background was elected, these hopes gave way to disillusionment and, in some quarters, bitterness and accusations of bad faith. The poverty of dialogue between the politicians and the ethnic minorities in Wales, both pre- and post-devolution, was exacerbated by the minorities' sense of exclusion from some of the discussions of nation and Welsh identity during the devolution campaign. This reminds us that inclusivity is not simply a matter for the Assembly but covers other areas of civic responsibility and public appointments within which a political culture of participation is engendered across social, cultural and economic domains. For people from minority ethnic communities in Wales such wider dimensions to involvement in public life have been very slow to develop.

The interviews with minority ethnic groups discussed by Williams and Chaney revealed some anxieties about the potential dangers of tokenistic consultation and careful gatekeeping of the various minority constituencies. Yet, there appear to be some encouraging signs that such groups are not overlooked in the policy process. The mainstreaming of a policy of race equality across Assembly subject committees is helping to 'equality-proof' a number of policies across education, housing, staffing and appointments in the public sector. In this context, the initiatives tend to lie within a service-orientated rather than a citizen-orientated approach to negotiating the meaning of diverse ethnic identities and interests across Wales.

In the early days of the Assembly ethnic minority groups appeared to be inadequately mobilized in relation to a community of interest that could articulate a shared position. It may be that such a community is not feasible and that what is needed are multiple forums in which ethnic diversity is given status and there are real opportunities to voice concerns. But the view from this study is that we can be cautiously optimistic that there is now a strong legislative and policy mandate for ethnic minority participation and emerging representative structures to promote the association of groups and individuals.

Clearly there is a considerable way to go to bolster the inclination and capacity of minority ethnic groups to engage in active citizenship after a history of some exclusion from the mainstream. Much will depend upon the energy and will of the Assembly to make inclusiveness an authentic and achievable goal for all. In this context the former First Secretary Alun Michael declared that active citizenship was one of his 'highest priorities' (Michael, 2000), and reference to recent Assembly policy documents and the pronouncements of politicians reveals that it remains a key objective for all citizens in Wales (for example, ETAG, 2000; NAW, 2000j; 2000s; 2000r; Murphy, 2000). Future analysis of the models of citizenship promoted by the Assembly will be necessary in order to ensure that this goal is realized in the most effective manner.

Chapters 3, 4 and 5 of this book highlight, *inter alia,* the centrality of issues of community, association and identity to the future success of the devolved government, and these topics constitute a major part of the future research agenda. Further work will be necessary to determine the relationship between citizenship, identity and a more participative mode of engagement in the policy process. The Welsh context therefore presents an ideal social experiment in which to test democratic theories of citizenship and activism. Conceptual work such as that of Barber (1984) sets out the relevant parameters in this respect:

to participate is to create a community that governs itself, and to create a self-governing community is to participate. Indeed from the perspective of strong democracy, the two terms are one aspect of a single social being: citizenship . . . participation without community merely rationalises individualism, giving it the aura of democracy. (1984: 155)

In addressing these questions there will be a need for the careful examination of nested 'national' identities (such as mediated notions of being Welsh, British, Asian, Bengali, European – and so forth) and of the way identity change in one part of the UK impacts on other parts. Determining how other dimensions of identity fit into this complex picture will be central to increased understanding: for example, to date there has been almost no relevant research into the sort of identities founded upon (dis)ability, faith, language, sexuality, lifestyle and gender.

The Assembly was founded upon the rhetoric of inclusive engagement with all the citizens of Wales and, as we have seen, some progress has already been made in this respect. However, more research will be necessary. We need this research in order to understand and shape the way in which the devolved systems of Welsh governance change to engage and mediate effectively and fairly between groups defined by multiple and sometimes competing identities. Further research will also be necessary if we are to understand if, or indeed how, devolution has shifted the gender parameters in UK politics. More specifically there is an obvious need for research which compares the roles that women played, and agendas they were able to promote, in the debates leading up to devolution and the quality of female representation in the politics and operation of the new Welsh legislature.

The study by Dicks, Hall and Pithouse suggests that perhaps the most articulated and well-developed of policies now in place is that which defines the Assembly's relationship with the voluntary sector. Here, UK government ambitions for a 'Third Way' response to the ideals of active citizenship and community renewal found clear expression in the Voluntary Sector Scheme. This sets out the framework for a closer collaboration over government policy between the Assembly and the multifarious world of 25,000 voluntary organizations in Wales which uniquely represent civil and community values. The scheme makes provision for a Partnership Council which consults with government over policy and advises on the working of the scheme. There are evident difficulties in representing the empirical diversity of the sector, and representatives to sit on the council are being drawn from but a fraction of the thousands of voluntary groups and organizations.

The Assembly is avowedly interventionist in its policy ambitions for the voluntary world and is intent on 'joining up' this agenda with the sectors of local government and business in order to create a new synergy that can tackle social exclusion and marginalized communities. While the scale of such aims appears highly ambitious (and generally 'untested') it would be wrong to assume that these are but lofty ideals which we will never see in practice. There are now in place clear structures and mechanisms for consultation and joint development of strategy. While we have yet to see major social development initiatives to regenerate communities via collaboration with business, local authority and voluntary groups, there are a growing number of smaller schemes that promote a synergistic approach, and these might act as important pathfinders for more extensive ventures in the future.

Messages about the early experience of devolution from the voluntary sector seem positive. It is clear from the study by Dicks, Hall and Pithouse that many groups prepared in earnest for the arrival of the Assembly by putting together policy, people and technology in order to engage effectively with new governance. The critical divide within the sector therefore is not defined so much by function, speciality, shape or constitution, but by the capacity and willingness to meet the costs of inclusiveness. Those costs include staff time, print and electronic technology, network skills, training in system know-how and the acquisition of political antennae. While geographical distance from the Assembly may be a disadvantage, the real difficulties over inclusiveness are more likely to relate to communication and information technology deficits that preclude monitoring and liaison with consultative machinery. These deficits cannot help but impact upon many small organizations and groups that cannot afford such investments and running costs.

Very many voluntary groups throughout Wales cannot be represented in some direct way, and inevitably consultation must operate through umbrella bodies or consortia that will emerge over time. In these early stages of the Assembly, the Wales Council for Voluntary Action has played a pivotal role in acting as a conduit and voice for the sector. It must somehow mediate a complex relationship between Assembly and sector without losing its campaigning voice or the important influence it has with government in Wales. The dangers of a small élite becoming the acceptable face of the sector are all too familiar to those concerned and are therefore unlikely to occur, but developing widely accessible and effective democratic machinery will take time. Time is not an elastic commodity in government, where pressing policy aims, personal ambitions and the need for election-winning public approval must trade off against the time-consuming ideals of inclusiveness.

It is unlikely that Assembly policy and practice involving the voluntary sector will await the full consultation of all interested parties before making progress towards stated aims. With a sector as large and diverse as this, it seems inevitable that some will have to play 'catch-up' in relation to policy developments that will affect the function, relationships and funding of many voluntary organizations. Closing this democratic gap presents a formidable challenge and we should not expect solutions in the short term.

Future research is essential if we are to map out and understand the way in which the 'third' sector, and civil society in general, are responding to the realities of a devolved Wales. We need to reach a better understanding of the nature and effects of the realignment of the voluntary sector in relation to government associated with devolution. Here a number of questions immediately pose themselves. What is the relationship between voluntarism, social capital and citizenship? What forms of representative bodies are most effective in engaging with the Assembly, and why? What is the impact of devolution on voluntary-sector finance and regulation? What is the place of the third sector in the political visions of the four main parties following devolution?

The early evidence is that important changes are taking place and that we might be witnessing the birth of something that might be tentatively called a *Welsh* civil society as opposed to 'civil society in Wales' (Paterson and Wyn Jones, 1999). The findings of chapters 5, 6 and 7 suggest that, in some quarters, new Welsh-focused organizational structures are emerging that are more autonomous and designed to engage in a distinct Welsh policy process. There is a nascent Welsh lobby in Cardiff Bay, yet it remains to be seen how issues of communications, resources, organizational cultures, and the complexities of the Westminster–Cardiff Bay relationship, will shape the development of a devolved civil society in Wales.

Much of the focus of the devolution debate has been on the assumed benefit of a more participatory democracy in which the Assembly promotes greater openness and accountability. For longer-term assessments to be made the key terms that featured in the rhetoric of devolution will need to be appraised in an independent manner (cf. Beetham, 1994; Weir and Beetham, 1999). Such analysis will test and measure the devolved policy process to determine whether the Assembly has introduced a truly participative (as opposed to solely consultative) mode of governance in which civic society is freely able to engage in the process of democratic decision-making and resource allocation. Within such an assessment, future research should explore the way in which the Assembly's embracing of new technology will further mass citizen participation and citizen involvement in the policy process (cf. Budge, 1996).

Disinterested observers might be forgiven for thinking that discussion of constitutional reform in Wales is limited to the way in which the citizen and civil society can benefit from devolution. The more cynical amongst them might even conclude that this is a part of the process by which devolution is cast as a self-evidently 'good' thing. They could point out that equating devolution with inclusion means that the only way in which devolution can fail will be if that promise is unfulfilled and citizens and communities remain excluded or insufficiently included. Judging whether the degree of inclusion that is eventually achieved is adequate will be a contentious business, and it may never be possible to decide whether the Assembly has failed in these terms. It is therefore fortunate that this book has also reported on research on other aspects of the Assembly, including its role in relation to the promotion of economic development and its regulatory function *vis-à-vis* the public services. Here one can identify specific tasks for the Assembly within which it appears, at least at first glance, to be a more simple job to evaluate the effectiveness of new governance.

Against the background of the devolutionary rhetoric of inclusivity, the chapter (6) by Morgan and Rees presented a preliminary evaluation of how far the Assembly has succeeded in instigating new forms of governance of economic development in Wales. In their analysis they focused on organizational networks and contrasted the earlier modes of 'raj'-style governance under the Welsh Office prior to 1997 and the transitional period 1997–9 with the new devolved structures centred on the National Assembly after May 1999. In so doing they explored the powers and structures that underpin the new system of Welsh governance and questioned the extent to which the Assembly has begun to foster changes in the nature and interrelationships of a range of organizations concerned with the formulation and delivery of economic development policies. Their analysis reveals how the effectiveness of democratized governance of Wales post-1999 depends not only on the character of the emerging relationships between business organizations and the Assembly, but also on the sort of relationships that exist *between* these business organizations.

Morgan and Rees raise the question of whether devolved governance structures necessarily make for a more effective system of regional policy-making. In answering this key question they bring to bear their research on the Partnership Council and the Business Partnership, together with the revised roles of the Welsh Development Agency and recent reforms in post-sixteen education and training. These case studies were examined in order to ascertain if earlier models of consultation have been replaced by more participative structures of economic governance. Initial analysis suggests that this transition *has* involved a shift in the structure of network relations between organizations. As with the findings of chapters 3, 4 and 5 in respect of 'minority' groups and the voluntary sector as a whole, this project found that it was the knowledgeable and well-organized groups that were in the best position to take advantage of the opportunities offered by new governance. The composition and disposition of the membership of the Assembly was highly influential in this respect. To date, the new structures of economic governance have been used to greatest effect by the Wales Council for Voluntary Action and Welsh local government. In contrast, AMs have displayed much less enthusiasm for business interests.

Whereas administrative devolution of economic development matters had produced a strongly hierarchical organizational network, focused vertically on the dominating Welsh Office (and WDA), since devolution proper this has shifted to a somewhat less hierarchical, but as yet still indeterminate pattern of network relationships. This, the authors argue, is the most significant aspect of new governance because the Assembly has created multiple points of entry into the political system, something that derives from the creation of wholly new organizational mechanisms.

Morgan and Rees found less evidence that there has been an equivalent change in the institutional regime of social rules, norms and conventions. Instead they assert that the persistence of an institutional regime from the era of administrative devolution constitutes the greatest obstacle to fulfilling the potential which more democratic forms of devolution offer. In this analysis the role of the Assembly civil service – simultaneously under-resourced and risk-averse in its approach to the policy process – is pivotal. Thus during the transitional phases of the Assembly's development reported on here (1999–early 2001), the civil service had 'exercise[d] a good deal of power and influence over its political masters in the Assembly'. Whilst the democratization of governance in Wales, and, in particular, matters relating to economic development, has to be an inherently good thing, new governance does not automatically improve the prospects for economic development. For Morgan and Rees democracy may be a good thing in itself but its implications for economic development are neither clear nor straightforward.

Morgan and Rees go on to assert that there is a limit to what government reforms can achieve in isolation. Rather, they argue, economic growth will depend upon successfully addressing the shortcomings of a weak civic capacity in Wales. Once more we return to the question of the capacities of citizens and organizations. Morgan and Rees think they will need to be 'tooled up' (and this involves the desire to participate along with more time, expertise and resources) to take advantage of the opportunities afforded by the Assembly. Within the wider picture of devolved govern-ance in Wales, Morgan and Rees conclude that that there is no simple relationship between, on the one hand, the greater openness and transpar-ency of governmental decision-making that democratic devolution brings, and, on the other, the development of more collaborative and inclusive forms of economic strategy, let alone actual improvements in economic well-being. Rather, the latter have to be worked for and constructed in a complex and demanding process of 'learning by doing'.

The chapter by Ashworth, Boyne and Walker (chapter 7) focused on an analysis of six regulatory regimes and allied instruments used by the former Welsh Office and taken on by the Assembly in respect of key public provisions in relation to economic development, social services, housing, higher education and local government. Interviews with key staff prior to and after devolution provided valuable insights that were then grounded within conceptual categories as applied generally to regulatory systems. From this analysis a number of factors arose that suggested limits and new possibilities for effective regulation. For example, it was recognized that the Assembly might not make much of a regulatory step-change in the short term because most mechanisms remained much the same as before. Secondly, the relocation of so many staff to new divisions in the Assembly, together with the demanding policy agenda of an ambitious new government keen to see many changes in public services, was likely to have an impact on effective regulation. Thus policy demands for speedy change on many service fronts do not sit easily with a more programmatic and paced cycle of regulatory business that often works best with some degree of stasis in the service environment.

Assembly-related change is most notable in relation to the new subject committees which now provide more visible political accountability by their formal scrutiny of public bodies. The subject committees' relationship with the executive is the key to their effective monitoring of public bodies, and the signs are that the committees will not act as some 'rubber stamp' for the wishes of the Cabinet. Greater oversight now comes from the Assembly's Audit Committee, the main function being to analyse statements of account and value-for-money reports in relation to Welsh public services.

The number of investigations by this committee will, it is thought, far exceed its pre-devolution counterpart, and there is an evident desire to broaden its remit in relation to local authorities and police authorities. How this will be received by local authorities when intention becomes reality is not yet clear, particularly when the mood music of 'partnership' and 'consultation' has been so ubiquitous in discussions of the intended relations with the public sector. Within this atmosphere a more muscular investigative stance would surely raise some hackles. While there is already greater visibility of the regulatory aspect via publication of committee proceedings on the internet, we may also see a more assertive Assembly keen to dispel any notion of some 'cosy' relationship with public bodies. We may also see the introduction of more explicit performance criteria by which to regulate, for example in relation to economic development, health and social care. There seems little evidence of reluctance by Assembly Members to use their committee powers and the early signs are that a new era of transparent and robust regulation may be dawning. We will soon know if this heralds a very different regulatory culture and practice than the more secluded system operated by the pre-devolution Welsh Office.

As with the earlier chapters in this book, chapters 6 and 7 raise a number of questions that can only be answered by further research. A number of these questions refer to the Assembly's role in promoting economic growth. One of the most interesting areas for future research on this topic lies in the policy process. It is clear from the chapter by Morgan and Rees that we need to know much more about the relative importance of open and democratic mechanisms for influencing Assembly policy, as opposed to closed and opaque, and sometimes secret, channels. The biggest item on the future research agenda is, however, not the policy process but evaluation of the major policy impacts. In the field of economic development the research priority may well be the study of the uses to which European Union financial assistance is put. In any event future research will increasingly be focused on the effectiveness of Assembly policies, and in this way we will begin to understand how big (or small) a difference the Assembly has made to the lives of people in Wales.

Several of the chapters in this book have suggested that the people who live in Wales will have to make some changes in the way they conduct themselves if they are to get the best out of their Assembly. One of the more intriguing questions raised in the chapter by Morgan and Rees concerns the extent to which business organizations may learn – perhaps by following the example of the local authorities or the voluntary sector – how to get their voices heard more effectively. Future research will also need to be conducted to find out if the make-up of the Assembly, and particularly the professional background of the AMs, continues to have an influence on the way business concerns are dealt with beyond the first few months in the life of the Assembly. It might be fairly easy to understand why AMs need to take time to come to terms with issues that they find alien and unfamiliar, but we would expect research conducted in a few years' time to tell a different story.

Morgan and Rees give an account of an Assembly which still functions in the shadow of its administrative predecessor, the Welsh Office – either in its pre-1999 incarnation under Ron Davies, or even the unreconstructed pre-1997 version – but memories of the Welsh Office are likely to dim rather quickly. Ashworth, Boyne and Walker would say there is evidence that this is happening already, but their research also raises a number of issues for future research.

Perhaps the biggest, and certainly the most interesting, question they raise concerns the issue of performance ambiguity and the steps that the Assembly might take to minimize it. In the near future, research will need to pay close attention to the outcome of the Assembly's own programme designed to review performance objectives in order to reflect policy outcomes. In effect, we need research to find out whether the move to an emphasis on measuring policy outcomes works. For example, does it lead to the provision of better data for assessing performance? We will be unable to judge whether the Assembly is having a positive effect unless we, and the civil servants and politicians, know how to recognize such an effect. This point is fairly obvious when we are discussing topics like inclusivity which are hard to define or operationalize, but there is, apparently, plenty of room for ambiguity elsewhere. Good research which looks at the way the Assembly sets targets, and then measures whether these targets are achieved, could be of great help in respect of all of those issues to which the Assembly claims competence: from the level of gross domestic product in Wales to the way local social service departments manage foster carers.

Finally, Ashworth, Boyne and Walker explain that reforms are needed if organizational accountability is to be improved in a way that will reduce the democratic deficit. Keeping a check on the effectiveness of the reform of regulation that occurred with devolution contributes to this end. As Ashworth, Boyne and Walker conclude, we do not yet know whether the people of Wales are better placed to hold public-service organizations to account as a result of devolution. It is going to take more research to fill this gap in our knowledge, just as we need more research to find out whether devolution really is good news for economic development in Wales.

LOOKING AHEAD

For social science, then, the process of devolution will continue to produce significant opportunities for new research. Research of the type reported in this book is needed to inform users and beneficiaries (within which categories we include the Welsh population as a whole), but researchers will also continue to wish to take advantage of the natural experiment of devolution. Simply because devolution represents a major change in the way things are done, it will continue to offer social scientists rare and sometimes unique opportunities to find answers to questions that cannot be pursued at all in another context. This will continue to be the case because, as described at the end of the previous section, research is needed in order to evaluate the effects of devolution, for example the outcomes of Assembly policies. But the natural experiment will also continue because the reforms will continue. It is to contemplation of the future of this great experiment that we now turn.

The findings we have presented here offer snapshots of the Assembly at work, and we have seen that there is much to commend in relation to early achievements and future potential. While popular perceptions of the Assembly will take their starting-point from the more racy and often combative politics and internal feuds that marred the early days of a minority Labour administration, it is clear that this picture has changed as we go to press in early 2001. A new, more inclusive executive of Labour and Liberal Democrat parties is, for the moment at least, operating in a more quiet and purposeful political climate. The Assembly's First Minister, Rhodri Morgan, is leading a more open administration which appears to be ready to 'learn by doing', instead of the conflict-based one-party approach of the early days. Such changes are not simply to be explained in terms of the ideals of inclusiveness, however. Politics is alive and well, and much inclusiveness might be explained simply in terms of the steps which have been seen as necessary to the survival of the Labour-dominated executive. Pragmatism is also at work in another way since coalition politics is also founded on the recognition that there is not an overflow of political talent in any of the main parties.

As we have seen in earlier chapters, in various quarters the Assembly enjoys much approval and good will, albeit that this good will is often conditional on future achievement. The desire to see this new government become confident, successful and closely identified with a more prosperous Wales surfaced frequently in the studies discussed above, and we finish this book with some general thoughts about the future of the Assembly derived from the insights of earlier chapters.

First, we return to the disappointing turnout for the Assembly elections and the narrowest conceivable majority for devolution itself. While this must be of real concern, there is still a democratic mandate from all who did vote. Whatever their motives and affiliations, we may conclude that most who voted believed devolution and the Assembly would make a difference for Wales. Keeping faith with this community of the hopeful while seeking to convert non-believers and the agnostic must be uppermost in the minds of most politicians and parties. The need to deepen the legitimacy of devolved government (even on the basis of political self-interest) will perhaps call forth the sort of political maturity and culture that will build loyalty for this infant government. Interestingly, it is worth trying to imagine what it might feel like to occupy a 'non-devolved Wales' still tied closely to Westminster at a time (now) when regional government is so clearly on the UK agenda. In this sense there is no conceivable turning back but no well-trodden path to follow either.

The Assembly must to some extent design its own future. Further research will be necessary to inform this process of self-development. Institutional theories of political support may assist in outlining the levels of trust and participation that the Assembly is able to foster amongst the Welsh citizenry (cf. Norris, 1999b), the effectiveness of the deliberative process and the success of policy outcomes (cf. Gargarella, 1998).

There have been concerns that subject committees may become, or have already become, overburdened. Significant demands have already been placed on some relatively inexperienced Assembly Members who have been much tested by agricultural crises and by damaging battles over economic development and European Union regional aid in the first year of government. Being blooded this early is perhaps no bad thing. The Assembly and its officers and members are perhaps much more resilient than some of the anxious guardians of the devolution dream give them credit for. Yet, as the full weight of their regulatory functions and second- ary legislative powers begins to expand, there may be some demanding times to come – and to anticipate.

For while there is no legislative devolution, there is substantial executive power to elaborate upon primary legislation and, depending upon the framing of laws, there can be wide-ranging discretion of real consequence for people in Wales. The control of the budget, significant by European regional standards, is of course an opportunity for the Assembly to prove its capacity for creative and effective stewardship. Powers to appoint to public bodies should offer full encouragement for people from excluded groups to seek civic and professional positions.

While not transcending the conventions of British party politics, the Assembly has moved some way from the Welsh Office model of governing, in which a few ministers and selected civil servants looked more towards Westminster-driven policies and priorities. Notwithstanding its limited powers, the Assembly has become the focus for considerable aspiration about a national identity and future for Wales. Perhaps too much is expected, as we have seen from the studies reported above. There are many policy agendas, many constituencies, and many expectations have been raised. In all of these cases the Assembly's failure to deliver may engender a loss of legitimacy.

But if there are disappointments these will be experienced differently by citizens, groups and corporate bodies, and there will be different con- sequences for the fortunes of the Assembly. Local government, for example, has been invited into 'partnership' but might become more wary of an Assembly that begins to question its performance more closely and direct public expenditure more precisely. Such developments are already evident in some policy areas and could become more widespread and impact upon relations between the Assembly and its partners. While closer regulation may upset some public-sector partners, it is unlikely to become a citizen-based issue on a par with public concern about health, transport, education and jobs.

With so many organizations and individuals involved across Wales, the Assembly's relations with civic society via the voluntary sector have considerable significance. Those working in this sector could become valuable ambassadors for the good work of the Assembly, or its antagonists who share their disaffection over Assembly ambitions for closer collaboration that for some reason turned sour.

The biggest challenge that faces the Assembly lies in the construction of the institutional framework needed to promote investment, enterprise, business support, training and sustainable and balanced development across Wales. Making inroads on this enormous task will be a decisive measure of Assembly success for many Assembly watchers. Much will depend upon capacities and energies in the Assembly to connect with the critical networks of power in European and UK governments. This is reflected in the emerging research agenda which must place the evolving structures of Welsh governance within a wider comparative research framework.

Norris observes that 'constitutional settlements which seemed frozen suddenly break and reform', and that

> during the last decade, partly in response to perceived problems of public trust, Italy, New Zealand and Japan have adopted radical reforms of their electoral systems for parliament while Israel introduced direct elections for the executive. The UK opted for a radical set of constitutional initiatives including devolution for Scotland and Wales. (1999a: 270)

Within this shifting global picture the political map of Europe is being re-drawn as new countries join the EU. The fast-moving and ever-integrating Union of Europe assumes much significance for law, policy and economy. The English regions demand some realignment of the traditional UK distribution of public expenditure in favour of their pressing needs. This wider environment of threats and opportunities means that the Assembly, far from distancing itself from London, must remain close to Whitehall, Westminster and Brussels where Wales's UK and European membership is defined. In short, the Assembly must look outward as well as inward to Wales, and do so with some acumen and determination. In doing so its identity will not be forged in *Cymreictod*[2] alone but founded in the twenty-first-century politics of an enlarged Europe and pluralist Britain in which devolution will still be a process, and the Assembly as we know it now will be but a particular phase in the evolution of democratic government in Wales.

Notes

[1] 'Worthwhile, despite the flaws', *The Economist*, 26 July 1997, 15.
[2] 'Welshness'.

Bibliography

Age Concern (2000). 'The facts: an ageing population', *http://www.ace.org.uk*

Alexander, W. (2000). 'Women and the Scottish Parliament', in Coote 2000.

Alibhai-Brown, Y. (2000). 'Ain't I a woman? The need for a new dialogue about gender and diversity', in Coote 2000, 66.

Amin, A. (1999). 'An institutionalist perspective on regional economic development', *International Journal of Urban and Regional Research* 23 (2), 365–78.

Andrews, L. (1999). *Wales Says Yes: The Inside Story of the Yes for Wales Referendum Campaign*, Bridgend, Seren.

Anthias, F. and Yuval-Davies, N. (1993). *Racialised Boundaries*, London, Routledge.

Anwar, M. (1986). *Race and Politics*, London, Tavistock.

AWEMA (1999). 'Foreword', *AWEMA Newsletter 1999* 1, 1.

Axelrod, R. (1984). *The Evolution of Co-operation*, London, Penguin.

Ayres, I. and J. Braithwaite (1992). *Responsive Regulation*, Oxford, Oxford University Press.

Balsom, D. (2000a). 'Poll confirms emergence of new Welsh politics', *Agenda*, Winter, 35–6.

Balsom, D. (2000b). 'The referendum result', in Jones and Balsom 2000.

Barber, B. (1984). *Strong Democracy: Participatory Politics for a New Age*, Berkeley, University of California Press.

Barnes, M. (1999). *Building a Deliberative Democracy: An Evaluation of Two Citizens' Juries*, London, Institute for Public Policy Research.

Barrow, M. (1996). 'Public services and the theory of regulation', *Policy and Politics* 24, 263–76.

Barton, L. (1996). *Disability and Society*, Harlow, Longman.

Baynes, K. (2000). 'Deliberative democracy, the public sphere, and global democracy', in Wyn Jones, R. (ed.), *Critical Theory and World Politics*, Boulder, Co., Lynne Rienner Publishers.

Beetham, D. (1994). 'Key principles for a democratic audit', in D. Beetham (ed.), *Defining and Measuring Democracy*, London, Sage.

Bellin, I. (2000). 'Television and the referendum', in Jones and Balsom 2000.

Bennett, R. (2000). 'Postal ballots found to deliver higher turnout', *Financial Times*, 2 November.

Betts, C. (1999). 'All paths lead to Michael', *Western Mail*, 26 November.

Betts, C. (2000a). 'Independence fight unites speakers', *Western Mail*, 16 February, 8.

Betts, C. (2000b). 'Morgan calls for a written constitution', *Western Mail*, 9 March, 8.

Bevan, A. (1952), *In Place of Fear*, London, Heinemann.

Blair, T. (1996). *New Britain: My Vision of a Young Country*, London, Fourth Estate.

Blair, T. (1998). *The Third Way: New Politics for the New Century*, Fabian Pamphlet 588, London, The Fabian Society.

Blair, T. (2000a). 'Britishness', speech by the Prime Minister, London, 28 March, *http://www.labour.org.uk/*

Blair, T. (2000b). Speech by the Rt. Hon. Tony Blair MP, Prime Minister and leader of the Labour Party, to the Labour Party Local Government Conference, Blackpool, 4 February.

Blais, A. and S. Dion (eds.) (1992). *The Budget Maximizing Bureaucrat*, Pittsburgh, University of Pittsburgh Press.

Borland, J., R. Fevre and D. Denny (1992). 'Nationalism and community in north west Wales', *Sociological Review* 40, 49–72.

Bowerman, M. (1994). 'The National Audit Office and the Audit Commission: co-operation in areas where their VFM responsibilities interface', *Financial Accountability and Management* 10 (1), 47–63.

Boyne, G. A., J. Gould-Williams, J. Law and R. M. Walker (2000). *The Evaluation Study on Best Value in Wales, Final Report*, Cardiff, Business School, Cardiff University.

Bozeman, B. (1987) *All Organisations are Public*, San Francisco, Jossey-Bass.

Bradbury, J., L. Bennie, D. Denver and J. Mitchell (2000). 'Devolution, parties and the new politics: candidate selection for the 1999 National Assembly elections', *Contemporary Wales* 13, 159–81.

Bradbury, J., D. Denver, J. Mitchell and L. Bennie (2000). 'Devolution and party change: candidate selection for the Scottish Parliament and the Welsh Assembly elections', paper to the PSA Conference, 11 April, University of London.

Bristow, G. and N. Blewitt (1999). *Unravelling the Knot: The Interaction of UK Treasury and EU Funding for Wales*, Cardiff, Institute of Welsh Affairs.

Brown, A. (1998). 'Deepening democracy: women and the Scottish Parliament', *Regional and Federal Studies* 8 (1), 103–19.

Brown, A. (1999). 'Taking their place in the new house: women and the Scottish Parliament', *Scottish Affairs* 28, 44–50.

Brown, A., A. Jones and F. Mackay (1999). *The 'Representativeness' of Councillors*, York, Joseph Rowntree Foundation.

Bryan, J. and C. Jones (2000). *Wales in the Twenty-First Century: An Economic Future*, London, Macmillan.

Bryson, V. (1999). *Feminist Debates: Issues of Theory and Political Practice*, London, Macmillan.

Budge, I. (1996). *The New Challenge of Direct Democracy*, Cambridge, Polity Press.

Caines, Sir John et al. (1993). *Inquiry into the Findings of the Committee of Public Accounts Concerning the 1991/92 Accounts of the WDA*, London, House of Commons Library.

Campaign for a Welsh Assembly (1988). *Strategy Paper 1*, Cardiff, CWA.

Carter, H. (1999). 'Adladd yr wythdegau', *Barn* 442, 16–19.

Carter, N., P. Day and R. Klein (1992). *How Organisations Measure Success*, London, Routledge.

Chaney, P. and R. Fevre (2001a). 'Ron Davies and the cult of "inclusiveness": devolution and participation in Wales', *Contemporary Wales* 14 (forthcoming).

Chaney, P. and R. Fevre (2001b). 'Inclusive government for minority groups: the case of the third-sector in Wales', *Voluntas* 12 (2), forthcoming.

Chaney, P., T. Hall, and B. Dicks (2000). 'Inclusive governance? The case of "minority" and voluntary sector groups and the National Assembly for Wales', *Contemporary Wales* 13, 203–29.

Chwarae Teg (ed.) (1999). 'Women's entrepreneurship', paper presented to the National Assembly Economic Development Committee, 29 September, *http://www.wales.gov.uk*

Clements, L. and P. Thomas (1999). 'Human rights and the Welsh Assembly', *Planet* 234, 23–8.

Coleman, J. S. (1988). 'Social capital and the creation of human capital', *American Journal of Sociology* 94, S95–S120.

Coleman, J. S. (1990). *The Foundations of Social Theory*, Cambridge, Mass., Harvard University Press.

Commission for Racial Equality Wales (2000). *Commission for Racial Equality Wales Annual Report*, Cardiff, Commission for Racial Equality.

Conservative Central Office for Wales (1992). *Conservative Manifesto for Wales*, Cardiff, CCOfW.

Cooke, P. and K. Morgan (1998). *The Associational Economy: Firms, Regions and Innovation*, Oxford, Oxford University Press.

Coote, A. (ed.) (2000). *New Gender Agenda*, London, Institute of Public Policy Research.

Coote, A. and J. Lenaghan (1997). *Citizen Juries: Theory into Practice*, London, Institute for Public Policy Research.

Council of Welsh Districts (1995). *Quangos in Wales*, Cardiff, CWD.

Crossman, R. (1976). *The Diaries of a Cabinet Minister*, London, Cape.

Davies, D. J. (1949). *Towards an Economic Democracy*, Cardiff, Plaid Cymru.

Davies, G. P. (2000). *Y Cynulliad Cenedlaethol: Blwyddyn o Osod Sylfeini*, Darlith Gyfreithiol Eisteddfod Genedlaethol Cymru, Llanelli, Caerdydd, Cymdeithas y Cyfreithwyr.

Davies R. (1992). 'Regeneration of the Valleys', speech by Ron Davies MP, shadow secretary of state for Wales, Treorchy, November 1992, reproduced in Parliament for Wales Campaign (1994), 10.

Davies, R. (1995). 'Shaping the vision', *Red Kite* (June), 14–17.

Davies, R. (1996). 'The economic case for a Welsh Assembly', *Welsh Democracy Review* 2, 6–7.

Davies, R. (1999a). *Devolution: A Process not an Event*, Gregynog Papers 2 (2), Cardiff, Institute of Welsh Affairs.

Davies, R. (1999b). 'Preface', in Taylor and Thomson 1999.

Davies, R. (2000a). 'We need a coalition of ideas', *Agenda*, Winter, 27–31.

Davies, R. (2000b). *In Search of Attitude*, paper circulated to the media on 4 December.

Day, G. (1998). 'A community of communities? Similarity and difference in Welsh rural community studies', *The Economic and Social Review* 29, 233–57.

Day, G., M. Fitton and M. Minhinnick (1998). 'Finding our voices', in J. Osmond (ed.), *The National Assembly Agenda*, Cardiff, Institute of Welsh Affairs.

Day, G., M. Fitton and M. Minhinnick (1999). *Finding our Voices: The Role of Local Participatory Democracy in the Governance of Wales*, Porthcawl, Sustainable Wales.

Day, G. and A. Thompson (1999). 'The politics of inclusion? National and ethnic repercussions of devolution and communal integration in Wales', unpublished paper presented to the Conference on Nationalism, Identity and Minority Rights, University of Bristol, September.

Day, P. and R. Klein (1987). *Accountabilities*, London, Tavistock.

Delanty, G. (1996). 'Beyond the nation state: national identity and citizenship in a multicultural society – a response to Rex', *Sociological Research Online* 1 (3), *http://www/socresonline.org.uk/socresonline/1/3/1.html*

Disability Rights Commission (2000). DRC Disability Briefing, August, Manchester, DRC, *http://www.drc-gb.org*

Disability Wales (1999a). *Disability Wales News* (Winter), 12.

Disability Wales (1999b). 'Economic development', *Disability Wales News* 33, 15.

Disability Wales (1999c). 'Industrial and economic development', paper presented to the National Assembly Economic Development Committee, 29 September, *http:www.wales.gov.uk*

Downs, A. (1967). *Inside Bureaucracy*, Boston, Little Brown.

Downs, G. and P. Larkey (1986). *The Search for Government Efficiency*, Philadelphia, Temple University Press.

Dunlop, A. (1993). 'United front? Anti-racist political mobilisation in Scotland', *Scottish Affairs* 3, 89–101.

Eisner, M. (1993). 'Bureaucratic professionalisation and the limits of the political control thesis: the case of the Federal Trade Commission', *Governance* 6, 127–53.

Elis Thomas, D. (2000). Dafydd Elis Thomas interview with Bethan Rhys Roberts, *The Point*, 15 June, BBC Wales, Cardiff.

Elis Thomas, D. (1999), quoted in 'A vision for Wales and for the National Assembly/Gweledigaeth i Gymru ac i'r Cynulliad Cenedlaethol', *Dialogues on Wales's Role* – Series Pamphlet, no attributed author, p. 1.

EOC (1998). *Facts About Women and Men in Great Britain*, Manchester, Equal Opportunities Commission.

ETAG (2000). *An Education And Training Action Plan for Wales: The Education and Training Action Group for Wales*, ETAG, Cardiff.

European Commission (1991). *Ex-Ante Evaluation of Community Support Programmes and Dependent Programmes for the Objective 2 Areas of South Wales and Bremen*, Brussels, European Commission.

Evans, D., and D. Trystan (1999). 'Why was 1997 different?', in Taylor and Thomson 1999, 95–117.

Evans, N. (1991). 'Internal colonialism? Colonization, economic development and political mobilization in Wales, Scotland and Ireland', in G. Day and G. Rees (eds.), *Regions, Nations and European Integration*, Cardiff, University of Wales Press.

Exworthy, M. and S. Halford (eds.) (1999). *Professionals and the New Managerialism in the Public Sector*, Buckingham, Open University Press.

Fahm, T. (1998). 'Remember the minorities', letters to the Editor, *Western Mail*, 16 February.

Farmer, K. and Y. Farmer (1999). 'Working with the Assembly', *Coalition News*, 9 December (Cardiff and the Vale Coalition of Disabled People).

Federation of Small Businesses (2000). *Barriers to Growth and Survival*, Cardiff, FSB.

Feld, V. (1999). 'Assembly must be given time to succeed', *Western Mail*, 16 November, 10.

Feld, V. (2000). 'A new start in Wales: how devolution is making a difference', in Coote 2000.

Femia, J. V. (1993). *Marxism and Democracy*, Oxford, Clarendon Press.

Fevre, R., J. Borland and D. Denny (1997). 'Welsh nationalism and Weberian theory', paper presented to the Annual Conference of the American Sociological Association, Toronto, Canada.

Finger, M. and S. Brand (1999). 'The concept of the "learning organization" applied to the transformation of the public sector: conceptual contributions for theory development', in M. Easterby-Smith, J. Burgoyne and L. Araujo (eds.), *Organizational Learning and the Learning Organization*, London, Sage.

Flegmann, V. (1986). *Public Expenditure and the Select Committees of the House of Commons*, Aldershot, Gower.

Flynn, P. (1999). *Dragons Led by Poodles: The Inside Story of a New Labour Stitch-up*, London, Politico Books.

Fryer, P. (1984). *Staying Power: The History of Black People in Britain*, London, Macmillan.

Fukuyama, F. (1996). *Trust: The Social Virtues and the Creation of Prosperity*, London, Penguin.

Gallent, N., R. Jones and C. Allen (1998). 'Local concerns and regional devolution: observations from Wales', *Regional Studies* 32, 181–6.

Gargarella, R. (1998). 'Full representation, deliberation and impartiality', in J. Elster (ed.), *Deliberative Democracy*, Cambridge, Cambridge University Press.

Garmise, S. and G. Rees (1997). 'The role of institutional networks in local economic development: a new model of governance?', *Local Economy* 12 (2), 104–18.

Gay, O. (1996). *The Quango Debate*, Research Paper 96/72, London, House of Commons Library.

Gellner, E. (1994). *Conditions of Liberty: Civil Society and its Rivals*, London, Hamish Hamilton.

Giddens, A. (1998). *The Third Way: The Renewal of Social Democracy*, Cambridge, Polity Press.

Gill, B. and A. Tarkowski (2000). *Winning Women: Lessons from Scotland and Wales*, London, Fawcett Society Research Paper.

Gilroy, P. (1987). *There Ain't No Black in the Union Jack*, London, Hutchinson.

Graber, D. A. (1992). 'Public sector communication: how organisations manage information', *Congressional Quarterly*.

Granovetter, M. (1985). 'Economic action and social structure: the problem of embeddedness', *American Journal of Sociology* 91, 481–510.

Great Britain (1991). *The Structure of Local Government in Wales: A Consultation Paper*, London, HMSO.

Great Britain (1998). *Government of Wales Act*, London, HMSO.

Gruber, J. (1988). *Controlling Bureaucracies*, Berkeley, University of California Press.

Grunig, J. E. and T. Hunt (1984). *Managing Public Relations*, Texas, Harcourt-Brace.

Habermas, J. (1994). 'Citizenship and national identity', in B. van Steenbergen (ed.), *The Condition of Citizenship*, London, Sage.

Hahn, H. (1986). 'Public support for rehabilitation programs: the analysis of US disability policy', *Disability, Handicap and Society* 21 (4), 740–51.

Hain, P. (1999). *A Welsh Third Way?*, London, Tribune Publications.

Hall, P. A. (1999). 'Social capital in Britain', *British Journal of Political Science* 29, 417–61.

Hann, C. and E. Dunn (eds.) (1996). *Civil Society: Challenging Western Models*, London, Routledge.

Hanson, D. (1995). *Unelected, Unaccountable and Untenable: A Study of Appointments to Public Bodies in Wales*, Cardiff, Welsh Labour Party.

Harris, S. (1999). 'Independent living', *Coalition News*, December (Cardiff and the Vale Coalition of Disabled People), 7.

Hassan, G. (1999). 'The changing debate in Scotland: devolution, home rule and self-government', *Soundings* 12 (Summer), 49–65.

Heath, A. (1999). 'Were the Welsh and Scottish referendums second-order elections?', in Taylor and Thomson 1999, 149–68.

Heclo, H and A. Wildavsky (1974). *The Private Government of Public Money*, London, Macmillan.

Hirschman, A. (1970). *Exit, Voice and Loyalty*, Cambridge, Mass., Harvard University Press.

Hirst, P. (1994). 'Associative democracy', *Dissent* (Spring), 241–7.

Hirst, P. and A. Barnett (1993). 'Introduction', in A. Barnett, C. Ellis, and P. Hirst (eds.), *Debating the Constitution: New Perspectives on Constitutional Reform*, Cambridge, Polity Press.

Hofstede, G. (1981). 'Management control of public and not-for-profit activities', *Accounting, Organisation and Society* 6, 193–211.

Hoggett, P. (1996). 'New modes of control in the public sector', *Public Administration* 74, 9–32.

Hood, C. and C. Scott (1996). 'Bureaucratic regulation and new public management in the United Kingdom: mirror-image developments?', *Journal of Law and Society* 23, 321–45.

Hood, C., G. James, G. Jones, C. Scott and T. Travers (1998). *Regulation Inside Government: Waste Watchers Quality Police and Sleaze-Busters*, Oxford, Oxford University Press.

Hornung, R. (2001). 'Scotland leaves Wales standing', *Western Mail*, 27 January.

Huggins, R., K. Morgan and G. Rees (2000). 'Devolution and development: the Welsh Assembly and the governance of economic development', Welsh Governance Centre Working Paper 1, Cardiff, Welsh Governance Centre, Cardiff University.

Hunt, R. C. (1984). *The Shape of Voluntary Action in Wales*, Caerphilly, Welsh Council for Voluntary Action.

Hurd, D. (1988). 'Citizenship in the Tory democracy', *New Statesman* 115, 14.

Hutt, J. (1999). Speech to the Disability Wales annual conference, 23 October, Port Talbot.

Hutt, J. and P. Bryant (1998). 'The voluntary sector', in J. Osmond (ed.), *The National Assembly Agenda*, Cardiff, Institute of Welsh Affairs.

ICM/*Scotsman* (2000). 'Wales devolution poll', March, *http://www.icmresearch.co.uk*

Industrial Committee of the South Wales Socialist Society (1919). *Industrial Democracy for Miners: A Plan for the Democratic Control of the Mining Industry*, Porth, South Wales Socialist Society.

International Parliamentary Union (2000). *International Classification of Parliaments, http://www.ipu.org/wmn-e/classif.htm*

Jackson, P. M. (1982). *The Political Economy of Bureaucracy*, Oxford, Phillip Allan.

James, M., and G. Mathias (1999). 'Coping with the fixed term', *Agenda*, Winter, 32–3.

John, H. (1998). 'The Welsh labour market: equal opportunities imperatives', in Chwarae Teg (ed.), *Integrating Equal Opportunities in the Structural Funds*, Cardiff, Chwarae Teg.

John, H. (1999a). 'Democratic renewal', *Disability Wales News* 30, 15–16.

John, H. (1999b). 'What the parties promised', *Disability Wales News* 31, 9–11.

Johnson, N. (1999). *Mixed Economies of Welfare*, Hemel Hempstead, Prentice-Hall Europe.

Jones, J. B. (2000a). 'Changes to the government of Wales 1979–1997', in Jones and Balsom 2000.

Jones, J. B. (2000b). 'Labour pains', in Jones and Balsom 2000, 194–212.

Jones, J. B. (2000c). 'Post-referendum politics', in Jones and Balsom 2000.

Jones, J. B. and D. Balsom (eds.) (2000). *The Road to the National Assembly for Wales*, Cardiff, University of Wales Press.

Jowell, R. and A. Park (1997). *Young People, Politics and Citizenship: A Disengaged Generation?* Report for a colloquium on the values, attitudes and behaviour of young people in the 1990s, London, Citizenship Foundation.

Keane, J. (1998). *Civil Society: Old Images, New Visions*, Cambridge, Polity Press.

Kearns, A. (1995). 'Active citizenship and local governance: political and geographical dimensions', *Political Geography* 14 (2), 155–75.

Kelly, S. and C. Rodden (1998). *From Watchdog to Guidedog? The Evolving Role of the Accounts Commission for Scotland*, Glasgow, Caledonian University.

Kendall, J. and M. Knapp (1996). *The Voluntary Sector in the UK*, Manchester, Manchester University Press.

Klingemann, H. D. (1999). 'Mapping political support in the 1990s: a global analysis', in P. Norris (ed.), *Critical Citizens*, Oxford, Oxford University Press.

Kymlicka, W. (1995). *Multicultural Citizenship*, Oxford, Clarendon Press.

Law, J. (1999). 'Accountabilities', in A. Rose and A. Lawton (eds), *Public Services Management*, London, Prentice Hall.

Lazare, D. (1998). 'America the undemocratic', *New Left Review* 232 (November–December), 3–40.

Lazare, D. (1999). 'The grand illusion of democratic nationalism: a reply to Michael Lind', *New Left Review* 235 (May–June), 135–52.

Lesly, P. (ed.) (1998). *Lesly's Handbook of Public Relations and Communications*, 5th edn, Illinois, NTC Business Books.

Levitas, R. (1998). *The Inclusive Society?*, Basingstoke, Macmillan.

Lind, M. (1999). 'Why there will be no revolution in the US: a reply to Daniel Lazare', *New Left Review* 233 (January–February), 97–117.

Luhmann, N. (1979). *Trust and Power*, Chichester, Wiley.

Lundvall, B.-A. and B. Johnson (1994). 'The learning economy', *Journal of Industry Studies* 1, 23–42.

McAllister, L. (1998). 'The Welsh devolution referendum: definitely maybe?', *Parliamentary Affairs* 51 (3), 149–65.

McCrudden, C. (1996). 'Mainstreaming fairness? A discussion paper on policy appraisal and fair treatment', Belfast, Committee on the Administration of Justice.

McGarvey, N. and A. Midwinter (2000). 'Scotland in transition: devolution, governance and accountability', Strathclyde, University Working Paper.

McPherson, A. and C. Raab (1988). *Governing Education: A Sociology of Policy since 1945*, Edinburgh, Edinburgh University Press.

Mansbridge, J. (1992). 'A deliberative perspective on neo-corporatism', *Politics and Society* 20 (4), 493–505.

Mansbridge, J. (1999). 'Should blacks represent blacks and women represent women? A contingent "Yes"', *Journal of Politics* 61 (3), 628–57.

Maskell, P., H. Eskelinen, I. Hannibalsson, A. Malmberg and E. Vatne (1998). *Competitiveness, Localised Learning and Regional Development*, London, Routledge.

MENCAP in Wales and SCOVO (1999). *Our Questions for National Assembly Candidates*, Cardiff, MENCAP in Wales/SCOVO.

Michael, A. (1999). Private letter to Roger Jones, Chairman of the Institute of Directors, Wales, 10 January.

Michael, A. (2000). *Questions to the First Secretary: Young People in Wales (Citizenship)*, answers to questions not reached in Plenary, 1 February, Cardiff, National Assembly for Wales.

Miles, R. and A. Dunlop (1986). 'The racialisation of politics in Britain: why Scotland is different', *Patterns of Prejudice* 20 (1), 23–33.

MIND Cymru (1999). *The MIND Cymru Manifesto*, Cardiff, MIND Cymru.

Morgan, G. (1990). *Organizations in Society*, London, Macmillan.

Morgan, K. (1994). 'Beyond the quangos: redressing the democratic deficit', *Welsh Agenda* 1 (1), 12–20.

Morgan, K. (1997). 'The regional animateur: taking stock of the Welsh Development Agency', *Regional and Federal Studies* 7 (2), 70–94.

Morgan, K. (1999a). 'Criticism vital for Assembly', letters to the Editor, *Western Mail*, 25 November, 12.

Morgan, K. (1999b). 'Towards democratic devolution: the challenge of the Welsh Assembly', *Transactions of the Honourable Society of Cymmrodorion 1998*, n.s. 5, 182–202.

Morgan, K. (2000). 'The developmental dilemmas of democratic devolution', *Town and Country Planning* 69 (5), 170–1.

Morgan, K. (2001a). 'A Europe of the regions? The multi-level polity and subsidiarity in the European Union', Report on Wilton Park Conference 617, Wilton Park, Sussex.

Morgan, K. (2001b). 'The new territorial politics: rivalry and justice in post-devolution Britain', *Regional Studies* 35.

Morgan K. and G. Mungham (2000). *Redesigning Democracy: The Making of the Welsh Assembly*, Bridgend, Seren.

Morgan, K. and C. Nauwelaers (eds.) (1999). *Regional Innovation Strategies: The Challenge for Less Favoured Regions*, Norwich, The Stationery Office.

Morgan, K. and G. Rees (1994). *Vocational Skills and Economic Development: Report to the Welsh Development Agency*, Cardiff, WDA.

Morgan, K., G. Rees and S. Garmise (1999). 'Networking for economic development', in G. Stoker (ed.), *The New Management of British Local Governance*, London, Macmillan.

Morgan, K. and E. Roberts (1993). *The Democratic Deficit: A Guide to Quangoland*, Papers in Planning and Research 144, Cardiff, Cardiff University Department of City and Regional Planning.

Morgan, K. O. (1970). *Wales in British Politics*, Cardiff, University of Wales Press.

Morgan, K. O. (1999). 'Welsh devolution: the past and the future', in Taylor and Thomson 1999.

Morgan, R. (2000a). Speech by the Rt. Hon. Rhodri Morgan AM, MP, leader of the Wales Labour Party, First Secretary, to Wales Labour Party Annual Conference, 25 March.

Morgan, R. (2000b). Statement on the review of Assembly procedures, National Assembly for Wales (The Record), Wednesday 12 July, Cardiff, NAW.

Morgan, R. (2000c). *Variable Geometry UK*, Cardiff, Institute of Welsh Affairs.

Morris, J. et al. (1999). Private letter to Alun Michael on post-sixteen education and training, 21 December.

Mouffe, C. (1998). 'The radical centre: a politics without an adversary', *Soundings* 9, 11–23.

Murphy, P. (1999). Speech by Rt. Hon. Paul Murphy MP, Secretary of State for Wales, Bournemouth, Wednesday 29 September, *http://www.waleslabourparty. org.uk*

Murphy, P. (2000). 'People first: the real test for Wales and new objectives, new partnerships, Wales, Britain and Europe', speech by the Rt. Hon Paul Murphy, Secretary of State for Wales, Swansea, Monday, 24 January.

Nagel, K. J. (1999). 'The "Europe of the Regions" and identity politics of nations without states', paper presented to the International Conference of the Regional Studies Association, University of the Basque Country, Bilbao, 18–21 September.

National Assembly Advisory Group (1998a). *National Assembly for Wales: Have Your Say in How it will Work* (consultation paper), Cardiff, Welsh Office.

National Assembly Advisory Group (1998b). *Recommendations of the National Assembly Advisory Group*, Cardiff, National Assembly Advisory Group.

National Assembly for Wales (1999–2000). Minutes of the Committee on Equality of Opportunity, Cardiff, National Assembly for Wales.

National Assembly for Wales (1999a). *The Approach to Equal Opportunities*, paper by the chair of the Committee on Equality of Opportunity, 22 July, Cardiff, National Assembly for Wales.

National Assembly for Wales (1999b). Briefing paper for the NAW Health and Social Services Committee, 24 November, on the National Carers Strategy for Wales, Cardiff, National Assembly for Wales.

National Assembly for Wales (1999c). *National Assembly for Wales: Standing Orders*, Cardiff, National Assembly for Wales.

National Assembly for Wales (1999d). 'National housing strategy for Wales', draft framework document, Cardiff, National Assembly for Wales.

National Assembly for Wales (1999e). 'Partnership with business', official report, 18 October, Cardiff, National Assembly for Wales.

National Assembly for Wales (1999f) Audit Committee Record of Proceedigns, 18 November 1999, Cardiff, National Assembly for Wales.

National Assembly for Wales (2000a). *A Better Wales*, Cardiff, National Assembly for Wales.

National Assembly for Wales (2000b). Committee on Equality of Opportunity: draft annual report, discussed in committee, Thursday, 25 May, Cardiff, National Assembly for Wales.

National Assembly for Wales (2000c). 'Equality Audit: equal opportunities baseline survey', 13 April, Cardiff, National Assembly for Wales.

National Assembly for Wales (2000d). 'Equality in education', paper for Pre-16 Education, Schools and Early Learning Committee, September 2000, Cardiff, National Assembly for Wales.

National Assembly for Wales (2000e). 'Equality in the public sector', Committee on Equality of Opportunity, May 2000, Cardiff, National Assembly for Wales.

National Assembly for Wales (2000f). *European Structural Funds Programme (Objective One) for West Wales and the Valleys*, Cardiff, National Assembly for Wales.

National Assembly for Wales (2000g). *The National Assembly for Wales: Arrangements to Promote Equality of Opportunity 1999–2000*, Annual Report 2000, Committee of Equality of Opportunity, Cardiff, National Assembly for Wales.

National Assembly for Wales (2000h). 'National Assembly "diversity"recruitment fair attracts big turnout', National Assembly for Wales. press release, 11 April, Cardiff, National Assembly for Wales.

National Assembly for Wales (2000i). 'National Assembly for Wales: plenary motions agreed between 1/5/99 and 20/4/00', Cardiff, National Assembly for Wales.; Edwina Hart launches final version of *A Better Wales*, press release, May 2000, Cardiff, National Assembly for Wales.

National Assembly for Wales (2000j). *The National Assembly for Wales Voluntary Sector Scheme*, Cardiff, National Assembly for Wales.

National Assembly for Wales (2000k). *National Housing Strategy Task Group 4 – Ensuring Decent Housing for All – Meeting the Needs of Vulnerable Households: Final Report to the National Assembly of Wales*, Cardiff, National Assembly for Wales.

National Assembly for Wales (2000l). *Objective One Single Programming Document: The Economic and Social Regeneration of West Wales and the Valleys*, Cardiff, National Assembly for Wales.

National Assembly for Wales (2000m). *Promoting Equality in Wales: Project Development Fund*, Cardiff, National Assembly for Wales.

National Assembly for Wales (2000n). *Review of Business Support and Development Services*, Cardiff, National Assembly for Wales.

National Assembly for Wales (2000p). 'Staff and other resources: the Equality Policy Unit', paper presented to the Committee on Equality of Opportunity, 3 April, Cardiff, National Assembly for Wales.

National Assembly for Wales (2000q). *Statistical Brief*, 15 December, Cardiff, National Assembly for Wales.

National Assembly for Wales. (2000r). 'Strategic priorities, Post-16 Education and Training Committee Papers', 12 July 2000, Cardiff, National Assembly for Wales.

National Assembly for Wales (2000s). *Teachers' Guide: National Assembly for Wales Workpack,* July 2000, Cardiff, National Assembly for Wales.

National Assembly for Wales. (2000t). Text of letter from Assembly Secretary for Education and Children to chair of Committee on Equality of Opportunity, Committee on Equality of Opportunity Papers, Thursday, 23 March, Cardiff, National Assembly for Wales.

National Assembly for Wales (2000u). *Audit Committee Report on National Museums and Galleries of Wales 1998/1999,* Cardiff, National Assembly for Wales.

National Assembly for Wales (2000v). Audit Committee evidence session, 11 May, Cardiff, National Assembly for Wales.

National Assembly for Wales (2001). *Audit Committee Annual Report 1999/2000,* Cardiff, National Assembly for Wales.

National Assembly for Wales Review Secretariat (2000/2001). National Assembly review of procedure, minutes of the first meeting, 6 December 2000; Minutes of the second meeting, 17 January 2001.

National Audit Office (1999). 'The audit of local authorities and local authority sponsored bodies in Wales', memorandum by Auditor-General for Wales, September, Cardiff, National Audit Office.

Nicolass, G., K. Thomson and P. Lynn (2000). *The Feasibility of Conducting Electoral Surveys in the UK by Telephone,* London, National Centre for Social Research.

Norris, P. (1999a). 'Conclusions', in P. Norris (ed.), *Critical Citizens,* Oxford, Oxford University Press.

Norris, P. (1999b). 'Institutional explanations for political support', in P. Norris (ed.), *Critical Citizens,* Oxford, Oxford University Press.

Norris, P. and J. Lovenduski (1995). *Political Recruitment: Gender, Race and Class in the British Parliament,* Cambridge, Cambridge University Press.

Nyoni, M. (2000). *From the Margins to the Centre: Assessing the Need for a Black and Minority Ethnic Housing Strategy in Wales,* Cardiff, National Assembly for Wales.

O'Dempsey, D. and A. Short (1996). *Disability Discrimination: The Law and Practice,* London, FT Law and Tax Publishing.

OECD (2001). *Cities and Regions in the New Learning Economy,* Paris: OECD.

Office of National Statistics (1996). *Social Focus on Ethnic Minorities,* Titchfield, Office of National Statistics.

Office of Population Census and Surveys (1992). *1991 Census County Reports, Parts One and Two,* Titchfield, OPCS.

Osmond, J. (1998). 'Introduction', in J. Osmond (ed.), *The National Assembly Agenda,* Cardiff, Institute of Welsh Affairs.

Osmond, J. (1999a). *Adrift but Afloat: The Civil Service and the National Assembly,* Cardiff, Institute of Welsh Affairs.

Osmond, J. (1999b). *Devolution: 'A Dynamic Settled Process'? Monitoring the National Assembly July–December 1999,* Cardiff, Institute of Welsh Affairs.

Osmond, J. (2000a). *Devolution in Transition: Monitoring the National Assembly February to May 2000,* Cardiff, Institute of Welsh Affairs.

Osmond, J. (2000b). *Devolution Relaunched: Monitoring the National Assembly December 1999 to March 2000*, Cardiff, Institute of Welsh Affairs.

Parekh, M. (2000). *The Future of Multi-Ethnic Britain*, Commission for the Future of Multi-Ethnic Britain, London, Profile Books.

Park, A. (2000). 'The generation game', in R. Jowell, J. Curtice, A. Park, K. Thomson, L. Jarvis, C. Bromley and N. Stratford (eds.), *British Social Attitudes: Focusing on Diversity, The 17th report: 2000–1 Edition*, London, Sage.

Parliament for Wales Campaign (1994). *Empowering the People: Response to the Labour Party's Consultation Paper 'Shaping the Vision – The Powers and Structure of the Welsh Assembly'*, Cardiff, PWC.

Pateman, C. (1970). *Participation and Democratic Theory*, Cambridge, Cambridge University Press.

Paterson, L. and R. Wyn Jones (1999). 'Does civil society drive constitutional change? The cases of Wales and Scotland', in Taylor and Thomson 1999, 169–97.

Pfeffer, J. and G. Salancik (1978). *The External Control of Organisations*, New York, Harper & Row.

Phillips, A. (1995). *The Politics of Presence*, Cambridge, Polity Press.

Phillips, A. (2000). 'Representing the difference: why should it matter if women get elected?', in Coote 2000, 58–66.

Piore, M. (1995). *Beyond Individualism*, Cambridge, Mass., Harvard University Press.

Pollit, C. and H. Summa (1997). 'Reflexive watchdogs? How supreme audit institutions account for themselves', *Public Administration* 75, 313–36.

Pollitt, C., X. Giries, J. Lonsdale, R. Mul, H. Summa and M. Waerness (1999). *Performance or Compliance? Performance Audit and Public Management in Five Countries*, Oxford, Oxford University Press.

Power, M. (1994). *The Audit Society*, Oxford, Oxford University Press.

Power, M. (1997). *The Audit Society*, Oxford, Oxford University Press.

Prys Jones, H. (1997). 'Dathlu o'r diwedd', *Golwg* 10 (4), 3.

Public Accounts Committee (1993). *WDA Accounts 1991/92*, House of Commons, London, HMSO.

Putnam, R., with R. Leonardi and R. Y. Nanetti (1993). *Making Democracy Work: Civic Traditions in Modern Italy*, Princeton, NJ, Princeton University Press.

Pyper, R. (1999). 'The civil service: a neglected dimension of devolution', *Public Money and Management*, April–June, 45–9.

Ramcharan, P., G. Roberts, G. Grant and J. Borland (1997). *Empowerment in Everyday Life*, London and Bristol, Jessica Kingsley.

Rawlings, R. (1998). 'The new model Wales', *Journal of Law and Society* 25 (4), 461–509.

Rawlings, R. (2000). 'Assembly subordinate legislation', in Osmond 2000b.

Rees, G. (1997). 'The politics of regional development strategy: the programme for the Valleys', in H. Thomas and R. MacDonald (eds.), *Nationality and Planning*, Cardiff, University of Wales Press.

Rees, G. and Thomas, M. (1994). 'Inward investment, labour market change and skills development: recent experience from south Wales', *Local Economy* 9, 48–61.

Rees, I. B. (1999). 'Cynulliad Cenedlaethol: "plus ça change" ynteu cychwyn proses', *Contemporary Wales* 12, 107–29.

Rees, T. (1999). *Women and Work: Twenty Five Years of Gender Equality in Wales,* Cardiff, University of Wales Press.

Rees, T. (2000). 'Teresa Rees, head to head interview', BBC Radio Wales, 19 March.

Rex, J. (1996). 'National identity in the democratic multi-cultural state', *Sociological Research Online* 1 (2), *http://www.socresonline.org.uk/socresonline/1/2/1.html.*

Rhodes, R. (1988). *Beyond Westminster and Whitehall,* London, Unwin Hyman.

Rhodes, R. (1997). *Understanding Governance,* Buckingham, Open University Press.

Rhodes, R. A. W. (1999). 'New Labour's civil service: summing up joining up', *Political Quarterly* 71 (2), 151–66.

Rico, A., P. González and M. Fraile (1999). 'Regional decentralisation of health policy in Spain: social capital does not tell the whole story', in P. Heywood (ed.), *Politics and Policy in Democratic Spain,* London, Frank Cass.

Ridley, F. and D. Wilson (1995). *The Quango Debate,* Oxford, Oxford University/ Hansard Society for Parliamentary Government.

RNIB Cymru (1999). *RNIB Cymru's National Assembly Manifesto,* Cardiff, Royal National Institute for the Blind Cymru.

Robinson, V. (1987). 'Race, space and place: the geographic study of UK ethnic relations 1957–1987', *New Community* 14 (1/2), 186–97.

Rousseau, Jean-Jacques (1968). *The Social Contract,* translated and introduced by Maurice Cranston, London, Penguin.

Sabel, C. (1994). 'Learning by monitoring: the institutions of economic development', in N. Smelser and R. Swedberg (eds.), *Handbook of Economic Sociology,* Princeton, Princeton University Press.

Sanderson, I. (1999). 'Participation and democratic renewal: from "instrumental" to "communicative rationality"?', *Policy and Politics* 27 (3), 325–41.

Scheuerman, W. E. (1994). *Between the Norm and the Exception: The Frankfurt School and the Rule of Law,* Cambridge, Mass., MIT Press.

Secretary of State for Wales (1997). *A Voice for Wales,* Cardiff: HMSO.

Seligman, A. B. (1997). *The Problem of Trust,* Princeton, Princeton University Press.

Sherlock, A. (2000). 'Born free, but everywhere in chains? A legal analysis of the first year of the National Assembly for Wales', *Cambrian Law Review* 31, 61–72.

Shipton, M. (1999). 'Yes Minister, leave it to me', *Wales on Sunday,* 5 September.

Silk, P. (1998). 'The Assembly as a legislature', in J. Osmond (ed.), *The National Assembly Agenda,* Cardiff, Institute of Welsh Affairs.

Skelcher, C. (1998). 'Reforming the quangos', *Political Quarterly* 69 (1), 41–7.

Skinner, Q. (1989). 'Language and political change', in T. Ball, J. Farr and R. L. Hanson (eds.), *Political Innovation and Conceptual Change,* Cambridge, Cambridge University Press.

Sparrow, A. (1995). 'Day of the quango over if Labour wins', *Western Mail,* 12 May.

Spicer, C. (1997). *Organizational Public Relations: A Political Perspective,* New Jersey, NJ, Lawrence Erlbaum Associates.

Squires, J. (1999). 'Rethinking the boundaries of political representation', in S. Walby (ed.), *New Agendas for Women,* London, Macmillan.

Stephenson, M. (1996). *Winning Women's Votes: The Gender Gap in Voting Patterns and Priorities,* London, Fawcett Society.

Stone, B. (1995). 'Administrative accountability in the Westminster democracies: towards a new conceptual framework', *Governance* 8, 505–26.

Task and Finish Group (2000). *Report of the Objective One Task and Finish Group*, Cardiff, National Assembly for Wales.

Taylor, B. and K. Thomson (eds.) (1999). *Scotland and Wales: Nations Again?* Cardiff, University of Wales Press.

Tester, K. (1992). *Civil Society*, London, Routledge.

Thomas, P. G. (1998). 'The changing nature of accountability', in B. Peters and D. Savoie (eds.), *Taking Stock: Assessing Public Sector Reforms*, Montreal, McGill-Queens University Press.

Tonkiss, F. and A. Passey (1999). 'Trust, confidence and voluntary organizations: between values and institutions', *Sociology* 33, 257–74.

Unofficial Reform Committee (1912). *The Miners' Next Step: Being a Suggested Scheme for the Reorganisation of the Federation*, Porth, Unofficial Reform Committee.

Vertovec, S. (1996). 'Multiculturalism, culturalism and public incorporation', *Ethnic and Racial Studies* 19 (1), 49–69.

Vertovec, S. (1999). 'Minority associations, networks and public policies: re-assessing relationships', *Journal of Ethnic and Migration Studies* 25 (1), 21–42.

Wales Council for the Blind (1999). *To Political Parties in Wales and National Assembly Candidates: Visually Impaired People and the National Assembly of Wales* (sic), Cardiff, WCB.

Wales Council for Voluntary Action (1998). *Annual Report: 1997–1998*, Caerphilly, WCVA.

Wales Council for Voluntary Action (1999). *Wales Voluntary Sector Almanac 1999: Key Facts and Figures*. Caerphilly, WCVA.

Wales Labour Party (1992). *Opportunity Wales*, Cardiff, WLP.

Wales Labour Party (1993). *Wales Labour Party Policy Commission's Interim Reports – A Welsh Assembly: The Way Forward*, Cardiff, WLP.

Wales Labour Party (1994). *Shaping the Vision: A Consultation Paper on the Powers and Structure of the Welsh Assembly*, Cardiff, WLP.

Wales Labour Party (1996). *Preparing for a New Wales: A Report on the Structure and Workings of the Welsh Assembly – WLP Conference 10th and 11th May 1996*, Cardiff, WLP.

Wales Labour Party (2000). 'Report of the Wales Labour Party election debrief team', *Wales Labour Party Centenary Conference Report*, Cardiff, WLP, 26–30.

Wales Office (2000) *The Government's Expenditure Plans 2000–01 to 2001–02*, London, HMSO.

Wales Women's National Coalition (1999). *Priorities for Further Action in Wales*, Cardiff, WWNC.

Waterhouse, R. (2000) *Lost in Care: Report of the Tribunal Inquiry into the Abuse of Children in Care in the former County Council Areas of Gwynedd and Clwyd since 1974*, London, HMSO.

Weinreich, P. (1998). 'Social exclusion and multiple identities', *Soundings* 9, 139–44.

Weir, S. and D. Beetham (1999). *Political Power and Democratic Control in Britain*, London, Routledge.

Welsh Affairs Committee (1995). *Wales in Europe*, House of Commons, London, HMSO.

Welsh Affairs Committee (2000). *The Work of the Committee Since Devolution*, London, HMSO.

Welsh Development Agency (2000). *Promoting Prosperity: Corporate Plan 2000-2003*, Cardiff, WDA.

Welsh Development Agency Economic Panel (1999). *Report of the WDA's Economic Panel*, Cardiff, WDA.

Welsh Local Government Association (1996). *Evidence to House of Lords Select Committee on Relations Between Central and Local Government*, London, HMSO.

Welsh Local Government Association (1998). *Building Prosperous Communities: A Local Government Economic Agenda for Wales*, Cardiff, WLGA.

Welsh Office (1997). *A Voice for Wales: Llais Dros Gymru, The Government's Proposals for a Welsh Assembly*, Cm 3718, London, HMSO.

Welsh Office (1998). 'Ron Davies raises profile of ethnic and minority groups in National Assembly', Welsh Office press release W98493-dev, 16 September, Cardiff, Welsh Office.

Welsh Office (1999a). *Building for the Future*, London, HMSO.

Welsh Office (1999b). *Making the Difference in Wales*, Cardiff, Welsh Office.

Welsh Office (1999c). *Standing Orders of the National Assembly for Wales made by the Secretary of State for Wales under Section 50(3) of the Government of Wales Act 1998*, Cardiff, Welsh Office.

Welsh Women's Aid (1999). *Domestic Violence: An Agenda for Action for Women and their Children*, Cardiff, Welsh Women's Aid.

White, F. and K. Hollingsworth (1999). *Audit, Accountability and Government*, Oxford, Clarendon Press.

Wilcox, D. L., P. Ault and W. Agee (1997). *Public Relations Strategies and Tactics*, 4th edn, New York, HarperCollins.

Wilkinson, H. and S. Diplock (1996). *Soft Sell or Hard Policies*, London, Demos Pamphlet.

Williams, C. (1995). 'Race and racism: some reflections on the Welsh context', *Contemporary Wales* 8, 113–31.

Williams, C. (1999). 'Passports to Wales? Race, nation and identity', in R. Fevre and A. Thompson (eds.), *Nation, Identity and Social Theory*, Cardiff, University of Wales Press.

Williams, C., G. Day, T. Rees and M. Standing (1999). *Equal Opportunities Study for Inclusion in the European Structural Fund Programme Document 2000–2006. Report for the National Assembly Office*, Cardiff, National Assembly for Wales.

Williams, D. (2000). 'Wales, the law and the constitution', *Cambrian Law Review* 31, 53–60.

Williams, G. A. (1988). 'A Welsh perestroika', an address given to the launch of the Campaign for a Welsh Assembly, Merthyr Tydfil, 26 November, in Campaign for a Welsh Assembly, *Agreeing an Assembly for the 1990s*, Cardiff, CWA, 2–5.

Williams, J. (1980). 'The coalowners', in D. Smith (ed.), *A People and a Proletariat*, London, Pluto Press.

Williams K. (2000). 'No dreads, only some doubts: the press and the referendum campaign', in Jones and Balsom 2000.

Wirth, W. (1986). 'Control in public administration: plurality, selectivity and redundancy', in F. Kaufman, G. Majore and V. Ostrom (eds.), *Guidance, Control and Evaluation in the Public Sector*, Berlin, De Gruyter.

Wood, B. and R. Waterman (1991). 'The dynamics of political control of the bureaucracy', *American Political Science Review* 85, 801–28.

Wooding, N. (1998). 'Equal opportunities', in J. Osmond (ed.), *The National Assembly: A Handbook*, Cardiff, Institute of Welsh Affairs.

Wright, A. (1996). *Citizens and Subjects: An Essay on British Politics*, London and New York, Routledge.

Wyn Jones, R. (1999). *Security, Strategy and Critical Theory*, Boulder, Co., Lynne Rienner Publishers.

Wyn Jones, R. (2000). 'Cyfyng-gyngor y Blaid', *Barn*, 444 (January), 8.

Wyn Jones, R. (2001). 'Barn ar Gymru', *Barn*, 458, 10–11.

Wyn Jones, R. and B. Lewis (1998). 'The Wales Labour Party and Welsh civil society: aspects of the constitutional debate in Wales', paper to the PSA annual conference, April 1998, Keele.

Wyn Jones, R. and B. Lewis (1999). 'The 1997 Welsh devolution referendum', *Politics* 19 (1), February, 37–46.

Wyn Jones, R. and D. Trystan (1999a). 'Chwyldro yng ngwleidyddiaeth Cymru', *Barn*, 436, 12–19.

Wyn Jones, R. and D. Trystan (1999b). 'The 1997 Welsh referendum vote', in Taylor and Thomson 1999, 65–93.

Wyn Jones, R., D. Trystan and B. Taylor (2000). 'Voting patterns in the referendum', in Jones and Balsom 2000, 161–75.

Index

Aberystwyth 108
accountability 3, 9, 12, 16, 17, 24, 25, 87,
    138, 172–3, 174, 176, 198, 201, 205, 212,
    219
Agri-Food Partnership 150
All Wales Black and Ethnic Minority
    Assembly Consultative and
    Participatory Association (AWEMA)
    82, 96, 99, 100
Amsterdam Treaty 70
Ashworth, Rachel 16, 222, 223–4
Assembly Information Service 115
Assembly Review Group 13–14
Assembly Sponsored Public Bodies
    (ASPBs) 97, 100, 151–2, 176, 180, 191,
    208; see also non-departmental public
    bodies (NDPDs), quangos
assembly workers' group 113–14, 115
'assumptive worlds' 42, 152, 154, 157,
    163, 166, 167
Audit Commission 179, 183, 184, 185,
    186, 187, 195, 199, 200, 208, 210
Audit Committee 115, 156–7, 176, 203,
    204, 205–7, 208, 209–10, 212, 222–3
Auditor-General for Wales (AGW) 176,
    205–7, 209

Balsom, Denis 4, 11
Barber, B. 216–17
Barnett formula 169
Basque country 170
BBC Wales 35
beef-on-the-bone ban 163
Bentham, Jeremy 21
Best Value 176
Better Wales, A 71
Betts, Sandra 15, 214–15
Bevan, Aneurin 22
Birmingham 83
black and minority ethnic
    groups/organizations (BMEs) 80, 84,

86–8, 91, 97, 101; see also ethnic
    minorities
Blair, Tony 7–8, 11, 103
Board of Celtic Studies 14
Borland, John 15, 214–15
Bosch 134
Bourn, Sir John 206–7
Bowerman, M. 207
Boyne, George 16, 222, 223–4
Bristol 108
Britain 8, 10, 89, 99, 128
Brown, Alice 53
Brussels 164, 227
Bryson, V. 75
Building for the Future 197
business community 133–4, 145, 147–9,
    150, 151, 159–61, 163, 165–6, 167, 168,
    170, 218, 220–1, 223
Business Partnership 145–6, 147–50, 160,
    164, 166, 220
Business Wales 147, 148, 149, 150

Cabinet 12, 13, 145, 146, 149, 150, 161,
    162, 164, 205, 222
Cadw 206
Caines, Sir John 152
calf-processing scheme 163
Campaign for a Welsh Assembly (CAW)
    6
Campbell, Betty 90
Cardiff 56, 63, 79, 80, 80, 116, 122, 131,
    138, 144, 164
Cardiff and Vale Coalition of Disabled
    People 69, 75
Cardiff Bay 11, 95, 121, 219
Cardiff Bay Development Corporation
    204
Care Council for Wales 180
Care Standards Act (2000) 180, 202
census (1991) 32
Chamber Wales 149

Chaney, Paul 15, 214–16
Chwarae Teg conference 55, 72, 75
Citizen's Charter 180
citizenship 16, 72, 74, 79–80, 84, 93, 96, 100, 101, 103, 104, 170, 215, 216–17, 219–20, 226
civil society 5, 6, 12, 15, 25, 85, 96, 103, 105, 120, 140–2, 163, 165, 166, 169–70, 219–20, 227
Code of Practice on Public Access to Information 114
Commission for Racial Equality (CRE) Wales 81, 82, 83–4, 88, 96, 97, 100
Community Consortia for Education and Training (CCETs) 159, 160
Compact between the Government and the Voluntary Sector in Wales 111
Comptroller and Auditor-General (C+AG) 193, 198, 206–7, 208
Compulsory Competitive Tendering (CCT) 181, 182, 183, 184
Confederation of British Industry (CBI) Wales 134, 145–6, 147, 148, 149, 159, 160
Conservative Party 5, 6, 7, 9, 28, 35, 36, 39, 44, 48, 92, 104, 132, 133, 135, 150, 155, 163; *see also* Welsh Conservative Party
Conservative Party Manifesto for Wales (1992) 7
Consultative Steering Group on the Scottish Parliament 52
Corus 167
County Voluntary Councils 116
Crossman, Richard 131
Cynon Valley 141

Dahl, Robert 21
Daily Post 25
Davies, D. J. 22
Davies, Ron 6, 7, 9, 11, 24, 48, 75, 79, 81, 84, 87, 96, 98–9, 103, 138, 139, 140, 141, 224
Day, G. 48, 85, 99
Democracy Declaration (1994) 6
'democratic deficit' 15, 79, 103, 136, 172, 212, 224
Denbighshire 194
Development Board for Rural Wales 139, 153, 191
devolution: administrative, 64, 126, 130–7, 140, 142, 162, 164, 165–6, 221; democratic, 26, 133, 136, 137–40, 142, 145, 148, 151, 157, 158–63, 164, 165, 166, 167, 169, 170, 172, 221; executive,

164, 202; referendum on (1997), 2, 4, 10–11, 15, 18, 19, 20, 22, 23, 25, 32–3, 36, 37, 42, 43; and *passim*
Devolution: A Process not an Event 24, 44, 81, 89, 102, 103, 140
Dicks, Bella 15, 217–18
Direct Service Organizations (DSOs) 181–3, 195, 196, 197, 198, 199, 200–1, 203
disability 15, 49, 50–1, 81, 82, 217
Disability Wales 63, 64, 65, 66, 67, 69, 75
Disability Wales News 64
disabled people 10, 15, 48–51, 62–75, 94, 97, 214, 215
Disabled Rights Commission in Wales 63
Disraeli, Benjamin 132
District Audit 183, 184–5
Downs, A. 175
Drake, Ashley 148
Dunlop, A. 84

Economic and Social Research Council (ESRC) 14, 27
economic development 6, 9–10, 16, 22, 126–71, 190–5, 200, 220, 222, 223, 224, 226
Economic Development Committee 11, 72, 203, 204, 205, 210
education 100, 137, 143, 144, 147, 158–63, 164, 176, 188–90
Education and Training Action Plan (ETAP) 158–60, 161
Education and Training Group for Wales (ETAG) 158, 159, 161, 164, 166
elections, Assembly (1999) 2, 10–11, 15, 18–19, 20, 23–34, 36–47, 53, 56, 57–8, 62–4, 78, 87, 88–9, 90–4, 95, 140, 141, 213–14, 225
elections, parliamentary (1987) 4; (1992) 5, 7; (1997) 9, 19, 26, 48, 140, 153, 158; (2001) 53
Elis Thomas, Dafydd (Lord) 13, 79, 114
England 5, 8, 32, 34, 41, 44, 46, 80, 89, 105, 111, 119, 131, 150, 151, 157, 160, 181, 193, 213
Equal Opportunities Commission (EOC) Wales 59
Equality Action Plan 70
'Equality Audit: Equal Opportunities Baseline Survey' 70, 83
equality of opportunity 49, 51, 54, 55–6, 78–9, 100, 112, 216
Equality Partnership Wales 81, 82
Equality Unit 49, 96
ethnic minorities 2, 6, 10, 15, 49, 78–101,

215–16; *see also* black and minority ethnic groups/organizations (BMEs), race
Europe 4, 53, 89, 93
European Commission 70, 135
European Convention on Human Rights 12, 49
European Equality Partnership (EEP) 70
European Structural Fund (ESF) 83, 135
European Union (EU) 13, 128, 132, 134, 135, 163, 164, 169, 223, 226, 227

Federation of Small Businesses (FSB) 134, 147, 149
Feld, Val 11, 66, 72
Financial Management and Performance Review 151
Fitton, M. 48
Flegmann, V. 194
Ford 134
Frankfurt School 21
Future of Multi-Ethnic Britain, The 89

Gargarella, R. 52
gender 15, 41, 49, 50–1, 52–3, 55, 59, 60, 81, 82, 97, 142, 217; *see also* women
Germany 127, 133
GM seeds, regulation of 163
Goldthorpe–Heath class schema 33–4
Government of Wales Act (1998) 3, 13, 49, 54, 67, 81, 82, 111, 143, 145, 209
Graber, D. A. 210
Green Paper (1991) 7
Green Party 29
Gwent 80

Hain, Peter 8, 24, 139, 159
Hall, Tom 15, 217–18
Hart, Edwina 66, 151
Haywood, Dr Elizabeth 148
Health and Social Services Committee 69, 204, 205, 210
Heath, Edward 132
Higher Education Funding Council for Wales (HEFCW) 16, 176, 188–90, 196, 199
higher education institutions (HEI) 188–90, 195, 196; *see also* institutions of higher education (IHE)
Hirst, P. 100
Hoggett, P. 174
Hollingsworth, K. 209
Hood, C. 174
housing 100, 183–8, 198, 199–200, 203, 216, 222

housing associations 185–8, 196, 198, 199, 200, 203
Housing for Wales 183, 187
Housing Revenue Account 184
Housing Strategy and Operational Plan 184
HTV Wales 35
Hunt, David 132
Hutt, Jane 49–50, 66, 72, 96, 104

inclusiveness 3, 5, 6, 10, 12, 15, 17, 24, 25, 48–75, 78–101, 102–4, 112–13, 114, 120, 127, 146, 165, 215, 216, 218, 220
Institute of Directors (IoD) 134, 147, 148, 149, 160, 161
Institute of Welsh Affairs 132
institutions of higher education (IHE) 203; *see also* higher education institutions (HEI)
Interim Consultative Report (1994) 9
Ireland 80
Islwyn 18, 141
Italy 227

Jackson, P. M. 173
Japan 227
John, Howard 69
'joined-up' government 119, 137, 144, 217–18
Joint Committee for Ethnic Minorities in Wales 81
Jones, Dr Gwyn 152
Jones, Helen Mary 66

Kearns, A. 84, 86
Kendall, J. 120
Kirchheimer, Otto 21
Knapp, M. 120

Labour Party 5–6, 7, 8, 9, 10, 15, 19, 24, 28, 29, 35, 36, 39, 44, 45, 48, 92, 132, 136, 138, 139, 141, 150, 151, 163, 169, 170, 189; *see also* New Labour, Wales Labour Party
Land Authority for Wales 139, 153, 191
Learning and Skills Bill 159
Learning and Skills Council 160
legitimacy 2, 3, 15, 17, 18–47, 52, 93, 140, 178, 214, 225, 226
Liberal Democrats 7, 10, 12, 19, 28, 35, 36, 39, 44, 92, 104; *see also* Welsh Liberal Democrats
Llanelli 18, 141
Llanwern 167
lobbying 59, 61, 64, 65, 67–9, 110, 112–13,

114, 118, 119, 124, 146, 147, 155, 162, 163, 165, 166
local authority social services departments (LASSDs) 178–81, 195, 196, 199, 200
local government 6, 7, 9, 16, 20, 42, 127, 133, 135, 137, 138, 139, 140, 141, 142, 143, 145, 146–7, 148, 151, 155, 157, 159, 161, 162, 166, 176, 177, 181–5, 199–200, 203, 206, 207–8, 212, 218, 221, 222, 223, 226
Local Government Act (1980) 181
Local Government Act (1998) 181
Local Government Act (2000) 202
Local Government and Housing Act (1989) 183
Local Government, Environment, Planning, Housing and Transport Committee 204
Lomax, Rachel 139
London 6, 26, 28, 81, 118, 131, 143, 164, 227

Macmillan, Harold 132
McPherson, A. 142
MacPherson inquiry 79, 82, 97
'mainstreaming' 51–2, 70–9, 98, 100, 215, 216
Major, John 9, 15
Mansbridge, J. 52, 96
'Memorandum of Understanding' 155
Merched y Wawr 59
Merthyr 141
MEWN (Minority Ethnic Women's Network) Cymru 87, 88
Michael, Alun 11, 18, 28, 82, 96, 104, 112, 118, 140, 141, 144, 147–8, 160, 161, 162, 216
Middleton, Tom 161
Mill, J. S. 22
Mill, James 21
Miners' Next Step, The 22
Minhinnick, M. 48
Monitoring Committee for Industrial South Wales 135
Morgan, Kevin 16, 106, 205, 220–2, 223
Morgan, Rhodri 11, 13, 14, 18, 29, 49, 73, 139, 141, 148, 154, 156, 225
Murphy, Paul 79, 82

National Assembly Advisory Group (NAAG) 3, 52–3, 81, 98, 103
National Assembly 'Diversity' Recruitment Fair 82
National Assembly Economic Development Committee 69

National Assembly Voluntary Sector Centre 113, 121–2
National Association of Carers Charter 59
National Audit Office (NAO) 193, 195, 197, 198, 206, 207, 208, 210–11, 212
National Council for Education and Training in Wales (CETW) 149, 158, 159, 160
National Council for Voluntary Organizations (NCVO) 119
National Curriculum for Wales 100
National Economic Development Strategy (NEDS) 168
National Health Service (NHS) 178, 205, 207, 210
national identity 24, 31–3, 42, 78, 79, 80, 85, 87–9, 98, 110, 172, 217, 227–8
National Museum of Wales 206
Neath 141
Neumann, Franz 21
New Deal 90
New Labour 4, 7, 26, 79, 103, 104, 138, 141, 161
new public management (NPM) 173
Newport 80
non-departmental public bodies (NDPBs) 126, 134, 136, 138–9, 151, 191, 192, 193, 194, 195, 197; *see also* Assembly Sponsored Public Bodies, quangos
Norris, P. 227
Northern Ireland 5, 8, 93
Nyoni, M. 80

Objective One Monitoring Committee 154
Objective One programme 83, 149, 150, 157, 168, 169
Objective Two programme 168
Objective Three programme 168
Office for National Statistics (ONS) 80
Office for Standards in Education (OFSTED) 174
openness 3, 17, 55, 87, 104, 113, 127, 137, 146, 162, 201, 219, 221
Operation Black Vote 82, 90, 96
Opportunity Wales 7
Osmond, John 204

Parliament for Wales Campaign (PWC) 6
participation 3, 5, 15, 10, 17, 18–47, 49, 72, 86, 90–4, 103, 112, 114, 146, 165, 214–15, 216, 217, 219
Participation and Democratic Theory 20, 21

partnership 102, 112, 104, 116, 117, 122, 123, 124, 145, 150, 151, 222, 226
Partnership Agreement 141
Partnership Council 145, 146–7, 148, 150, 164, 166, 208, 217, 220
Pateman, Carole 20, 21
performance audit 173
performance indicators (PIs) 189
Phillips, Anne 53
Piore, M. 145
Pithouse, Andrew 15, 217–18
Plaid Cymru 5, 7, 10, 12, 18, 19, 22, 29, 35, 36, 39, 44, 53, 64, 92, 94, 104, 141, 142, 156, 206
Policy Commission (1993) 9
political culture 18, 34, 101
Pontypridd 141
Post-sixteen Education and Training Committee 158, 160, 161, 162, 203
Preparing for a New Wales 9
Priorities for Further Action in Wales 59
Programme for the Valleys 132
Public Accounts Committee (PAC) 152, 176, 191, 193–4, 195, 197, 203, 205, 206, 209
public sector 16, 100, 163, 166, 167, 168, 172–212

Quality Assessment Audit 190
quangos 5, 6, 63, 97, 100, 126, 136, 138–9, 151–2, 153, 154, 172, 176, 209; *see also* non-departmental public bodies (NDPBs), Assembly Sponsored Public Bodies (ASPBs)
Quinquennial Review 151, 153, 157, 205

Raab, C. 142
race 79, 81, 82, 83, 87, 92, 93, 96, 97, 100, 216; *see also* ethnic minorities
Race Equality Councils (RECs) 81, 82, 84
Race Relations Act 79
Redwood, John 132–3, 138, 153
Rees, Gareth 16, 220–2, 223
Rees, Teresa 72
Referendum Bill (1997) 9
regional committees 25, 65, 122, 144–5, 159, 160, 164, 201
Regional Development Division (RDD) 191, 192, 195
regional economic forums 144, 159, 160
Regional Selective Assistance 134, 155
Regional Technology Plan 132
regulation 16, 17, 139, 172–212, 220, 222, 223
Report to Tenants regime 184

Research Assessment Exercise (RAE) 189
Rex, J. 86
Rhodes, R. 174
Rhondda 18, 141
Rhondda Cynon Taff 141
Right to Vote Campaign 82, 91
'risk-averse culture' 131, 132, 153, 166–7
Riverside (Cardiff) 80, 92
Rousseau, Jean-Jacques 21–2

Schumpeter, Joseph 21
Scope 67, 68
Scotland 1, 5, 8, 13, 25, 80, 81, 84, 93, 111, 119, 140, 169, 170, 172, 193, 213, 227
Scott, C. 174
Scottish Labour group 169
Scottish Office 131
Scottish Parliament 8, 13, 26, 53, 143, 204
Select Committee on Domestic Violence 59
Shadow Voluntary Sector Partnership Council 112
Short, Cherry 88, 93–4
Shortridge, Jon 210
Sianel Pedwar Cymru (S4C) 139
Silk, P. 202
Skelcher, C. 195
Smith, John 7
Social Housing Grant 186
social service inspectorate (SSI) 179, 180, 199
Social Services Division 197
Sony 134
South Glamorgan 80
Squires, Judith 53, 74
Standing Committee on Equality of Opportunity 49, 55, 59, 69–70, 82, 97
Stephens, Elan Closs 139
Strategic Plan 157, 168
Straw, Jack 79
subject committees 144–5, 163, 164, 201, 203, 204–5, 212, 216, 222
subsidiarity 6, 128, 163–4
Swansea 79

Teaching Quality Assessment 190
'Team Wales' 138, 155
Thatcher, Margaret 15, 132, 153
'third way', the 7–8, 24, 79, 103, 161, 217
'thirds principle', the 165, 167, 219
Thomas, P. G. 173
Thomas, Roger 147, 148
Thompson, A. 85, 99
three-Wales model 4
Torfaen 179–80

Towards an Economic Democracy 22
Toyota 134
trade unions 127, 140, 161, 166
Training and Enterprise Councils (TECs)
    127, 135, 155, 159, 160, 161–2
Trystan, Dafydd 5, 14–15, 48, 213, 214

United Kingdom (UK) 2, 5, 7, 8, 13, 19,
    21–2, 24, 25, 26, 30, 39, 42, 45, 46–7, 49,
    68, 72, 84, 89, 93, 104, 105, 119, 127,
    132, 134, 135, 145, 154, 163, 168, 172,
    174, 192, 195, 202, 217, 226, 227
United States of America 20
University of Wales 1, 14
Urban Investment Grants 191

Vale of Glamorgan 180
'value for money' (VFM) 173–4, 186, 193,
    207, 212, 222
Vertovec, S. 86
Video Nation 81
Voice for Wales, A 3, 9–10, 11, 49, 172, 201,
    204, 206
voluntary sector 10, 15–16, 57, 58, 59, 61,
    62, 67, 84, 102–24, 127, 145, 147, 160,
    164, 165, 166, 217–19, 220–1, 223, 227
Voluntary Sector Partnership Council
    118, 121, 123
Vountary Sector Scheme 15–16, 111–12,
    113, 121, 123, 217

Wales Assembly of Women 59
Wales Council for Voluntary Action
    (WCVA) 59, 65, 67, 102, 105, 107, 109,
    110, 112, 116, 118–21, 123–4, 165, 218,
    221
Wales Labour Party (WLP) 6–7, 9, 11, 12,
    18, 19, 53, 87, 88, 91–2, 93, 102, 104,
    118, 119, 141, 142, 151, 154, 162, 166,
    203, 204, 205, 213–14, 225; *see also*
    Labour Party
Wales Labour Party Conference (1996) 9
Wales Tourist Board 204
Wales Trades Union Council (TUC) 149,
    150, 160–1
Wales TUC Women's Advisory
    Committee 59
Wales Voluntary Sector Almanac 105
Wales Women's National Coalition 59, 75
Wales Yearbook (1998) 107
Walker, Peter 132, 152
Walker, Richard 16, 222, 223–4
Waterhouse inquiry 180
Weinrich, P. 99

Welsh Affairs Committee (WAC)135–6,
    191, 194, 195, 197, 198, 200, 203, 209
Welsh Conservative Party 53, 104, 142;
    see also Conservative Party
Welsh Development Agency (WDA) 16,
    126, 127, 129, 132, 134, 136–7, 139, 144,
    152–7, 159, 160, 166, 176, 190–5, 196,
    197, 198, 203, 204, 205, 210, 220, 221
Welsh Industrial Estates Corporation 190
Welsh language 31, 32, 40, 41, 44, 89, 100
Welsh Liberal Democrats 53, 141–2, 203,
    225; *see also* Liberal Democrats
Welsh Local Government Association
    (WLGA) 135, 138, 146, 155, 161–2, 166,
    177
Welsh National Assembly Election
    Survey (WNAES) 14–15, 19, 27–42
Welsh Office 6, 7, 8, 10, 16, 19, 64, 66, 82,
    83–4, 87, 96, 105, 117, 119, 120, 126, 129,
    130–3, 134–5, 136–7, 138, 139, 144, 145,
    150, 151, 152, 154, 155, 162, 164, 166,
    167, 172, 176–80, 182, 183–4, 186, 189,
    190, 191, 192–3, 194, 195, 197, 198, 199,
    200, 201, 203–4, 205, 207–8, 211, 220,
    221, 223, 224, 226
Welsh Office Further and Higher
    Education Department 188
Welsh Office Housing Division 184, 185,
    186, 187, 188, 195
Welsh parliament 1, 6, 214
Welsh Referendum Survey (1997) 31, 37
Welsh Third Way, A 24
Welsh Women's Aid (WWA) 59
West Glamorgan 80
Westminster Parliament 3, 7, 13, 24, 25,
    42, 46, 54, 56, 118, 138, 143, 159, 173,
    192, 193, 195, 202, 203, 204, 208, 209,
    214, 219, 226, 227
White, F. 209
Whitehall 25, 46, 130–1, 138, 150, 155,
    202–3, 227
Wigley, Dafydd 156
Williams, Charlotte 15, 215–16
Williams, Professor Gwyn Alf 6
Willott, Brian 155, 156–7
women 2, 6, 10, 15, 30, 48–61, 67, 69,
    70–3, 74–5, 94, 214–15, 217; *see also*
    gender
Women Say Yes 81
*Work of the Committee since Devolution,
    The* 209
Wyn Jones, Richard 5, 14–15, 48, 213, 214

'Yes for Wales' campaign 103